CRISIS SYSTEM

This book throws light onto the nature and causes of three different but strongly interconnected crises in contemporary societies worldwide: an economic crisis, an ecological crisis and a normative (moral and political) crisis. These crises are reflected in the profoundly inequitable distribution of wealth, resources and life opportunities around the world. If we follow the causal roots of these crises, we are led back to an inherent dynamic in the capitalist economic system itself, discursively expressed as neoclassical, mainstream economics. For instance, by conflating human needs with market demand, mainstream economics disregards the needs of those who do not have sufficient purchasing power, as well as any needs that cannot be quantified or monetised in some way. Mainstream economics also ignores the notion of natural limits. Furthermore, it seems that everything that is quantifiable is potentially for sale and this results in the substitution of nature, indigenous cultural traditions and various life forms with commodities and 'human capital'. The latter is defined as the skills instrumental in continual economic growth. Besides critiquing the academic discipline of economics, this book points to a number of dysfunctional and crisis-prone structures and practices of substantive economic life. It will be of interest to students and scholars working in philosophy, economics and environmental studies.

Petter Næss is Professor of Planning in Urban Regions at the Norwegian University of Life Sciences, Norway.

Leigh Price is Research Associate at Rhodes University, South Africa, and visiting Research Associate at University College London, UK.

Ontological Explorations

Other titles in this series:

The Politics of Childhoods Real and Imagined
Volume 2: practical application of critical realism and childhood studies
Priscilla Alderson

Critical Realism, Environmental Learning and Social-Ecological Change
Edited by Leigh Price and Heila Lotz-Sisitka

Metatheory for the 21st Century
Critical Realism and Integral Theory in Dialogue
Edited by Roy Bhaskar, Sean Esbjörn-Hargens, Nicholas Hedlund and Mervyn Hartwig

The Post-Mobile Society
From the Smart/Mobile to Second Offline
Edited by Hidenori Tomita

Enlightened Common Sense
The Philosophy of Critical Realism
Roy Bhaskar

A Complex Integral Realist Perspective
Towards a New Axial Vision
Paul Marshall

Crisis System
A critical realist and environmental critique of economics and the economy
Edited by Petter Næss and Leigh Price

Structure, Culture and Agency
Selected Papers of Margaret Archer
Edited by Tom Brock, Mark Carrigan and Graham Scambler

For a complete list of titles in this series, please visit www.routledge.com/Ontological-Explorations-Routledge-Critical-Realism/book-series/OE

CRISIS SYSTEM

A critical realist and environmental critique of economics and the economy

Edited by Petter Næss and Leigh Price

Routledge
Taylor & Francis Group
LONDON AND NEW YORK

First published 2016
by Routledge
2 Park Square, Milton Park, Abingdon, Oxon OX14 4RN

and by Routledge
711 Third Avenue, New York, NY 10017

Routledge is an imprint of the Taylor & Francis Group, an informa business

British Library Cataloguing in Publication Data
A catalogue record for this book is available from the British Library

Library of Congress Cataloguing in Publication Data
Names: Næss, Petter, editor. | Price, Leigh, editor.
Title: Crisis system : a critical realist and environmental critique of economics and the economy / edited by Petter Næss and Leigh Price.
Description: New York : Routledge, 2016. | Series: Ontological explorations
Identifiers: LCCN 2016004654 | ISBN 9780415818735 (hardback) | ISBN 9780415818742 (pbk.) | ISBN 9781315563138 (e-book)
Subjects: LCSH: Economic policy. | Capitalism–Environmental aspects. | Socialism–Environmental aspects. | Economic development–Moral and ethical aspects.
Classification: LCC HD87.C754 2016 | DDC 330–dc23
LC record available at http://lccn.loc.gov/2016004654

ISBN: 978-0-415-81873-5 (hbk)
ISBN: 978-0-415-81874-2 (pbk)
ISBN: 978-1-315-56313-8 (ebk)

Typeset in Bembo
by Out of House Publishing

CONTENTS

FIGURES

TABLES

CONTRIBUTORS

Robert Biel teaches Political Ecology at University College London, the Development Planning Unit, UK.

Bob Jessop is Distinguished Professor of Sociology and Co-Director of the Cultural Political Economy Research Centre at Lancaster University, UK.

Tony Lawson is Professor of Economics and Philosophy at the Faculty of Economics, University of Cambridge, UK.

Petter Næss is Professor in Planning in Urban Regions at the Norwegian University of Life Sciences, Department of Landscape Architecture and Spatial Planning, at Ås, Norway.

Leigh Price is the Secretary of the Centre for Critical Realism and a Research Associate of the Environmental Learning and Research Centre, Rhodes University, South Africa.

David Tyfield is Reader in Environmental Innovation and Sociology at the Lancaster Environment Centre, Lancaster University, UK, and Director of the International Research and Innovation Centre for the Environment (I-RICE) in Guangzhou, China.

Arne Johan Vetlesen is Professor of Philosophy at the University of Oslo, Norway.

Jin Xue is Associate Professor in Urban and Regional Planning at the Norwegian University of Life Sciences, Department of Landscape Architecture and Spatial Planning, at Ås, Norway.

1

INTRODUCTION

Petter Næss and Leigh Price

Informed by critical realist ontology, this book throws light onto the nature and causes of three different but strongly interconnected crises in contemporary societies worldwide: an economic crisis, an ecological crisis and a normative (moral and political) crisis of the profoundly inequitable distribution of wealth, resources, and life opportunities. Arguably, these crises are at the base of the violent conflicts that currently beset many countries. Moreover, the global system of production and consumption is on a highly unsustainable trajectory measured against all dimensions of sustainable development. This book follows the roots of the different manifestations of the global crisis back to an inherent dynamic in the capitalist economic system itself, discursively expressed as neoclassical economics. Exhibiting an unshakable faith in questionable axioms, mainstream economic theory has been immune to critical inputs from other disciplines. Notably, by conflating human needs with market demand, mainstream economics disregards the needs of those who do not have sufficient purchasing power, as well as any needs that cannot be quantified or monetized in some way. Mainstream economics, and the globalized economy it serves, also ignores the notion of natural limits. It seems that everything quantifiable is potentially for sale, and any piece of nature, indigenous cultural tradition, or life form is susceptible to being substituted with commodities and "human capital," the latter understood mainly as skills instrumental in continual economic growth.

While the authors of this book are strongly critical of the academic discipline of economics, they do not assume that this exhausts the problem. It is also necessary to critique substantive economic life, which has a set of ontological structures and practices that, among other things, assumes continual and limitless growth and leads inevitably to social and economic crises. Orthodox economics, for the most part, merely reflects and justifies these structures and practices and takes them as an unalterable given. That is, it assumes that there is no alternative. Nevertheless, we can criticize economics as a discipline in so far as it a) fails to provide an explanatory critique of the basic structures of economic life, thus it fails to guide agents in their attempts to transform dysfunctional structures, and b) fills the void of genuine explanatory critique with misinformation about the practices in which we seek to describe, explain, navigate, and change our material being and circumstances. In these ways economics acts as a source of mystification, or causally efficacious illusion, of what critical realists have called "demi-reality."

The book aims to unveil this "demi-reality" and takes as its point of departure two different, but complementary, theoretical approaches. First, it offers a critique of the ontological and epistemological assumptions of economic theory from the point of view of critical realism. Second, it offers a critique of the ways in which economic theory deals with nature and ecological systems, based on theoretical contributions from the fields of ecology, environmental studies, and environmental philosophy. Bridging these two theoretical positions, a number of contributions elaborate on various more or less concrete aspects of the global crisis.

It follows that an interdisciplinary approach is crucial to grasp the multi-faceted aspects of this combined economic, ecological, social, and moral/political crisis. Whereas many of the most influential positions within the philosophy of science, if taken seriously, prohibit or at least strongly hamper interdisciplinarity, critical realism readily accommodates it. Indeed, it emphasizes the need for contributions from a variety of disciplines to deal with the multitude of causal mechanisms that together produce the complex phenomena that we observe in the natural and the social world. This book, with its contributions from authors from several academic disciplines, is an attempt to achieve such interdisciplinarity.

All of the chapters in this book are written by authors who are, explicitly or implicitly, informed and inspired by a critical realist meta-theoretical position. The book follows the main theme of the 14th International Association for Critical Realism Conference held in Oslo in September 2011, "A world in profound change – welfare and nature in crisis." The book also elaborates upon several of the issues addressed in the two preceding books: *Interdisciplinarity and Climate Change* (Bhaskar *et al.*, 2010) and *Ecophilosophy in a World of Crisis: Critical realism and the Nordic contributions* (Bhaskar *et al.*, 2012). En route to completion of the manuscript of this book, two PhD courses on "Critical realism, environmentalism, interdisciplinarity and the critique of economics" were organized in Oslo in November 2012 and September/October 2014, both with Roy Bhaskar as the central presenter (with contributions from Petter Næss and Leigh Price). The latter course, where Roy gave his lectures through interactive Skype displayed on a big screen, was probably his last teaching event for an academic audience.

The contents of the book can be roughly divided into two sections focusing on, respectively, critiques levelled against the discipline of economics (Chapters 2–5), and critical analyses of and normative responses to the interrelated environmental, social, economic, and moral/political crises (Chapters 6–12). In Chapter 2, Tony Lawson argues that the widespread and long-lived failings of academic economics are due to an over-reliance on largely inappropriate mathematical methods of analysis. This is an assessment Lawson has long maintained. Many heterodox economists, however, appear to hold instead that the central problem is a form of political–economic ideology. Specifically, it is widely contended in heterodox circles that the discipline goes astray because it takes an abstract idea – of the market economy as a smoothly or efficiently functioning system – and assumes that this reflects the way that the economy works in reality. In his chapter, Lawson critically assesses the evidence in favour of this contention and concludes that it does not fare well. Lawson does not, however, deny that ideology of some sort has a major impact on the output of the modern economics academy. Nevertheless, he considers this to be of a different nature to the form typically discussed, and that it works in somewhat indirect and complex ways. Having raised the question of the impact of ideology, Lawson thus explores the way that it plays out in the economics academy more generally.

In Chapter 3, David Tyfield uses an aspect of the economy itself – specifically the knowledge-based economy – as a case for raising a more general critique of mainstream economics. In the wake of the global financial crisis and amidst continuing global economic malaise, mainstream economics continues to reign supreme despite its inability to explain these challenges. Tyfield's critique of mainstream economics offers both a political challenge and an epistemological one. In his political challenge, he strategically assesses issues in the "knowledge-based" economy, including the heightened importance of innovation, technological change, and socio-economic "rhythms" thereof, including socio-technical systems transitions, the interaction of economy and "nature," and the commercialization of research. In his epistemological challenge, he reframes the paradigm of "economics" such that it can furnish critical and explanatory, not just axiomatic and ahistorical, knowledge of these inherently temporal, complex, and systemic phenomena. Tyfield begins his chapter by describing the substantive problem of developing an economics of research capable of illuminating the commercialization of research and its interaction with and implications for broader social crises, and showing how critical realism is a crucial component in this theoretical project.

In Chapter 4, Petter Næss uses the meta-theoretical perspective of critical realism to critically discuss the use of cost–benefit analyses of transportation infrastructure investment. Næss contends that such analyses are based on a number of untenable ontological assumptions about social value, human nature, and the natural environment. The reliance of the cost–benefit analyses on exact, quantified predictions of future situations ignores measurement problems and inevitable forecasting uncertainty. For instance, the method requires precise input data, but in practice traffic forecasts are inaccurate and often also biased. The valuation of many impact categories is arbitrary, and the discounting rules entail an untenable diminishing of long-term and irreversible negative environmental impacts. The willingness-to-pay principle on which the method is based represents ethical bias against the poor, future generations, and affected parties outside the local context. Due to its reliance on market demand, the method tends to undermine political objectives of changing current trends of traffic growth. The opaqueness of the method makes it difficult for outsiders to evaluate the credibility of the results. The chapter concludes that the method is inadequate for assessing whether or not to build a proposed project (although it may be less inappropriate when comparing different design alternatives for an already adopted project). Næss briefly introduces alternatives to cost–benefit analysis, which avoid some of its flaws.

In Chapter 5, Jin Xue critically scrutinizes economic, social, environmental, and ethical arguments for and against economic growth as a strategy to deal with the contemporary socio-economic and ecological crises. From an economic perspective, it has been argued that capitalism has an inherent growth compulsion, and technological advancement, escalating consumer demand, and debt-based money creation constitute the drivers of economic growth. However, opponents argue that the economy is inclined to stabilize due to biophysical, human, and social limits. From a social perspective, critics of growth employ theoretical arguments and empirical evidence to rebut the conventional belief that economic growth is essential to human progress after growth has reached a certain point. From an environmental perspective, growth advocates believe that economic growth can be sustained through decoupling growth from environmental impacts, while growth critics argue that decoupling is not sufficient to reduce resource consumption and environmental impacts to a level within the limits of ecosystems' biocapacity. Arguments from a moral perspective provide ethical justification to the arguments against growth. The chapter concludes that perpetual economic growth in already affluent countries is neither socially desirable nor environmentally possible.

In Chapter 6, Bob Jessop, after reviewing "critical realism in general," notes the challenge of developing "particular critical realisms" to address particular sets of explananda. Crises are an interesting test case for four reasons: (1) they invite the critical realist question, "What must the world be like for X to have occurred?"; (2) actual symptoms have no one-to-one correspondence to real causes; (3) this requires retroduction to relate crisis symptoms to causal mechanisms; and (4) these diagnoses can be tested through efforts to resolve crises. Jessop considers that critical realism could benefit from developing particular crisis symptomatologies that address the asymmetry between diagnosis and prognosis in dealing with open systems, especially where the action of social forces can shape their development. This indicates a distinction between scientifically adequate explanations of crisis and conjuncturally "correct" readings of the potential for transformative action in response to crisis. It also underlines the emancipatory potential of critical realism as well as its relevance to crisis management, crises of crisis management and lessons drawing from crisis. Building on Marx, Jessop then examines the abstract possibility of crisis in capitalism and how it is overdetermined in specific cases. He concludes by emphasizing the need to integrate critical semiotic analysis into critical realism to facilitate its further development.

In Chapter 7, Leigh Price revisits the idea of wicked problems first introduced in 1973 by Horst Rittel and Melvin Webber. Rittel and Webber arrived at the idea of wicked problems in their attempt to explain why, despite twenty years of first-generation, functionalist systems thinking, scientists were unable to adequately address complex bio/socio/economic problems. While much of Rittel and Webber's critique of mainstream science prefigured the critical realist critique, they differ significantly in terms of what they suggest that we can do about it. Specifically, they argue that science is irrelevant to discussions of values, and that it is not designed to cope with the open system of real-world problems; thus it is unfit for purpose. They therefore suggest that we reduce the role of science significantly in policy-making, replacing it with a relativist, consensualist version in which consensus trumps reality. In her chapter, Price argues the opposite: that science can and should be used in discussions of values and that by assuming a stratified ontology it can and should be used to address complex, open-system problems. She also tries to give practical advice about how we can achieve this. Specifically, Price suggests a version of evidence-informed decision-making, based on retroductive theorizing, that is both more democratic and more likely to be "fit for purpose" than current mainstream versions.

In Chapter 8, Petter Næss and Jin Xue illuminate social distributional aspects of non-growth or de-growth in the overall economy in affluent countries, using the housing sector as an example. Smarter designs of dwellings and cities can reduce negative environmental impacts of growth in the housing stock, but the possible "decoupling" is only relative, not absolute. In order to prevent cities in affluent countries from becoming increasingly environmentally unsustainable, a shift toward non-growth or de-growth in the building stock seems necessary. A national "ceiling" for the housing consumption per capita implies that increased floor space for those who already live in a spacious dwelling comes in direct competition with the wish to build for those who are lacking a dwelling or who live in a substandard residence. If we intend to secure a decent housing standard for everyone while not exceeding the "ceiling" on per capita consumption, it is necessary to practice a principle of selective standard improvement, setting minimum as well as maximum standards for housing consumption. These standards should be based on conceptions of human needs, welfare rights, distributional ethics and environmental capacity. The introduction of such standards would, however, be contradictory to the growth imperative of capitalism as well as its incentive system.

In Chapter 9, Robert Biel broaches the question of "crisis" from the perspective of general systems/complexity theory, illustrating his argument with the world's food production systems. Although some critical realists have suggested that complexity theory is simply the new name for irrealism in social science, some recent theorists of complexity theory seem to have implicitly adopted an essentially critical realist ontology. For example, they have a version of emergence that allows structures to come into being that are more than the sum of their parts. Following resilience systems thinkers, Biel argues that the Marxist assumption that crisis leads to revolution is inadequate. Significant fluctuations (which appear as crises) resulting from disturbances may not only fail to lead to regime change but may play a useful role in preventing stagnancy and creating advantageous circumstances that benefit the current regime. However, this is not to say that a disturbance might not be large enough to create a regime change; this is known as a tipping point. Since we are currently seeing an increase in volatility in the world systems, Biel suggests that we should use this opportunity to push the system in the direction that we want it to go.

In Chapter 10, Petter Næss contends that the ideas of green growth and green capitalism are illusory. The idea of green growth is based on flawed conceptions of the diversity of environmental impacts, the possibilities for efficiency-increasing technologies and recycling schemes, and the scope for compensating for growth in the volume of consumption through changes in its composition. At the same time, capitalism depends on growth in order to avoid running into severe crises. The assumptions of mainstream economists about infinite economic growth (and infinite dematerialization) represent a false ontology according to which the powers and mechanisms of the natural world are considered controllable by humans as if they were mere epiphenomena of the human world. Meanwhile, the assumptions of certain ecological economists about the possibility of steady-state capitalism disregard the relation between capital and surplus value, which, together with the competition on which the capitalist system is based, makes up a strong mechanism driving the capitalist economy toward limitless growth. Næss argues that the growth compulsion of capitalism is plausibly the main reason for the widespread but illusory belief in unlimited, green growth.

In Chapter 11, Jin Xue argues for the limits of the "growth and ecological modernization paradigm" as a path to a sustainable future in China. Specifically, she critiques China's National Functional Zones Planning (2011), whose objective is to strategically restructure China's territorial development in accordance with the ecological modernization model. By employing basic concepts of critical realism, Xue analyses the limitations of this plan in terms of its ability to achieve long-term sustainability in the Chinese context. She argues instead that the achievement of sustainable development depends on de-growth in the affluent parts of China and an ecological restructuring all over the country toward ecosocialism. The past and ongoing economic reforms in the pursuit of a modern capitalist liberal society are at odds with the ecosocialist paradigm. However, China's economic–political conditions and traditional philosophies provide possible resources for such a transformation.

In the final chapter, Arne Johan Vetlesen contends that in the critical analysis of capitalism pursued within Western Marxism, the contradiction between capital and labor is privileged over that between capital and nature. Vetlesen argues that the work of David Harvey is a case in point and seeks to show that the costs of underestimating the truth of the slogan "no planet, no business" are increasingly severe. In disputing that there are barriers in nature, or "pure natural limits," to the profit–growth imperative of capitalism, Harvey remains loyal to the notion that the limiting factor is, and will remain, manmade capital, not natural capital. The fact of overshoot belies this notion, however, since capital's exploitation of nature destroys – spoils, degrades, depletes – the various ecosystems that capital itself, not to mention its alleged "primary" contradiction with labor, depends upon. Invoking the work of Herman Daly and Karl Polanyi, Vetlesen argues that Harvey exemplifies a Marxist critique of capitalism marred by ecological blind spots.

The editors of this book regard an interdisciplinary and environmentally conscious critique of the discipline of economics and the economy as such as vital for the future of the species and the planet. The philosophy of critical realism is particularly suitable for the development of such a critique, due to its ontological inclusiveness and hence its openness to richer and more nuanced analyses of the complex and interrelated crises facing humanity. We hope this book will enhance the originality, integrity, and coherence of the intellectual understanding of, as well as the political responses to, these challenges.

This book has had a lengthy and painful birth. The original editorial team was made up of Karl Georg Høyer, Roy Bhaskar, and Petter Næss. Karl Georg Høyer came up with the idea of putting the book together but, sadly, he died from cancer at the age of 66 in the late autumn of 2012. Roy Bhaskar passed away in November 2014, struck by a heart attack at the age of 70, only a few days before a scheduled meeting to discuss the updated composition of chapters. At the beginning of 2015, Leigh Price joined Petter Næss as co-editor. We are therefore extremely indebted to Roy Bhaskar and Karl Georg Høyer and dedicate this book to both of them.

References

Bhaskar, R., Frank, C., Høyer, K. G., Næss, P. and Parker, J. (eds) (2010). *Interdisciplinarity and Climate Change*. London/New York: Routledge.

Bhaskar, R., Høyer, K. G. and Næss, P. (eds) (2012). *Ecophilosophy in a World of Crisis: Critical realism and the Nordic contributions*. London/New York: Routledge.

2

IDEOLOGY AND ECONOMICS[1]

Tony Lawson

Introduction

One positive consequence of the ongoing economic crisis is that the intellectual malaise of the modern academic discipline of economics is becoming ever more widely recognised. Economics is a discipline that is marked by significant explanatory failure stemming from wildly unrealistic formulations, and has been for many years now (see Lawson, 2003, Chapter 1).

The reference to specifically *academic* economics here is not incidental; I want to stress that throughout the discussion my concern is not economics in all its forms or manifestations but economics as it is pursued within the modern academy, which after all is the site from which most strands of the subject emanate.

Elsewhere I have put forward an explanation of the noted academic malaise that draws significantly on ontological theorising, i.e. on theorising the *nature* of (social) reality. Because my focus here is on examining the power of, and support for, an alternative explanation, I do not want to rehearse my own position at length. But in brief, the explanation I maintain elsewhere is that the fundamental problem of modern economics is that certain methods of a restricted kind are repeatedly applied in conditions for which they are not appropriate (see Lawson, 1997, 2003). Specifically, modern academic economics is dominated by a mainstream tradition whose defining characteristic is an insistence that various methods of mathematical modelling be more or less always employed in the analysis of economic phenomena, and are so in conditions for which they are not suitable.

Fundamental to my argument is an assessment that the application of mathematics involves more than merely the introduction of a formal language. Of relevance here is recognition that mathematical methods and techniques are essentially tools. And as with any other tools (pencils, hammers, drills, scissors), so the sorts of mathematical methods that economists wield (functional relations, forms of calculus, etc.) are useful under some sets of conditions and not others.

The specific conditions required for the sorts of mathematical methods that economists continually wield to be generally applicable, I have shown, are a ubiquity of (deterministic or stochastic) closed systems. A closed system is simply one in which an event regularity occurs. Notice that these closures are as much presupposed or required by the 'newer' approaches to mathematical economics, those often referred to as non-linear modelling, complexity modelling, agent-based modelling, model simulations and so on (including those developed under the head of behavioural or neuro-economics), as they are by the more traditional forms of micro, macro and econometric modelling.

The most obvious scenario in which a prevalence of such closures would be expected is a world 1) populated by sets of atomistic individuals or entities (an atom here being an entity that exercises its own separate, independent and invariable effect, whatever the context), and 2) where the atoms of interest exist in relative isolation (so allowing the effects of the atoms of interest to be deducible/predictable by barring the effects of potentially interfering factors). Not surprisingly, the latter two (ontological) presuppositions are easily shown to be implicit in almost all contemporary economic modelling contributions (see Lawson, 2003, Chapter 1).

However, explicit, systemic and sustained (ontological) analysis of the nature of social reality reveals that the social domain is *not* everywhere composed of closed systems of sets of isolated atoms. Rather, social reality is an open, structured realm of emergent phenomena that, among other things, are processual (being constantly reproduced and transformed through the human practices on which they depend), highly internally related (meaning constituted through (and not merely linked by) their relations with each other, for example employer/employee or teacher/student relations), value-laden and meaningful, among much else (see Lawson, 2003, Chapter 2).

Clearly, if social phenomena are highly internally related they do *not* each exist in isolation. And if they are processual in nature, being continually transformed through practice, they are *not* atomistic. So the emphasis on the sorts of mathematical modelling methods that economists employ necessarily entails the construction of economic narratives – including the sorts of axioms and assumptions made and hypotheses entertained – that, at best, are always but highly distorted accounts of the complex phenomena of the real open social system (for lengthy elaborations of all this see, for example, Lawson, 1997, 2003; Edward Fullbrook, 2009). It is thus not at all surprising that mainstream contributions are found continually to be so unrealistic and explanatorily unsuccessful.

Employing the term *deductivism* to denote the thesis that closed systems are essential to social scientific explanation (whether the event regularities, correlations, uniformities, laws, etc. are a priori constructions or a posteriori observations), I conclude that the fundamental source of the discipline's numerous, widespread and long-lived problems and failings is precisely the emphasis placed upon forms of mathematical deductivist reasoning (in conditions where the latter are inappropriate).

So much for my own assessment. Many heterodox economists clearly demur, and most of these seemingly hold to the view that a superior explanation of the state of modern economics is provided by focusing on the prevalence of a form of political–economic ideology. The real source of all the failings of the mainstream academic project, according to advocates of this view, is that ideology about how the economic system works gets in the way of explanatorily successful or realistic analysis.

Ideology is a term I have rarely employed, as various heterodox critics have pointed out.[2] Here I address the claim that ideology provides a better, or even an alternative, explanation of the modern academic economics malaise than the one I have advanced and have briefly sketched above. In so doing I take the opportunity to explore the role of ideology in the practices and output of the modern economics academy more generally.

Ideology

The term *ideology* was seemingly coined by Count Destutt de Tracy in the late eighteenth century to define a 'science of ideas'. Few interpret the category in this way today, however. Almost universally, the current understanding is that the term *ideology* refers not to the study but rather to the content of certain sets of ideas, along with their consequences.

Thereafter, however, interpretations diverge, with many alternatives to be found in the contemporary literature.[3] Even so, with a little systematising I think most interpretations within current debates among heterodox economists can be seen either to presuppose or to reduce to special cases of two broad systemic conceptions:

1. Ideology$_1$: a relatively unchallenged set of (possibly distorted or misleading) background ideas that every society or community possesses which forms the basis of, or significantly informs, general opinion or 'common sense', a basis that remains somewhat invisible to most of its members, appearing as 'neutral', resting on preconceptions that are largely unexamined. A consequence is that viewpoints significantly out of line with these background beliefs are intuitively seen as radical, nonsensical or extreme, no matter what may be the actual content of their vision.
2. Ideology$_2$: a set of ideas designed, or anyway intentionally employed, in order to justify, preserve, reinforce, develop or transform some existing state of affairs, where the intended outcome is preferred for any of a number of reasons, perhaps because it facilitates or legitimates various advantages for some dominant or privileged or even some disadvantaged group, and where these ideas mostly work in the manner described by way of intentionally masking or misrepresenting the nature of reality or what is actually taking place.

Whether or not these two conceptions are sufficiently comprehensive with regard to the literature on ideology in general, as far I can discern they do cover the interpretations found in the economics literature (and are clearly apparent in the contributions of those who emphasise my apparent neglect of the role of ideology in modern economics). They also cover the viewpoints of many that never mention the term *ideology*. I should note, though, that those who adopt such positions, including those who explicitly emphasise ideology, frequently refer to (what I am calling) modern mainstream economics as neoclassical. The latter is again a term I rarely use, though I take it for the purposes of the current chapter that both expressions are intended to refer to the same project, even if there is disagreement as to its nature.[4]

The ideology theorists

The version of the first conception of ideology that regularly figures in heterodox accounts of the failures of modern economic theory is as follows. Many academic economists continually act upon, but fail seriously to think about, challenge or treat as other than given, a set of background intuitions/ideas of efficiently functioning markets, or of the optimality of the capitalist system, or of the status quo, or the validity of certain traditional ways of maintaining the latter, or some such. It is these intuitions/ideas that constitute the content of the ideology in question. Mainstream theories, it is held, are grounded in such intuitions, and it is just because such intuitions are inadequate to real-world processes, but so unquestioningly and almost unthinkingly maintained, that economics goes so wrong.

The version of the second conception of ideology that also regularly figures in purported explanations of the failures of modern economic theory is the following. Mainstream economists are agents (rather than subjects) of ideology, adopting notions of efficiently functioning markets that are knowingly unrealistic but used for purposes of sustaining the basic underlying economic (capitalist or competitive market) system or status quo, albeit perhaps facilitating a modifying of features of it here and there in ways that serve certain vested interests. Thus, the failings of the modern discipline are held to be explained just by this desire of mainstream economists to maintain/achieve a preferred economic state of affairs using theories that are knowingly inappropriate to the world as it actually is.

These two contentions, though connected, are clearly not identical. In the first case, mainstream economists are viewed as the hapless dupes of the prevailing ideology. In the second case, these same economists are viewed as knowingly and indeed conspiratorially providing, maintaining and promoting the ideology. In both cases, though, the ideology is grounded in a conception of advantageous market competition or of an efficiently functioning beneficent capitalist economic system, or something similar at the system level. Let me briefly give examples of each interpretation.

Ideology$_1$

A version of the former mainstream-as-manifestation-of-background-ideology interpretation is advanced by, for example, Bernard Guerrien (2004). Criticising my own contributions in particular, Guerrien writes:

> I am only going to consider Lawson's main criticism of neoclassical economics: its 'lack of *realism*'. I think that it is not the appropriate objection: *all* theories lack realism, as they take into consideration only some aspects of reality. Everyone agrees on this, even neoclassical economists. The real problem with neoclassical theory is not its 'lack of *realism*' but the 'ideology' (a word Lawson never uses) that it smuggles in and carries with it.

Having suggested that the real problem is not a lack of realism or (a better term) realisticness, Guerrien proceeds by agreeing that a lack of realisticness nevertheless is a problem, albeit, he supposes, mostly one that lies in the mainstream formulation of structure rather than its accounts of human agency. Guerrien understandably finds the formulations that abound to be somewhat absurd; in fact, he goes as far as to talk of 'irrelevant' and 'stupid' models. His main concern, though, is not with the lack of realisticness *per se* but with the extreme nature of it; with why anyone – and specifically intelligent academics – would choose to reproduce and study constructions that can only be regarded as 'stupid':

> The question is [...]: how such intelligent people can propose – and endlessly study – such *stupid* models?

Guerrien answers his own question as follows:

> I only see one reason for that: *ideology* (intuitive beliefs which render them blind).

This is Guerrien's only elaboration of his understanding of the term. But it does suggest that Guerrien means something like a certain set of beliefs held by the community that is so intuitive in its appeal that its holders rarely reflect upon them and are mostly blinded to the possibility that the beliefs in question might be wrong or even open to valid criticism.[5]

What is this set of intuitive beliefs that Guerrien has in mind? Following his brief outline of what he means by ideology, Guerrien writes:

> Here, the belief alluded to is that 'market mechanisms' [...] produce 'efficient' results – if you abstract from 'frictions', 'failures', etc. (ignoring these 'imperfections' being, for neoclassical theorists, the principal reason of 'lack of realism'). As there is a strong link between competitive equilibrium (that is, with auctioneer, etc.) and efficient states – link given by the two Welfare Theorems – then competitive equilibrium *must be* identified with 'perfect market' (as both are supposed to be efficient). In some books (especially those on growth, in the 'macro' mood – as those of Romer and Barro and Sala-I-Martin), perfect competition and an 'omniscient' 'representative agent' (or planner) choice are presented as giving the same results. How can a normal person make any sense of this?

Guerrien's answer to the question posed in the last sentence, in effect, is that we make sense of this by seeing mainstream economists as essentially cultural or economic dupes, unable to rise sufficiently above or beyond the prevailing ideology of their times.

Ideology$_2$

A rather more conspiratorial view of mainstream theory as itself a form of ideology is perhaps more common. A colourful statement of it is provided by Rajani Kanth (1999). Kanth, indeed, is quite explicit in the view that (mainstream) 'economics is the ruling ideology of the capitalist system' (p. 191). Writing of (mainstream or 'neoclassical') economics as 'this crown jewel of capitalist ideology' (p. 191), of 'the inherent charlatanism of economic ideology' (p. 189), and so forth, Kanth elaborates as follows:

> To state the moral: *the entire enterprise of neo-classical economics is rigged to show that laissez-faire produces optimal outcomes*, but for the disruptive operation of the odd externality (a belated correction) here and there.
>
> *(Kanth, 1999, pp. 191–2, emphasis in the original)*

How is this rigging achieved? One component of the strategy is everywhere to stipulate that human beings are rational (meaning optimising) atomistic individuals. A second is the construction of theoretical set-ups or models specified to ensure that (typically unique) optimal outcomes are attainable.

There are indeed very many economists who do adopt the individualist framework and assumption that individual behaviour is optimal (in the sense of always deriving from optimising decisions in conditions where optimal outcomes are to be had). Perhaps most do. But this is not yet enough to show that the overall economic system is itself optimal in any way. If the claim is that mainstream economists seek to defend the economic system *per* se, something more is required to guarantee the result that the system is in a sense 'optimal'. This, it is supposed, is achieved by the commonplace construction of an equilibrium framework, the latter being so specified that the actions of isolated optimising individuals somehow (tend to) work to bring about an equilibrium position. Thus Kanth, for example, refers to the 'economic science of capitalism' as:

> simply *irrelevant* for being a fantasy world of an ideal rational, capitalism where all motions are mutually equilibriating, in a Newtonian co-ordination of the elements.
>
> *(Kanth, 1999, p. 194)*

In sum, two competing interpretations of the nature of ideology and how it connects to the mainstream tradition of modern economics can be found. The first supposes that mainstream economics is the more or less unrecognised product of ideology, the second sees mainstream economics itself as an ideology knowingly concerned with promoting deception.

If the two interpretations radically underpin accounts of the motivations of mainstream economists, the two sets of explanations supported do, to repeat, have something significant in common. They both characterise the mainstream project as primarily concerned with producing theories that express capitalism as, in its basics, an efficiently functioning, or otherwise desirable or optimal, system. Thus, according to both sets of accounts, the lack of realisticness and so forth of mainstream economics arises just through that project's portrayal of the economic system, in its fundamentals at least, as somehow advantageous to all, a portrayal that is regarded as being inconsistent with the way the real world really is.

In this manner the two interpretations ultimately provide somewhat similar explanations of the enduring failings of the modern mainstream, even if their accounts of the intentions of economists and the way in which ideology impacts are quite different.

An assessment of the political–economic ideology explanations

My own view is that neither of these explanations of the state of modern economics – explanations that dominate current heterodox thinking – is sustainable. Remember, the phenomenon before us is the generalised explanatory failure and lack of realisticness of formulations across the totality of the mainstream (macro, micro and econometric) output over a large number of years (again see, for example, Lawson, 2003, Chapter 1).

It is one thing to suggest that mainstream economists mostly suppose that capitalism, or a market-centred system, is somehow natural or normal or the best that can be achieved, but it is quite another thing to suppose that much of the output of these economists is even mainly concerned with such issues of political economy. In truth, the social system that is capitalism is, *qua* social system, barely ever even considered.

Moreover, in those cases where economists do focus on questions of market or competitive equilibrium, etc., the formulators of the models in question are often careful to stress that their theorising has little connection with the real world anyway and should not be used to draw conclusions about the latter, whether in terms of efficiency or for policy or whatever. Thus, Frank Hahn, a major contributor in this field, writes:

> It cannot be denied that there is something scandalous in the spectacle of so many people refining the analyses of economic [equilibrium] states which they give no reason to suppose will ever, or have ever, come about. It probably is also dangerous. Equilibrium economics [...] is easily convertible into an apologia for existing economic arrangements and it is frequently so converted.
>
> *(Hahn, 1970, pp. 88–9)*

Elsewhere, Hahn reveals in rather dramatic fashion what he feels should happen if people contemplate using such models for policy:

> When policy conclusions are drawn from such models, it is time to reach for one's gun.
>
> *(Hahn, 1982, p. 29)*

In fact, in those cases where mainstream assumptions and categories are couched in terms of economic systems as a whole, they are mainly designed to achieve consistency at the level of modelling rather than coherence with the world in which we live.

This concern for a notion of consistency in modelling practice is true, for example, of the recently fashionable rational expectations hypothesis, originally formulated by John Muth (1961) and widely employed by those who focus on system-level outcomes. The hypothesis proposes that predictions attributed to agents (being theorised about) are treated as being essentially the same as (consistent with) those generated by the economic model within which the same agents are theorised. As such the proposal is clearly no more than a technique for (consistency in) modelling, albeit a bizarre one. Significantly, any assertion that the expectations held (and so the model in which they are imposed) are essentially correct is a step that is *additional* to assuming rational expectations.

It is a form of modelling consistency (albeit a different one) that underpins the notion of equilibrium itself. In modern mainstream economics the category equilibrium has nothing to do with the features of the real economy (say, with the balance of supply and demand – see, for example, Lawson, 2005, 2006). Economic models often comprise not single but sets of equations, each of which is notoriously found to have little relation to what happens in the real world. One question that nevertheless keeps economists occupied with such unrealistic models is whether the equations formulated are mutually consistent in the sense that there 'exists' a vector of values of some variable, say one labelled 'prices', that is consistent with *each and all* of the equations. Such a model 'solution' is precisely the meaning of equilibrium in this context. As such, the notion is not at all a claim about the world but merely a (possible) property that a set of equations may or may not be found to possess.

The mainstream economist Huw Dixon gets it right when he summarises matters as follows: 'At its most general, we can say that "equilibrium" is a method of solving economic models. At a superficial level, an equilibrium is simply a solution to a set of equations' (Dixon, 1990, p. 356). In short, when mainstream economists question whether an equilibrium 'exists', they merely enquire as to whether a set of equations has a solution.

More to the point, however, the substantive content of mainstream theorising is far wider and more dynamic than a fixed focus on market mechanisms or on conceptions of competitive equilibrium and claims that the market mechanisms lead to efficiency, and such like.

In fact, most mainstream economists, as I say, have never concerned themselves much with the workings of the economic system as a whole (whether via an equilibrium framework or otherwise). Rather, the dominant concern has been, and remains, with specific or partial analyses of some highly restricted sectors or forms of behaviour. Very often the focus is on 'micro' decision making or 'behaviour'. Even (or perhaps especially) here, though, the contributions have more or less always been unrealistic and have rarely, if ever, generated (as opposed to imported) insight.

To the extent that it has ever been meaningful for the various disparate results or theorems of these economists to be considered as a whole, the clearest conclusion that can be drawn is that they are mostly wildly inconsistent with each other. So long as the assumptions are tractable, mainstream theorists are free to posit anything they want, no matter how unrealistic. Competing hypotheses abound, even by the same contributors in different contributions.

If we focus on empirical contributions specifically, it is clear that there are few attempts to repeat the results of others, progress the results of others, or even acknowledge the results of others. Even econometricians using identical, or almost identical, data sets are regularly found to produce quite contrasting conclusions, usually with little attempt at explanation. The systematic result here, as the econometrician Edward Leamer (1983) observes, is that, in the academy at least, 'hardly anyone takes anyone else's data analysis seriously' (p. 37).

Furthermore, far from being a conspiracy or a uniformly misled project, there is little agreement among mainstream economists even as to the project's purpose or direction. As one of its leading practitioners, Ariel Rubinstein, acknowledged more than a decade ago:

> The issue of interpreting economic theory is [...] the most serious problem now facing economic theorists. The feeling among many of us can be summarized as follows. Economic theory should deal with the real world. It is not a branch of abstract mathematics even though it utilises mathematical tools. Since it is about the real world, people expect the theory to prove useful in achieving practical goals. But economic theory has not delivered the goods. Predictions from economic theory are not nearly as accurate as those by the natural sciences, and the link between economic theory and practical problems [...] is tenuous at best. Economic theory lacks a consensus as to its purpose and interpretation. Again and again, we find ourselves asking the question 'where does it lead?'
>
> *(Rubinstein, 1995, p. 12)*

In short, the modern mainstream is not a project whose emphases and explanatory failures are mainly direct manifestations either of intentions to maintain attachment to the existing economic system or of a blindness to its real nature. At the level of substantive theory, there is far more heterogeneity within mainstream theorising than Guerrien, Kanth and others allow, with relatively little attention focused on the economic system as a whole, let alone given over to the theorising of its optimality.

Indeed, at the level of substantive theory the project is marked by overall incoherence and lack of cohesion among its various strands, and by significant uncertainty even as to what is worth pursuing.

The one (and as far as I can see only) feature that has persistently and comprehensively marked all mainstream contributions, and continues to dominate, is the insistence that methods of mathematical modelling always be employed. Significantly, this emphasis is by itself sufficient to explain the mainstream deficiencies at all levels, including that of economic content. Specifically, and unlike explanations that seek to make ideology at the level of economic content the central factor, explanations in terms of the misplaced emphasis on mathematical modelling can account for mainstream inadequacies, whether couched in terms of explanatory failure, unrealistic formulations, or the project's lack of direction; whether the economic focus is the system as a whole or very partial 'micro' situations; whether the modellers are or are not supporters of the status quo; whether or not data are employed; whatever the substance of the latest fad and fashion to preoccupy; and so on. In consequence, I see little reason in all of this to reject yet the assessment that the misplaced emphasis on mathematical deductivist reasoning provides the better (and indeed only adequate) explanation of the rather unhappy state of modern economics.

An alternative conception of ideology in the economics academy

I have considered the two conceptions of ideology that are most often associated with modern academic economists and I have argued that, in the political–economy garb in which these ideologies are usually presented by opponents of the mainstream, they do not serve easily to account for the explanatory failings of the discipline.

However, in so concluding I must stress that it by no means follows that I suppose either that ideology is entirely absent from the modern economics academy, and specifically mainstream economics, or that questions of ideology have no bearing on the latter project's lack of explanatory power. Indeed, I am of the definite view that ideology is rife and with significant consequences for mainstream explanatory performance. There are various issues to consider though.

First and foremost, I want to indicate briefly an alternative ideology, a version of ideology$_1$ (a set of background views manifest unquestioningly as if normal or neutral) that I believe does pervade the economics academy, one that is extremely widespread and indeed plays a significant contributory role in the failings of the discipline. But this is a set of beliefs that does not bear directly upon the nature of the underlying economic system at all. Rather, it is precisely the doctrine that all serious economics must take the form of mathematical modelling.

This ideology, as I am suggesting it to be, usually involves a presumption of an event-regularity-seeking (and so prediction-oriented) conception of science along with the complementary belief that mathematics is closely aligned with, and indeed essential to, such a science.

I must stress that the contention I am advancing here is not an arbitrary add-on adopted just because the focus of discussion is ideology. If I am right that the problems of modern economics stem first and foremost from the misplaced attachment to mathematical reasoning despite the record of failure so far, there must be a reason for this emphasis. That reason, I want to suggest, is, in large part at least, the unquestioning, uncritical, taken-on-trust-as-normal, blinkered orientation to employing mathematical techniques characteristic of most of those who pursue it. It is blindness to, or an unreasoned dismissive resistance to any suggestion of, any alternative to the idea that wielding mathematical techniques is both essential to science and compulsory if economics is to make a proper contribution. Such a stance amounts precisely to a system of beliefs that is itself a form of ideology (ideology$_1$).

Let me emphasise that I am quite aware that there are forms of mathematical systems, methods and techniques beyond those currently and/or traditionally prosecuted by economists. Deductivist forms, presupposing closures of the sort defined above, just happen to be those that economists (so far) find easiest to wield or otherwise most convenient. I do not argue that all forms of mathematical method (including those yet to be invented) must necessarily be inappropriate to social analysis – though I strongly doubt that any will ever prove of general use for addressing/illuminating the sort of capitalist social system in which we currently live. But this is not the issue. My point, rather, is that far from even contemplating, let alone exploring, alternative non-mathematical approaches – where various available alternatives are easily shown to be relevant to, and fruitful for, illuminating the real social system (for illustrations see, for example, Lawson, 2009a; 2003, Chapter 4; 1997, Chapter 18) – modern mainstream economists continually seek out mathematical techniques of some kind. It is, to repeat, this unwillingness or apparent inability to contemplate the idea that a serious, fruitful and explanatorily successful (science) of economics might be developed that does not rely upon the application of mathematical methods and techniques of some form that indicates the dominant form of the actually prevalent ideology.

Ideology in action

It can be easily seen that the unquestioned emphasis on mathematical modelling is indeed a form of ideological blindness if a brief examination is made of cases where, for whatever reason, mainstream economists, whether in the form of a few critical contributors or as a collective body, have come to critically address the explanatory failings of their project. For it is evident that the one feature that is almost never addressed in such endeavour is precisely the emphasis on the employment of mathematical techniques. Even in the very few cases where mainstream contributors recognise or acknowledge that criticisms of the mathematical modelling emphasis have been made from outside their project, the latter criticisms tend to be summarily dismissed either without serious consideration, or at most with some vague referencing, of alternative, more appropriate mathematical techniques yet to be developed.

Let me first briefly consider examples of the latter, cases where the issue of the mathematical emphasis itself is at least broached in published mainstream commentaries. Among the very few examples I can find are those by the 'theorists' Alan Kirman and Frank Hahn, surely among the most open-minded and reflective of mainstream economists. However, even in such cases, any notion that the mathematical emphasis might be the problem is quickly dismissed rather than seriously entertained.

Kirman, for example, in critically examining the nature and poor performance of mainstream theorising, focuses on the individualist emphasis of the enterprise. But in suggesting alternative ways for the mainstream to proceed it is clear that he regards methods of mathematical modelling *per se* as effectively indispensable. Thus, he writes:

> The argument that the root of the problem [...] [is] that we are confined by a mathematical strait jacket which allows us no escape, does not seem very persuasive. That the mathematical frameworks that we have used made the task of changing or at least modifying our paradigm hard, is undeniable but it is difficult to believe that had a clear well-formulated new approach been suggested then we would not have adopted the appropriate mathematical tools.
>
> *(Kirman, 1989, p. 137)*

I noted above that Frank Hahn does not hesitate to acknowledge that equilibrium theory tells us little about economic reality, and he is especially ill-disposed towards those who would seek to use mainstream models to draw policy conclusions or as a guide to practical action. But the idea that mathematics might be dispensable to economic thinking, or anyway overly emphasised, or commanding too high a proportion of the resources available for economic research, is not afforded serious reflection. On the contrary, he dismisses any suggestion that the modern emphasis on mathematical modelling may be misplaced as 'a view surely not worth discussing' (Hahn, 1985, p. 18). In a major speech to the Royal Economic Society he even counsels that we 'avoid discussions of "mathematics in economics" like the plague' (Hahn, 1992a; see also Hahn, 1992b).

If mainstream economists tend to be blind to, or ignore, or at best dismiss, external critiques of the mathematical emphasis, how do they react in situations where they at least acknowledge explanatory failure? The ongoing economic crisis perhaps provides a unique insight to this. Recently, possibly the largest numbers of mainstream self-critics ever have been driven to reassess their own practices as a result of the ongoing economic crisis and widespread suspicion of, and concern for, if not outright condemnation of, academic economic output. Notably, even among mainstream economists there have been increased calls for change and numerous claims advanced that changes have indeed been, or are being, made. The situation thus affords an unusual opportunity to assess which parts of academic economic practice are most readily regarded as open to transformation and which are treated, consciously or subconsciously, as beyond, or anyway not in need of, critique.

A useful concentration or grouping of this unusually large set of mainstream critical reflections on the nature of modern academic economics is provided by the various contributions to the inaugural (2010) conference (held in King's College, Cambridge) of the Institute for New Economic Thinking (INET), an organisation set up precisely to transform economics in the light of the failings of the economics discipline to provide much understanding of the crisis.

Many economists attended the conference, all apparently concerned critically to reconsider the nature of academic economics. It is in such a forum if anywhere that we might hope to find mainstream economists challenging all but the most obviously acceptable aspects of their theories, approaches and activities.

Although George Soros, who sponsors the Institute, shows some awareness that the reliance upon mathematics may at least be something to question (see, for example, Soros, 2009; Lawson, 2013b), for most of his close associates the idea that there might be something problematic about the emphasis on forms of mathematical technique does not appear even to cross their minds (all the numerous contributions are posted on the INET website or can be found on Youtube).[6]

Consider, for example, the presentation by Joseph Stiglitz (2010[7]), a central contributor associated with the Institute. Stiglitz quickly focuses on the failure of most models to predict the crisis, he emphasises the need for predictive accuracy, then he proposes a strategy of experimenting with different model assumptions, most of which are accepted as unrealistic, in order to come up with a best model in terms of forecast accuracy. Or rather, Stiglitz makes reference to a 'standard model' and declares that the critical question for 'research strategy' is to decide which of the model's 'many unrealistic assumptions' we 'want to drop'. Indeed, emphasising the need for pluralism, Stiglitz suggests that we 'investigate a number of different models where different assumptions are dropped'. Stiglitz stresses that, in his view, dynamic models and stochastic models and general equilibrium models remain important for economics, even if it is necessary to revise some of their specifications. His overall preference is seemingly for analytic models or more complex stochastic models that can, at least in principle, accommodate human interactions (though other preferences for model specifications are listed).

Of relevance here is that, in all this, Stiglitz is seemingly open to entertaining an array of different modelling assumptions (albeit mostly unrealistic ones) and so is also open, to a degree, to policy stances and so forth that might be adopted. The one issue that is not even hinted at, however, is that we might also question the very emphasis on mathematical modelling itself. Indeed, the discussion throughout his presentation is only and continually about how economists should go about finding 'better' mathematical models. This uncritical stance typifies the presentations made throughout the conference, as recorded on INET's website.

Of course, mainstream economists like Stiglitz rarely explore in a sustained, serious or systematic way the issues of philosophy/methodology on which they sometimes pronounce (and perhaps they have little opportunity to do so). But the same reaction to the crisis is found even by methodologists of the mainstream who might be expected to look deeper and further. Thus, in an influential paper entitled 'The financial crisis and the systemic failure of academic economics',

Colander *et al.* (2008) offer an assessment that again questions anything and everything except the emphasis on formalistic mathematical modelling (see Lawson, 2009b, 2009c).

Heterodoxy and mathematical modelling

In fact, so apparently compelling is the belief system in question (that mathematical modelling is the proper way to do economics) that many heterodox economists too seemingly fall under its sway. Although heterodox modellers do not follow the mainstream in dogmatically insisting that we all everywhere adopt a mathematical orientation, it remains the case that many heterodox economists fail to recognise that the conceptions they find to be inadequate in mainstream theory owe something to the mainstream modelling emphasis, and these heterodox economists continue excessively (and often exclusively) to explore alternative mathematical models and forms of mathematical reasoning in the face of explanatory failures and unrealistic formulations.

The heterodox *Real-World Economics Review* has even seen fit to create a Revere Award for Economics, given in large part for success in predicting the global financial collapse, a move that may well further encourage the uncritical reliance on formalistic models and the predictive criterion of success. While that journal and its associated blog carry articles and comments that critically focus on the use of mathematics in economics, the dominant emphasis seems to be on the exploration of novel, or currently non-standard, forms of mathematical technique.

Of course, I do not wish to (and indeed do not – see, for example, Fullbrook, 2009, especially Chapter 12) discourage all experimentation with mathematical models and methods in all contexts, and certainly cannot insist that the use of methods of mathematical modelling must always be devoid of insight, even if the arguments I have laid out lead me to believe that the current emphasis is largely wasteful of resources (again see Lawson, 1997, 2003). My point, rather, is that the reliance on mathematical modelling, and on criteria such as predictive accuracy, goes almost unquestioned throughout much of the economics academy, certainly within the mainstream, and sometimes even beyond. This is so despite the unrealistic concoctions that so far have almost always resulted from this endeavour, along with the severe limitation of explanatory insight generated by (as opposed to being tagged on to) such activities. And it is so despite the ongoing crises leading economists of all persuasions to critically reflect upon the now-all-too-apparent failings of the academic discipline. All such features I suggest are strongly supportive of the contention that the belief/conviction that 'the only proper economics is a mathematical economics' is a prevailing form of ideology.

Explaining the ideology of mathematical technique in modern economics

If I am right about all this then the ideology I am identifying itself requires an explanation. This is easy enough to provide. But notice first that a feature (I believe it to be a strength) of the explanation of the state of modern economics that I am advancing is that I do not need to invoke a conspiratorial view of ideology (ideology$_2$) and specifically I do not at all view the mainstream as a body of dishonest individuals setting out to pull the wool over anyone's eyes.

Nor, of course, do Guerrien and others who also emphasise the first interpretation of ideology (ideology$_1$), but who suppose that mainstream economists are 'blind' to the unrealisticness of their presumption that the political economic system is an efficiently functioning one. But unlike these contributors I also do not need to suppose that mainstream economists or anyone else continue to be blind to the increasingly all-too-apparent crisis-ridden state of capitalist economies.

Still, I need to give some reason why mainstream economists may indeed be blind to the possibility that their methods of mathematical modelling are inappropriate to social analysis.

A large part of the explanation, I suggest, is simply that mathematics has been so successful in the history of human endeavour, and especially within (non-social) natural science, that its centrality to all science and serious and systematic investigation is taken as an article of faith throughout wide sections of society. Certainly a perception that all serious research requires a mathematical form, especially where measurable quantities are involved, has been widely in evidence since the Enlightenment. Economics is, more than any other social discipline, commonly interpreted as being concerned with measurable quantities (quantity of money, prices, output[8]). As such, it is not surprising to find many economists both supposing that forms of mathematics are essential to economic science and optimistic that economics can equally achieve significant mathematical successes eventually.

Thus, while Guerrien posits a blindness of mainstream 'intelligent' contributors even when he regards the content of their models as so obviously 'stupid', I posit a blindness only in a situation where it may be understandably difficult for many to see clearly. With the neglect of ontological reasoning, recognition that the current emphasis on formal mathematical modelling in economics is misguided is not so obvious. This is especially the case in the light of the just noted and often emphasised post-Enlightenment historical record of mathematical success throughout the various disciplines.

In fact, an acceptance of the idea that mathematics is essential to grounded knowledge has been a factor in sections of popular culture for rather longer even than the post-Enlightenment period. In the interests of brevity, let me recall how Morris Kline sums up the introduction to his majestic *Mathematics in Western Culture*:

> In this book we shall survey mathematics primarily to show how its ideas have helped to mould twentieth-century life and thought. The ideas will be in historical order so that our material will range from the beginnings in Babylonia and Egypt to the modern theory of relativity. Some people may question the pertinence of material belonging to earlier historical periods. Modern culture, however, is the accumulation and synthesis of contributions made by many preceding civilisations. The Greeks, who first appreciated the power of

> mathematical reasoning, graciously allowing the gods to use it in designing the universe, and then urging man to uncover the pattern of this design, not only gave mathematics a major place in their civilisation but initiated patterns of thought that are basic in our own. As succeeding civilisations passed on their gifts to modern times, they handed on new and increasingly more significant roles for mathematics. Many of these functions and influences of mathematics are now deeply imbedded in our culture.
>
> *(Kline, 1964)*

The influence of mathematics is now so deeply ingrained within our culture that many people appear to suppose that anything stated in mathematics must be correct, while for things to be correct, reliable, insightful or scientific (or at least conferring of scientific status), they must be stated in mathematics.[9] For so many people it seems to be simply an unquestionable matter of faith that if a field of study is to be scientific or accorded status as a knowledge-producing activity, or otherwise regarded as serious, it must take a mathematical form.

Of course, the Enlightenment gave an important boost to this long-in-evidence perception. In fact, ever since Newton succeeded in uniting heaven and earth in equations, and Kant announced that the study of social phenomena requires its own Newton, the programme of mathematising economics has been under way (see Lawson, 2003, Chapter 10).

Interestingly, John Henry (1997) observes that following the publication of Newton's *Principia*, readers 'took for granted the validity of mathematics for understanding the working of the world'. He stresses that 'although his book met with some fierce criticism, not a murmur was raised against it in [...] regard [to its emphasis on mathematical reasoning]' (p. 21).

Actually, from the point of view of understanding the acceptance of the emphasis on mathematisation as ideology, even more interesting is a critical response to Henry provided by Yves Gingras (2001) in his wide-ranging commentary on the history of mathematics. Addressing Henry's assessment that 'murmurs' of dissent against the mathematical formalism were absent from *Principia*, Gingras writes:

> As we will see, this was far from being the case but to recover these murmurs, one must look at actors who are now unknown precisely because they rejected the mathematization of physics and were thus excluded from the field (and its history) as it evolved in the eighteenth and nineteenth centuries.
>
> *(Gingras, 2001, p. 385)*

The point, then, is that a belief that mathematics is central to all science and serious study is a widespread cultural norm of long standing, one that emerged in the face of, and has been continually reinforced through, successes with mathematics throughout the disciplines. If the successes of mathematics have grounded a society-wide cultural belief in the general relevance of, and indeed need for, mathematics for scientific and all serious study, it is not surprising that economists enamoured of the idea of pursuing a serious and scientific economics have too fallen under its sway.

So, in sum, my contention is that the modelling emphasis of modern mainstream economics is explained by a largely unquestioning, society-wide conviction (a form of ideology$_1$) that mathematics is fundamental to all science, a conviction or ideology that itself is in large part explained by the successes of mathematics in so many other domains.

The modern mainstream and the economic system

I have argued that the malaise of modern economics is not primarily due to ideology at the level of substantive political economy. I have also argued that ideology is present in the economics academy nonetheless, albeit at the level of methodology. Finally, I want to stress that in maintaining these views I do not at all suppose there is no relation between the mainstream stance (that is, the insistence that mathematical techniques be everywhere employed) and the underlying economic system. Specifically, and despite the foregoing discussion, I do not at all deny that the mainstream practices can serve the purposes of sustaining the workings of the economic system. But let me be clear on how I think the two relate.

First, I do not doubt that political–economic and cultural ideological factors in the sense of prevailing background beliefs (ideology$_1$) are in play in all societies or communities, and are manifest in the contributions and practices of us all. We are all situated in and products of our time, place and culture, etc. Such background ideology of this sort bears on the kinds of questions we ask, the orientations we adopt, the assumptions, including absences, we take for granted, the states of affairs we regard as 'normal', and so on. However, I do not think the very real ideological beliefs that prevail regarding the benefits or 'normality' of the existing political–economy system are primarily or even significantly responsible for the perpetual failings and acknowledged fictions of contemporary academic economics. This is just to repeat the foregoing. Most economists as academic researchers do not even seem interested in the economy as such anyway. Far more important is their prowess in manipulating mathematical models and such like. The dominant ideology in the economics academy, I am maintaining, is precisely the extraordinarily widespread and long-lasting belief that mathematical modelling is somehow neutral at the level of content or form, but an essential method for science, underpinning any proper or serious economics.

Second, and following on from the above, the scandal of modern economics is not that it gets so many things wrong but that it is so largely irrelevant. However, in being irrelevant, and yet using significant resources that could have been used for research into the way the economy really works, then, at a time that the economy is in crisis and proving largely dysfunctional, the mainstream modelling orientation cannot but serve to deflect criticism from the nature of the status quo at the level of the economy and thereby work to sustain it (and would do so whatever that status quo happened to be). As Leamer (already noted above) observes, no one in the academy takes anyone else's data analysis seriously. In truth, few take any mainstream analyses seriously, except in economics faculties' promotion exercises.[10]

Third, if, however, anyone were to pay much attention to mainstream analysis, it would serve to sustain, if not reinforce, the status quo in an additional way. The point here is that the emphasis on event regularities (necessitated by a reliance on forms of mathematical modelling), and so attachment to an implicit ontology of closure and atomism, entails that any references to social relationality, and so to (relational) issues of power, discrimination, domination, oppression and conflict generally, are effectively masked over or hidden, or at best trivialised. For the framework is ill equipped even to allow such categories to be seriously considered. Thus the very emphasis on mathematical modelling renders analyses of real conflict, power relations and social transformation effectively if inadvertently precluded.

The persistence of mathematical reasoning

I am accepting, then, that although the generalised malaise of modern economics does not reflect any ideological attachment to specific economic theories, the persistent irrelevance of academic mainstream economics, resulting from the emphasis on formal modelling, is nonetheless inhibiting of analysis capable of constituting meaningful constructive criticism of existing political–economic states of affairs. Moreover, this consequence – which, I stress, I take to be largely unintended – does, I believe, contribute to explaining how the mathematical project persists in maintaining institutional power in the face of, and despite, its repeated failures and fictitious constructions. For government-sponsored funding bodies and the like are actually less likely to withdraw funds from a project that provides no serious criticism of the government's actions.

Parenthetically, I believe this inability of the mathematical modelling project to challenge anything seriously or convincingly is a major factor in understanding how the project has survived as long as it has in the economics academy, and even how it originally came to dominate. Elsewhere, I address at length the reasons for the rise and persistence of a mainstream tradition that so clearly lacks a history of explanatory successes (see especially Chapter 10 of Lawson, 2003).

I stress once more, however, that in all this I am not suggesting that those who contribute to the mathematising project in economics do so, in the main, opportunistically. Rather, I merely point out that whatever its advocates' intentions, the mainstream project (with its emphasis on mathematical deductivist modelling and lack of criticality) may appear – and at times has indeed proven to be (see Lawson, 2003, Chapter 10) – conducive to those, especially outside the academy, seeking, for whatever reason, to deflect or minimise intellectual challenges to the underlying economic system. As such, this mathematical project, itself underpinned by methodological ideology, and not formulated by those pushing, or duped by, a political–economy ideology, might nevertheless be said to contribute ultimately to sustaining the status quo.

Conclusion

My contention, in short, is that contemporary academic mainstream economics is indeed often underpinned by ideology. But this ideology is first of all methodological in nature, being in effect the widespread cultural view that mathematics is essential to science. Incidentally, I argue elsewhere not only that this ideology covers a false view in that successful natural science does not actually rest on the application of mathematics, but also that a non-mathematical economics can actually yet be a science in the sense of the successful natural sciences (see Lawson, 1997, 2003 and especially 2012).

I have suggested, too, that a possible, and indeed likely, reason the mathematical emphasis of the mainstream project does not come under more critical scrutiny from outside the academy is that the project's continuing irrelevance actually renders it harmless to political defenders of any prevailing status quo who might otherwise be drawn to more critical considerations in connection with funding and the like.

Although I have attempted here to explain the continuing misplaced emphasis on techniques of mathematical modelling in the economics academy, I might add that I do not suggest that there are not yet factors at play additional to those I have identified. Among other things, the longish recent history of mainstream perseverance with the deductivist modelling techniques in the face of repeated failure has suggested to some that there may also be something pathological to what is going on, and that a psychological explanation is likely also of some relevance. Also, the pattern of behaviour in question seems to be gendered, with the mathematical modelling and prediction activities being relentlessly pursued largely by those gendered as men. This, too, seems to warrant explanation (again see Lawson, 2003, Chapter 10). These are issues that are receiving attention elsewhere and in illuminating ways.[11] But that is another story, as they say.

For now it does seem safe to conclude that the primary explanation of the numerous, long-lived and continuing failings of modern academic economics is the (misplaced) emphasis on mathematical modelling. It is an emphasis underpinned by the cultural belief that a reliance on mathematical technique in science is somehow so normal or neutral or natural that any questioning of this emphasis can be ignored or swiftly dismissed as obviously far too radical or nonsensical for serious consideration.

Notes

1 The writing of this chapter has benefited from the financial support of the Independent Social Research Foundation. For helpful comments on some or other draft of the chapter I am grateful to Jānis Bērziņš, Frederico Botafogo, Thomas Bowen, Dick Burkhart, Lynne Chester, Donald Gillies, Egmont Kakarot-Handtke, Roy Langston, Bruce Littleboy, Jamie Morgan, Petter Næss, Leigh Price and Patrick Spread.

2 Brian O'Boyle and Terrence McDonough (2011), for example, suggest that a 'lack of an ideological-critique is perhaps the most glaring lacunae for the Lawsonian project, in light of its own philosophical project of critiquing mainstream economics'. They add that 'the Lawsonian project is unable (or unwilling) to entertain the possibility of an ideological function for mainstream economics' and, worse, that 'to follow Lawson in his particular critique of the mainstream is to relinquish the very tools that are needed to uncover "the anatomy and ideological function of orthodoxy" or indeed its contribution to neoliberal ideology'. Other such critics include, for example, Kanth (1999) and Guerrien (2004) – see below.
3 Terry Eagleton (1991, p. 2), for example, lists the following interpretations found in the recent literature: a process of production of meanings, signs and value in social life; a body of ideas characteristic of a particular social group or class; ideas that help to legitimate a dominant political power; false ideas that help to legitimate a dominant political power; systematically distorted communication; that which offers a position for a subject; forms of thought motivated by social interests; identity thinking; socially necessary illusion; the conjuncture of discourse and power; the medium in which conscious social actors make sense of their world; action-oriented sets of beliefs; the confusion of linguistic and phenomenal reality; semiotic closure; the indispensable medium in which individuals live out their relation to a social structure; the process whereby said life is converted to a natural reality.
4 Elsewhere (Lawson, 2013a) I critically question all prominent interpretations of the term *neoclassical economics*. Though I do uncover a conception that is coherent, I nevertheless give various reasons for concluding that it is a term that is best dropped from the literature.
5 Of course, when or where most people in a community think alike about certain matters, and even 'forget' that there are alternatives to the current state of affairs, we also arrive at Antonio Gramsci's concept of *hegemony*.
6 See, for example, http://ineteconomics.org/initiatives/conferences/kings-college or www.youtube.com/watch?v=SdZgD1DCNq4.
7 See http://ineteconomics.org/video/conference-kings/agenda-reforming-economic-theory-joseph-stiglitz.
8 As early as 1871 we find Jevons writing (p. 3): 'My theory of Economics, however, is purely mathematical in character [...] To me it seems that our science must be mathematical simply because it deals with quantities.'
9 Of course, this view means turning a blind eye to (or forgetting) the clear scientific successes of the largely non-mathematical disciplines of chemistry and biology in the nineteenth century and indeed much of modern chemistry and bio-medical research (on all this and much that relates to the current chapter, see Donald Gillies, 2004).
10 Remember, my focus here is on what goes on in the academy, not how others may use economic tools to justify some goal or other.
11 See, for example, Vinca Bigo (2008).

References

Bigo, Vinca (2008), 'Explaining modern economics (as a microcosm of society)', *Cambridge Journal of Economics*, 32(4): 527–554.

Colander, David, Hans Föllmer, Armin Haas, Michael Goldberg, Katerina Juselius, Alan Kirman, Thomus Lux and Brigitte Sloth (2008), 'The financial crisis and the systemic failure of academic economics', unpublished mimeo, available at: www.debtdeflation.com/blogs/wp-content/uploads/papers/Dahlem_Report_EconCrisis021809.pdf.

Dixon, Huw (1990), 'Equilibrium and explanation', in John Creedy (ed.), *Foundations of Economic Thought*, Oxford: Basil Blackwell.

Eagleton, Terry (1991), *Ideology: An Introduction*, London: Verso.

Fullbrook, Edward (2009) *Ontology and Economics: Tony Lawson and his critics*, London and New York: Routledge.

Gillies, Donald (2004) 'Can mathematics be used successfully in economics?' in Edward Fullbrook (ed.), *A Guide to What's Wrong With Economics*, London: Anthem Press, pp. 187–197.

Gingras, Yves (2001) 'What did mathematics do to physics?' *History of Science*, xxxix: 383–416.

Guerrien, Bernard (2004) 'Irrelevance and ideology', *Post-autistic Economics Review*, 29, 6 December, article 3.

Hahn, Frank H. (1970) 'Some adjustment problems', *Econometrica*, 38, January; reprinted as pp. 1–17 in *Equilibrium and Macroeconomics*, Oxford: Basil Blackwell.

Hahn, Frank H. (1985) 'In praise of economic theory', the *1984 Jevons Memorial Fund Lecture*, London: University College.

Hahn, Frank H. (1994) 'An intellectual retrospect', *Banca Nazionale del Lavoro Quarterly Review*: 245–258.

Hahn, Frank H. (1982) *Money and Inflation*, Oxford: Basil Blackwell.

Hahn, Frank H. (1992a) 'Reflections', *Royal Economics Society Newsletter*, 77.

Hahn, Frank H. (1992b) 'Answer to Backhouse: Yes', *Royal Economic Society Newsletter*, 78: 5.

Henry, John (1997) *The Scientific Revolution and the Origins of Modern Science*, New York: Palgrave Macmillan.

Jevons, W. Stanley (1965 [1871]) *The Theory of Political Economy*, New York: Reprints of Economic Classics, Augustus M. Kelley.

Kanth, Rajani (1999) 'Against Eurocentred Epistemologies: a critique of science, realism and economics', in Steven Fleetwood (ed.), *Critical Realism in Economics: Development and debate*, London and New York: Routledge.

Kirman, Alan (1989) 'The intrinsic limits of modern economic theory: the emperor has no clothes', *Economic Journal*, 99(395): 126–139.

Kline, Morris (1964) *Mathematics in Western Culture*, Oxford: Oxford University Press.

Lawson, Tony (1997) *Economics and Reality*, London and New York: Routledge.

Lawson, Tony (2003) *Reorienting Economics*, London and New York: Routledge.

Lawson, Tony (2005) 'The (confused) state of equilibrium analysis in modern economics: an (ontological) explanation', *Journal for Post Keynesian Economics*, 27(3), Spring: 423–444.

Lawson, Tony (2006) 'Tensions in modern economics. the case of equilibrium analysis', in Valeria Mosini (ed.), *Equilibrium in Economics: Scope and Limits*, London and New York: Routledge. Reprinted in Lawson (2015).

Lawson Tony (2009a) 'Applied economics, contrast explanation and asymmetric information', *Cambridge Journal of Economics*, 33(3), May: 405–420.

Lawson, Tony (2009b) 'The current economic crisis: its nature and the course of academic economics', *Cambridge Journal of Economics*, 33(4), July: 759–788. Reprinted in Lawson (2015).

Lawson, Tony (2009c) 'Contemporary economics and the crisis', *Real-World Economics Review*, 50: 122–131. Reprinted in Lawson (2015).

Lawson, Tony (2012) 'Ontology and the study of social reality: emergence, organisation, community, power, social relations, corporations, artefacts and money', *Cambridge Journal of Economics*, 36(2), March: 345–386.

Lawson, Tony (2013a) 'What is this "school" called neoclassical economics?' *Cambridge Journal of Economics*, 37(5): 947–983. Reprinted in Lawson (2015).

Lawson, Tony (2013b) 'Soros's theory of reflexivity: a critical comment', *Revue de Philosophie Economique*, 14(1). Reprinted in Lawson (2015).

Lawson, Tony (2015) *The Nature and State of Modern Economics*, London and New York: Routledge.

Leamer, Edward E. (1978) '*Specification searches: ad hoc inferences with non-experimental data*', New York: John Wiley and Sons.

Leamer, Edward E. (1983) 'Let's take the con out of econometrics', *American Economic Review*: 73(1): 31–43.

Muth, John F. (1961) 'Rational expectations and the theory of price movements', *Econometrica*, 29(3), July: 315–335.

O'Boyle, Brian and Terrence McDonough (2011) 'Critical realism, Marxism and the critique of neoclassical economics', *Capital and Class*, 35, February: 3–22; also found at http://goliath.ecnext.com/coms2/gi_0199-14565044/Critical-realism-Marxism-and-the.html.

Rubinstein, Ariel (1995) 'John Nash: the master of economic modelling', *Scandinavian Journal of Economics*, 97(1): 9–13.

Soros, George (2009) *The Crash of 2009 and What It Means: The new paradigm for financial markets*, New York: Public Affairs.

Stiglitz, Joseph (2010) *An Agenda for Reforming Economic Theory*, presentation at 2010 INET Conference at King's College, Cambridge. See http://ineteconomics.org/video/conference-kings/agenda-reforming-economic-theory-joseph-stiglitz.

3

THE ECONOMICS OF RESEARCH

The contribution of critical realism

David Tyfield

Introduction

The capitalist 'global economy' continues to hobble along, especially in the global North, which remains racked by recurrent crisis (financial, debt, fiscal). Nevertheless, the crisis of mainstream economics – which spectacularly failed to foresee the looming problems – may yet prove to be a major opportunity for the heterodox political economy. Unfortunately, to date, an alternative economics remains embryonic at best (e.g. Chakrabortty 2012), despite the slew of books critiquing mainstream economics and the invigoration of economic debate, as in the surge of economic blogs, websites and listserve emails (*The Economist* 2011).

There are at least two elements to this challenge to mainstream economics. First, there is a political challenge. The multiple, overlapping crises – at least a 'triple crisis' of political economy, ecology/resources and knowledge production – have shifted the ground on which political economy must (and 'economics' *should*) be able to comment informatively. This shift has been away from the traditional focus on industry and trade towards a more diverse set of issues in a 'knowledge-based' economy (in crisis), such as innovation *per se* and its broader socio-economic 'rhythms' and conditions, the commercialisation of research, socio-technical system transitions and the interaction of economy and 'nature' (often mediated by science and technology). These are all inter-related in complex and overlapping ways and so call for a research programme that is capable of illuminating these connections as well as, preferably, ways to minimise the suffering associated with the triple crisis. These issues come together within an 'economics of research' that assumes a broad, systemic perspective. Second, there is an epistemological challenge. Mainstream economics is incapable of furnishing an economics of research that is critical and explanatory, rather than axiomatic and ahistorical. It therefore fails to ask key questions such as: Why these changes? Why now? Why here? And what are the consequences (for science, innovation, society, political economy)? The patterns of funding of research, based on questionable assumptions of 'good' science, are thus a test case for economics and its transformation.

The pathological state of mainstream economics is not news for many. Since the mid-1990s at least, Tony Lawson and other critical realists have argued for a fundamental 'reorientation' of economics so that it actually examines the economic reality it purports to illuminate in an 'ontological turn' (Lawson 2003). In this context, the economic and economics crisis should be a golden opportunity to make definitive strides towards this laudable goal. Yet there seems to have been a lack of commentary from critical realists regarding an alternative economic analysis, both of how to respond to the crisis and its aetiology. Much, if not most, work in the 'ontological turn' of economic methodology is conducted at the level of philosophical argument alone. By contrast, there has been little space for these more abstract concerns in post-crisis debates about an alternative economics, perhaps due to the urgency of concrete, substantive economic issues. Meanwhile, the critics of mainstream economics amassing the greatest attention are those who debunk its substantive theoretical positions. This is especially true of authors who can claim to have predicted the crisis (e.g. Keen 2011). Nevertheless, confronted with this opportunity, we might ask: How can critical realism contribute to the construction of alternative perspectives that are compelling, both epistemically and politically? Or to phrase this more polemically, why waste time with abstract discussion of ontology if we could directly challenge and change economics?

This chapter therefore aims to demonstrate rather than merely argue for the contribution of critical realism to political economy.[1] We thus start with the substantive problem of developing an economics of research capable of illuminating the commercialisation of research and its interaction with and implications for broader social crises, and showing how critical realism is a crucial component in this theoretical project. The inadequacies of mainstream economics for such a project show that an economics of research demands profound rethinking of the science of 'economics'. Political economy also has much to learn from a productive synthesis with disciplines that have engaged with these issues for many years, including evolutionary economics of innovation.

We therefore highlight three key ways in which critical realist analysis makes a unique contribution to the development of an alternative economics:

1. Directly, via substantive transcendental argument (retroduction) and the relational Marxism that follows.
2. Indirectly, following this, by directing attention to and legitimating (hence 'underlabouring') specific substantive work for critical comparison and synthesis (elimination of competing theories via judgemental rationality).
3. Indirectly as ontological/epistemological ground for productive synthesis with empirical bodies of work that offer considerable insight into the contemporary science and/or innovation.

The problem of the 'economics of research'

There has been a broad process of commercialising science for more than thirty years, most obviously in the US, but also across the global North and even recently in the emerging global powers of the BRIC countries (Brazil, Russia, India and China). For example:

- Privatisation of research funding. Private funding of scientific research in the US grew 3.8 times in real terms (8.7 in nominal terms) from 1980 to 2010 as against increases of federal government funding of 1.5 times (3.5). Private funding of total R&D grew to 65–70 per cent of total national R&D expenditure in the decade from 1998 to 2008 from just under 50 per cent in 1980 (NSF 2010), with most of this funding being directed to research itself conducted by private industry. At universities, too, commercial funding increased dramatically.
- Commercial 'accountability' and 'relevance'/'impact' criteria in competitive public funding. Public funding also has increasingly come with strings attached that test the commercial relevance of research, an 'auditing culture' that seeks to quantify research achievements (e.g. Shore 2008).
- Growth in university–industry relations (UIRs) and direct incorporation of scientific research into commerce. These range from privately funded centres or entire departments to smaller projects and collaborations and, especially in fields relating to hi-tech industries such as biotechnology or information technology, spin-off firms. At the most successful research universities, this has created a revolving door between university and commerce.
- Growth in patenting, especially at universities and in life sciences. Since the early 1970s (before the passing of the US Bayh–Dole Act allowing patenting of publicly funded research (Mowery *et al.* 2004)), patenting at universities, especially in the US, has grown rapidly. Moreover, this growth has been particularly marked in high-growth sectors of science-intensive high technology, such as biotechnology.
- Commodification of higher education. Science education has also become progressively privatised, with student fees an increasingly important source of revenue and transforming students into 'consumers' of higher education (Slaughter and Rhoades 2004). In the US, in particular, there has been a significant growth in for-profit higher education, rising 59 per cent in three years to 3.2 million students at 3,000 colleges in 2008–2009 and representing 11.7 per cent of all American students (*The Economist* 2010: 130).
- Strong, global intellectual property rights, especially for life sciences and ICT. Finally, the 1995 'Trade-Related Aspects of Intellectual Property' agreement (TRIPs) instituted strong IPRs that would benefit only a handful of (largely US-based) transnational corporations, particularly those in the IP-sensitive industries of pharmaceuticals, agribusiness, ICTs and entertainment (Sell 2003). This trumped historical precedent in which nation-states have tended gradually

to strengthen IP law to reflect the strength of domestic industries dependent upon them (May and Sell 2006).

Some may argue that there is no clear *ex ante* or philosophical reason why the increasing prevalence of scientific research done within or funded by private industry should be seen as a problematic phenomenon (Shapin 2008). For instance, it is increasingly difficult to maintain any neat correlation between the institutional location of scientific research and the kind or standard of research: Nobel prize-winning science is conducted in private laboratories while universities conduct important applied research. Nevertheless, together all these changes have raised serious concerns about the future of scientific research and its institutions. Radder (2010: 14), for example, lists eight issues that have attracted critical comment:

1. The potentially undesirable influence of commercial interests on research methods and results.
2. Higher levels of secrecy as scientific findings are transformed into commercial secrets.
3. Downgrading of research disciplines not seen as relevant from the perspective of profitable economic activity.
4. A short termism in research agendas, as commercial investment demands quick pay-off, to the detriment of longer-term 'basic' research or other socially beneficial projects.
5. Assorted objections (ethical, legal, philosophical, religious and so forth) to the patentability of academic research, especially that associated with the life sciences.
6. Conflicts of interest and exploitation of public funds for private gain by entrepreneurial scientists.
7. Detrimental effects on public trust in science more generally and the (seemingly) 'disinterested' epistemic authority of scientific findings.
8. General concerns regarding the 'justifiability of the privatization and economic instrumentalization of public knowledge'.

Moreover, as Kleinman (2010) stresses, these impacts need not be the effect only of direct private investment but may also, if not primarily, arise from a more pervasive and indirect transformation of academic research cultures.

These exceptionally broad and far-reaching changes (and on a global scale) have generated a pervading sense of crisis. They have also been implicated in the global economic crisis, via an investment strike due to over-propertisation of knowledge (Pagano and Rossi 2009). It is no surprise, therefore, that there has been a proliferation of projects devoted to understanding the 'economics of research'. Yet none of the projects that have received widespread attention is concerned with exploring and explaining the changing economic underpinning of scientific research as a historical process with profound social repercussions. In other words, the crucial issues of 'why *these* changes in the economics of research, in *these* places and *now*' are almost entirely elided by such work. Instead, these projects employ mainstream economic analysis to investigate the institutional conditions for the optimal allocation of resources in order to maximise output of scientific research. They are 'economics' not in the sense of exploring economic aspects of science but rather in employing forms of (mainstream) economic analysis (Sent 1999).

Yet such a project has failed even on its own terms, despite some fifteen years of intense research activity regarding related issues. As Mirowski (2009) puts it, 'the landscape [of the mainstream economics of information], far from being crowded with monumental theorems and general models, is merely dotted with abandoned half-finished shells'. These problems hinge on the intrinsic difficulty, if not impossibility, of exploring the economics of research (or knowledge or information) using mainstream economic models built upon market exchange. Boyle (1996), for instance, notes that market models investigating the equilibrium of supply and demand for a commodity are built upon the assumption that individual agents have perfect information. When the commodity is itself information, therefore, models run up against intractable contradictions with their very assumptions (Mirowski 2009: 138–9).

Similar conclusions may also be reached by consideration of the second half of this phrase, namely, what is the economics of research an economics of? This question shifts our attention to a slightly different literature on the commercialisation of research. Assuming a mainstream economic perspective, and hence seeking to understand 'science' in terms of a market, necessarily demands that there be some 'thing' that is produced by science and that it is self-evidently a social good to maximise. From this starting point, it is extremely hard not to proffer models that reduce science to a familiar commodity, at least not without bringing the usefulness of this approach fundamentally into question.

Unfortunately, however, much of the literature on the commercialisation of research is just as problematic regarding its perspective on the nature of science and the interaction of 'science' and 'money'. Mirowski and Van Horn (2005) describe this literature in terms of a debate between 'Economic Whigs' and 'Mertonian Tories'. The former are simply concerned with maximising the productivity of 'science' and, true to their Whiggish (neo-)liberalism, tend to promote the commercialisation of research as a progressive development without any complications or problems for scientific research.[2]

Conversely, the latter adopt the Mertonian perspective of science being dependent upon social norms that leave it in splendid isolation from the corrosive influences of commerce and self-interest.[3] The commercialisation of research is thus treated as the catastrophic passing of a former Golden Age (i.e. the post-war period of the *trente glorieuses* of 1945–1975) in which the state 'wisely' chose to fund science generously for the public good. Although this approach shows a much clearer concern regarding the interaction of changing economic arrangements and scientific research, it too is highly problematic. In particular, the notion of 'science' it employs systematically excludes socio-political concerns except insofar as they are distortions or corruptions of the scientific enterprise. The Mertonian perspective is thus merely the flipside of the errors of the Economic Whigs, both frameworks effectively ruling out the investigation of the actual effects of different funding arrangements on science, if for diametrically opposed reasons. In neither case, therefore, is there any need for (let alone possibility of) empirical investigation into the actual effects, both negative and positive, on science of changing economic arrangements because the answer is already known.

It is clear, therefore, that if we are interested in actually investigating questions such as 'how is/are science/s funded?', 'how and why has this changed?' and 'how have these changes affected that/those science/s?', we must employ a completely different conception of science, just as we must employ a different economics. This perspective would not only recognise the variety of social practices designated 'science' – or, more accurately, research and innovation – and attend to their concrete particularities, it would also acknowledge that science is itself constituted as an irreducibly socio-historical process, with all the economic, cultural and political 'thickness' this entails. This vision of science is closely akin to that developed with science and technology studies (STS) under the rubric of 'co-production' of science and 'society', i.e. the mutual constitution of relatively autonomous social phenomena (e.g. Jasanoff 2004).

Such a redefinition of 'science', however, brings with it significant consequences for the form of economics that is capable of studying it in at least two obvious respects. First, the very subject matter of an economics that is relevant to the study of the economics of research (as opposed to the various reified definitions of Economic Whigs and Mertonian Tories) demands that we employ an economics that is capable of exploring economic aspects of an inseparably socio-political and cultural reality. The second challenge is methodological and arguably more profound. Since co-production posits a social ontology of science in which the very nature of science develops alongside that of its broader socio-economic context, it becomes epistemologically impossible to employ a framework that must first define what science is before proceeding to examine its economics. Whereas the co-production analysis is thus concerned to develop our understanding of the nature of research and innovation through analysis of its interactive development with its socioeconomic context – i.e. to stretch towards a 'definition' of science as its conclusion – the axiomatic and 'deductivist' structure of mainstream economics requires the 'science' it is investigating be defined *ex ante* and so reified.

Quite simply, then, mainstream economics cannot illuminate the commercialisation of research and the knowledge economy more broadly, yet demand for just such understanding can only grow, especially in the context of crisis and discontent such as the present. Taken together, therefore, these two challenges illustrate how an economics of research offers a singular opportunity and motivation for a broader substantive project to develop an alternative economics that breaks with the mainstream discipline and addresses issues that will be at the very heart of economic concerns for future generations (consider Sent 1999 for similar sentiments).[4]

We now turn, therefore, to a brief illustration of the difference critical realism makes, regarding formulation of a critical, explanatory political economy of research and innovation through engagement with the evolutionary economics of innovation. In doing so, we will highlight the three contributions of critical realist analysis listed above.

From EEI to critical realist economics of research

The school of thought that is variously called innovation studies or (as we shall call it here) the evolutionary economics of innovation (EEI) has contributed most to current understanding of the processes of technological change and innovation. Its inclusion in any research programme on the 'economics of research' is thus hardly short of obligatory. From the perspective of a critical realist economics, five strengths, in particular, stand out.

First, EEI does indeed share a *prima facie* compatibility with neo-Gramscian political economy, affording comparison that brings out differences that are informative. Conversely, the latter has not paid the same due heed to issues of scientific and technological change as has EEI. Much of this connection may be explained by the foundational influence on EEI of the works of Schumpeter. For Schumpeter not only stands alone in the 'canon' of Great Economists in his emphasis upon the importance of an economic sociology (Swedberg 1987), hence calling for an economics that is more akin to Lawson's (1997) critical realist 'economics as social theory'. He is also exceptional in the importance he placed upon the works of Marx and the Marxian argument for the quintessential dynamism of a capitalist economy and hence the central role of (technological) innovation (Bottomore 1992).

The second key strength of EEI is its empirical attention to actual processes of technical change and innovation, together with an attractive scepticism and reflexivity on how little is known about these phenomena (see, for example, Freeman 1994: 473–4). Among the most important of these has been the growing body of work that has comprehensively dismantled the dominant idea of science and innovation policy of the 'linear model' of innovation (Kline and Rosenberg 1986; Mowery and Sampat 2006), which posits the sequence of basic science → applied science/ technology → innovation and diffusion → economic growth.

The third significant strength follows directly, regarding EEI's theoretically sophisticated and empirically grounded critique of the two key arms of the economic argument for the commercialisation of research and strong intellectual property rights, namely the linear model (as just discussed) and the public good argument.[5] The core insight undercutting the latter is the increasingly undeniable evidence against the presumption of the non-rivalry and non-appropriability of knowledge. The conjunction of insights regarding the much greater importance of tacit knowledge, together with the diverse roles and stages of the contribution of science to innovation, leads to a much more complex picture regarding the economic incentives, or lack thereof, for private production of scientific knowledge, and hence the case for public subsidy. For instance, building up tacit knowledge may take a long time, with only uncertain prospective and medium- to long-term benefits promised in return, while the relevant personnel are not contributing to profitability in the meantime. It is also difficult to measure and so assess or purchase, and in many cases (for example, encultured and embedded organisational or management 'knowledges') it adheres to the individual, not to the firm.

The fourth reason that EEI is so important for a political economy of research and innovation resides in multiple fundamental insights that provide both (a) an expansive approach to innovation, as the process that mediates between scientific research and economic growth (insofar as there is such a link in a particular case), and (b) a broad set of factors that must be taken into account in any detailed research programme. These insights would include:

1. First and foremost, innovation and technical change are evolutionary processes, a 'groping' (Nelson and Winter 1982), and their outcomes are fundamentally uncertain and unpredictable (Rosenberg 1994; Dosi 1988).
2. Second, therefore, EEI is also explicitly critical of the cursory way mainstream economics 'black-boxes' technological (and scientific) change, since it cannot incorporate such change into its models (Rosenberg 1982). Similarly, against the fetishism for mathematical modelling and deductive 'rigour' for EEI, study of actual technological and economic change demands a much greater (inter-disciplinary) role for history (Freeman and Louça 2002) and qualitative or 'appreciative' theories (Nelson and Winter 1982).

The fifth reason concerns the EEI literature on long-wave theories of the economics of techn(olog)ical change (ETC) (Perez 1983, 2002; Freeman and Perez 1988; Freeman and Louça 2002; Freeman 1994; Freeman and Soete 1997), following the seminal work of Kondratieff. This work is of particular interest for an economics of research since it provides a meso-level historical context for understanding changing economic conditions of, and demand for, research and innovation. ETC, like EEI, has significant strengths. First, it too is an explicit critique of neoclassical economics, notably New Endogenous Growth Theory (NEGT), which 'endogenises' technological change (or rather productivity increase through modelling the R&D process) into its models, thereby reducing technological change to a one-dimensional variable of rate of change.[6] Conversely, ETC uses (Kuhnian) concepts of 'technoeconomic paradigm' and 'technological revolution' (Perez 2002; Kuhn 1970) and the cycle associated with these conceptions to incorporate technological change seriously into economic explanation. These concepts posit a model of 'long waves' of such paradigms.

For the duration of a paradigm, then, not only the rate but also the direction of the technological change is fairly straightforward for all to see, resulting in technological complementarities and path dependence. Technologies outside the paradigm, however, are excluded from development as not promising the same return on investment; the intrinsically uncertain nature of innovation privileges established patterns and processes that are known to be productive and to complement the parallel innovation of others on whom a given innovation's success significantly depends. The paradigm thus lends a cyclical temporality to innovation, in which there is first a surge of activity, then a steadying off to 'normal' growth (as per Kuhn's normal science) and then a gradual maturity and decline as the paradigm's technological fecundity approaches exhaustion. At that point, new technologies will be favoured instead, this in turn precipitating the next technological revolution, a turbulent Schumpeterian process that is at no point characterised by equilibrium.

Second, ETC also recognises the crucial and singular role of finance in the growth of the economy (Perez 2002: 21, Orsenigo 1989: 26), which is left out of neoclassical accounts in which money is simply a more efficient means of exchange, a financial market is just another commodity market, and finance does not have any emergent effects on the development of the economy (Keen 2011).

Finally, ETC, like its close disciplinary cousin STS, has a much more sophisticated hold on the importance of social factors in the shaping of technologies and in the actual trajectories of successful technoeconomic paradigms. Indeed, these are 'technoeconomic' paradigms, not merely 'technological' ones, for Perez, precisely in order to stress the overall social context and its interaction with technology.[7] One particularly important feature of this is the period of political and social turbulence that inevitably follows from the emergence of a new revolutionary technology (Freeman and Perez 1988: 59; Perez 2002: 4, 24–6).

The overall picture provided by ETC, therefore, is a credible and comprehensive systemic account of the coevolution of economic and technological change. Empirically, this yields a series of discrete paradigms or 'ages', as outlined in Table 3.1.

On this conception, then, the period of the contemporary commercialisation of research coincided with one of 'irruption', passing into 'frenzy' (from 1987) in which the technological successes in the new paradigm, ICTs (information and communication technologies), led to a bubble of financial speculation built on the continuing growth of the revolutionary technology.

EEI thus conclusively shows that there is, and can be, no such thing as a single, abstract 'economics of research'. Moreover, regarding prospects for a vigorous and robust academic school, in the likes of Nelson, Freeman, Rosenberg and Pavitt, EEI is a school of unarguable stature and economic seriousness. As such, it has as good a chance as any body of economics to challenge and transform the notoriously, unapologetically unreconstructed 'zombieconomics' (Fine 2010) mainstream.

Nevertheless, for all the strengths of EEI, there are also significant differences to the neo-Gramscian perspective and significant weaknesses. A critical, explanatory economics of research brings these out particularly clearly. A key question here is: How does the periodicity of techno-economic paradigms help explain the recent commercialisation of science? The neo-Gramscian perspective places politics (and culture) as constitutive of technological and economic change in the form of spatio-temporal fixes and modes of regularisation and societalisation that constitute the (transitory, constructed) settlement of a political–economic space. As argued in detail elsewhere (Tyfield 2012b), therefore, this leads to a compelling explanation for the commercialisation of research as the accumulation by dispossession of an as-yet-uncapitalised sphere of social activity, namely 'knowledge production', so

TABLE 3.1 [a]Five successive technological revolutions, 1770s–2000s

Year of irruption	*Technological revolution*	*Popular name for the period*	*Core country or countries*	*Big-bang initiating the revolution*
1771	First	The 'Industrial Revolution'	Britain	Arkwright's mill opens in Cromford
1829	Second	Age of Steam and Railways	Britain (spreading to Continent and US)	Test of the 'Rocket' steam engine for the Liverpool–Manchester railway
1875	Third	Age of Steel, Electricity and Heavy Engineering	US and Germany forging ahead and overtaking Britain	The Carnegie Bessemer steel plant opens in Pittsburgh, Pennsylvania
1908	Fourth	Age of Oil, the Automobile and Mass Production	US (with Germany at first vying for world leadership), later spreading to Europe	First Model-T comes out of the Ford plant in Detroit, Michigan
1971	Fifth	Age of Information and Telecommunications	US (spreading to Europe and Asia)	The Intel microprocessor is announced in Santa Clara, California

Source: Perez (2002: 11)

[a] Compare similar tables in Dosi (1982), Freeman and Louça (2002: 141), Freeman and Perez (1988) and Freeman and Soete (1997).

that capital accumulation may continue. The timing is then explained in terms of a persistent overaccumulation crisis since the 1970s, leading to financialisation and the aggressive search for a new settlement of expanded capitalist relations of production. The commercialisation of research is thus an intensely political phenomenon, not just a techno-economic one associated with the emergence of a 'new (knowledge-based) economy'.

Perez also stresses the importance of politics in the setting of technoeconomic trajectories and the 'mutual shaping' of politics and technology (ibid.: 19). But when turning to the analysis itself, ETC places technology at its centre and so treats politics as the epiphenomenon of the autonomous technoeconomic trajectory. Hence 'each technology does then indeed lead to a "new economy" [and] … technology is behind the transformations' (ibid.: 145 and 147, 24, 155). In particular, politics is seen either as the *ad hoc* context for particular technoeconomic developments (ibid.: 115, 123, 126) or as a functionalist safety valve that inevitably evinces the (generally socially progressive) change in regulatory framework necessary for the optimal exploitation of the technoeconomic paradigm (ibid.: 19, 99, 129–36). The irreducible contribution of willed political struggle in such progressive concessions is thus significantly downplayed. Moreover, the explicit acknowledgement of the importance of politics is belied by its total absence in the explanation of the creation of the new economy, as opposed to the social response to it, and hence in the explanation of the cycle itself. As a result, the commercialisation of research (including, for example, TRIPs) must be understood – implausibly in both cases – either as the old economy's political intransigence or as the essentially progressive forces of the new economy.

These problems, however, point to deeper problems with the ETC framework, which revolve around its largely 'neo-Kantian' ontological perspective (Bhaskar 2008: 9, 25–6), in which the 'surplus' of theoretical terminology beyond empirical observation is construed as the idealised heuristics that best afford intelligible organisation of the empirical data. According to Bhaskar, such a stance can be distinguished from, on the one hand, a purely empiricist position and, on the other, a transcendental realist position for which theoretical terminology, when justified, may be legitimately, if defeasibly, understood to refer to real phenomena.

It is clear, first of all, that ETC *is* a neo-Kantian framework, with its explicit invocations of heuristic ideal types. This is equally apparent in its wholesale assumption of the Kuhnian conceptual apparatus of revolutions and paradigms (applied here to the technoeconomy instead of to scientific knowledge). But it follows that all the familiar problems associated with Kuhn's argument are similarly taken on. In particular, ETC necessarily overstates the discontinuity, at the total expense of continuity, of one paradigm from the next in the exogenously given 'technological revolutions' (Dosi 1982: 90; Perez 2002: 25, footnote 33).

Certainly, the timing of these shifts is integrated into the framework, on the basis that the maturity and decline of the existing paradigm set up the conditions for the shift in investment to the next one. But this does not answer the fundamental problem of 'whence the next technology?' because ETC's argument rests on a central circularity. On the one hand, finance is attracted to the new technology because of its promise of greater profitability (Perez 2002: 11). But, *ex hypothesi*, the new technology takes off in a revolution only when finance is already investing heavily in it (ibid.: 33), or else the timing remains a mystery. The only way to resolve this is to presume *ex ante* that there is a next technology 'waiting in the wings' (ibid.: 32) and that all that is required is for one paradigm to end for another to begin. But this is to place technology as an exogenous given, the driving force of the whole economy, *pace* express statements against such technological determinism (ibid.: 22).

This fundamental problem, however, is inherited from ETC's other major inspiration, Schumpeter. For while it rightly focuses on the importance of technological innovation for the economy, and the resultant turbulent business cycle of economic growth, ETC, like Schumpeter, simply assumes that innovation will naturally occur (consider, for example, Fagerberg 2006: 1) and does not ask the question: 'What are the social presuppositions of a systemic subjective drive, across economic life, to innovate?' The effects of a new technological revolution are thus explained in terms of how it 'fires the imagination' of prospective entrepreneurs and engineers and produces a new business common sense (i.e. paradigm), completely neglecting the objective social context (Freeman and Perez 1988: 48; Perez 2002: 16). Similarly, ETC explanations are couched in terms of a subjective profit motive, but the objective (and exceptional) social context that is presupposed by this is not examined (Perez 1983: 358, 360, 366).

As such, like Schumpeter, ETC overlooks the fact that even if innovation (as opposed to invention) is the *differentia specifica* of a capitalist economy, it has not itself emerged miraculously from nowhere in the modern world (Bottomore 1992). Conversely, a neo-Gramscian perspective highlights how a systemic imperative to innovate presupposes the dominance of the social relations of production by the capital relation, which sets up the law of value that forces businesses to compete and innovate on pain of economic failure (Fine and Saad-Filho 2004).

This critical weakness is also evident regarding the key issue of the role of finance. Comparison with ontologically underlaboured neo-Gramscian argument (e.g. Arrighi 1994, 2008) thus also allows a comparison regarding ETC's explanatory power of the historical record. Both the ETC and critical realist frameworks accord finance a crucial role in the transformation of the economy and the shift from one phase of growth to another. Both parties also agree that finance assumes dominance over the economy, in particular through 'making money from money' (ibid.: 98, 100) or the 'financialisation' of the economy (Arrighi 1994, 2003; Blackburn 2006) respectively. Yet the significance of finance in the ETC schema is primarily its sponsorship of the new technologies, which will be at the heart of the emerging 'new economy' (Perez 2002: 33–5). Conversely, for the critical realist conception, such investment is the result of a much broader shift in the balance of power from productive to finance capital as the expansion of the former comes up against the limits of the existing political economic hegemonic settlement and its associated spatio-temporal fixes.

Two differences follow that are particularly striking. First, as we have seen, for the critical realist theory the pivotal role of finance revolves around its power to enforce a round of primitive accumulation in phases of financialisation (Arrighi 2003). Conversely, ETC sees no role for politics (beyond *ad hoc* national idiosyncrasy) in the creation of the new economy, with repercussions for the role accorded to finance in the cycle of growth of the world economy. This is also clear in the bizarre decision to omit global wars (e.g. 1914–1918, 1939–1945) from the ETC schema of explanation (see Table 3.1), when it is surely obvious that such wars are both hugely significant geopolitically (and hence indirectly for innovation/long waves) and periods of intense innovation *per se*.

Second, because technological change is placed at the heart of its analysis, ETC sees the growth of finance as dependent on new technologies. While it acknowledges that bubbles occur through the investment of finance in finance, it nevertheless places the new technology as the fundamental cause of financial dominance. Conversely, the critical realist theory treats the growth in finance as a *sui generis* phenomenon of which new technology investment is merely one consequence. And, taking the two points together, it focuses on the crucial interaction between finance and politics: the dependence of the former on political order, the political shift involved in its rise to dominance and its political effects.

These differences have conspicuous implications for the explanation of actual events. Perez (2002: 77) is unequivocal that the end of the 'frenzy' phase of a financial bubble economy is based on technology-based crashes:

> There is one type of collapse, though, which is directly connected with technological revolutions. It is the crash – or series of mini-crashes – that tends to close the casino bubble at the end of the frenzy phase.

Furthermore, she is clear that just such a crash occurred in 2000 and that such crashes precipitate 'prolonged recession' (ibid.: 7) that then triggers the political backlash and safety valve of painful reform to accommodate the new paradigm. Contrary to her analysis, however, following the dotcom bust (as well as the – geopolitical – shock of 9/11 the following year), the US (and world) economy did not collapse but GDP growth recovered: to 2.5 per cent in 2003, 3.9 per cent in 2004 and 3.2 per cent in 2005 (data from US Bureau of Economic Analysis). Moreover, as Blackburn (2006) has shown, the subsequent growth was still based on continuing financialisation, if not its acceleration. Indeed, the continuing growth of such derivatives markets was a major factor in the subsequent Great Crash of 2008. In short, it is clear that the bursting of the technology bubble did not solve the underlying economic problems, nor did it chasten finance capital more generally and bring it to heel, nor did it place meaningful financial regulation on the political table.

But on the critical realist conception, why should it? If it is acknowledged that the dominance of finance over the economy is dependent primarily on political support and stability, then there is no reason why it should not be able to withstand any number of financial crashes and shocks so long as its political dominance is not fundamentally undermined.

An alternative strategy for Perez, of course, has arisen with the Great Crash of August/September 2008 and the subsequent economic crisis. Hence, in a recent update on her position, Perez (2009) seeks to square this circle by claiming that 'this time' the technological and financial crashes were 'two episodes rather than one'. But she can do so only at the cost of the credibility of this central pillar of her argument that the power of finance and the developmental phase of the global economy itself are primarily dependent on the fortunes of paradigmatic technologies, in this case, ICT.

Moreover, and as further evidence for the neo-Gramscian theory and against Perez, even this almighty financial crash has not yet derailed the financialisation of the global economy and the political dominance of neoliberalism. But this is because there has still not been the fundamental political uproar and movement against finance capital's dominance. Only such a political change will spell the end of financialisation, but this moment's emergence cannot be predicted, at least on the basis of such abstract cyclical models alone.

While many ETC scholars are not uncritical of new technological developments and their potential social repercussions (e.g. Perez 2002: 4; Freeman 2001), therefore, the ETC framework they employ cannot fundamentally question the likelihood, possibility or even benefit of an emerging paradigm, let alone that of the cycle as a whole. Instead, it focuses its practical efforts on providing policy advice to minimise the economic problems caused by the inevitable birth – what Perez (2002: 113, 158) calls 'adaptive regulation' in order to 'restrain the excesses' of these cycles. Conversely, on the critical realist conception, it remains an open question whether or not there will be an emerging paradigm and whether or not it, and hence the cycle itself, is good for all groups and classes, let alone for humanity as a whole, or even fundamentally compatible with the ecological conditions of human survival, i.e. precisely the open questions of contemporary politics of science, technology and innovation that we have stylised above in terms of 'triple crisis'.

ETC thus carefully avoids the neoclassical errors of reifying economic states as static equilibria, but itself necessarily reifies the processes and trajectories it identifies. Conversely, the critical realist analysis identifies real, transfactual tendencies that condition but do not determine the possible courses of future political action (including but not limited to government policy) to alter or construct the course of history, not merely to adapt to it. And it does this not through identification of heuristic ideal types but through examination of the presuppositions of our actual, given understanding of the social world.

This illustration thus demonstrates the three ways in which critical realism may contribute to an alternative economics appropriate to the challenges, political and epistemic, of the present in the form of a critical, explanatory economics of research. First, by providing a relational Marxism through substantive transcendental argument, it sets a theoretical and methodological position that allows the contextualisation and strengthening (not abandonment) of the many insights of EEI, incorporating ETC. Second, by comparing its concrete explanations with those offered by substantive theories compatible with a 'value theory of labour' (in this case, neo-Gramscian IPE), this allows further criticism and development of explanations. Last, but by no means least, while EEI is fundamentally neo-Kantian in perspective, the development of a third philosophy that can incorporate and go beyond this perspective presents the ontological and epistemic grounds on which to build a productive synthesis of this tradition of economics and a Marxian political economy that has to date paid insufficient attention to detailed empirical study of science and innovation.

Conclusion

Economics has been a key starting point for the critical realist programme in general – both in actual history (viz. Bhaskar, Lawson, Sayer, Jessop *et al.*'s early and/or abiding interest in economic issues) and conceptually, regarding a turn to philosophy of science in order to open up alternative economic explanations. Yet in an age of multiple crises, including of capitalist political economy and the mainstream economic discipline purporting to study it, it is palpably no longer adequate – notwithstanding the major contributions of these philosophical arguments to date – to continue responding to demands to show the difference critical realism makes by pleading that such demands are to misunderstand the argument. This is so not just for epistemic reasons but also for political ones: in a rapidly changing and profoundly unstable social context that is crying out for a different economics, critical realism must now 'show its hand' in this respect.

Here, we have explored significant contributions, direct and indirect, of critical realism to an economic project of considerable contemporary importance: a critical, explanatory economics of research or, more accurately, a cultural political economy of research and innovation (Tyfield 2012a, 2012b). This thus begins to furnish a fitting response to those who would argue such analysis is simply a diversion from the real work of constructing such an alternative economics. For it highlights how, far from being a distraction, critical realism is a crucial parallel project and one that yields major gains at the level of substantive understanding of our contemporary situation – and thus the significant contribution it could make to charting a course beyond the 'triple crises'.

Notes

1 For more detail, see Tyfield (2012a, 2012b).
2 See, for example, Etzkowitz *et al.* (2000).
3 See, for example, Krimsky (2003).
4 For a collection of the growing body of work taking this issue seriously, see Tyfield *et al.* (forthcoming).
5 Though it must be noted that, in fact, it may be plausibly argued that EEI has been most influential in the corridors of power in just the opposite direction (Mirowski and Sent 2008; Godin 2006).

6 See, for example, Verspagen (2006).
7 Though compare Freeman and Perez (1988: 47) with Dosi (1982).

References

Arrighi, G. (1994) *The Long Twentieth Century*, London: Verso.

Arrighi, G. (2003) 'The social and political economy of global turbulence', *New Left Review*, 20: 5–71.

Arrighi, G. (2008) *Adam Smith in Beijing*. London: Verso.

Bhaskar, R. (2008) *A Realist Theory of Science* (2nd edition), London: Routledge.

Blackburn, S. (2006) 'Finance's fourth dimension', *New Left Review*, 39: 39–72.

Bottomore, T. (1992) *Between Marginalism and Marxism – The Economic Sociology of J.A. Schumpeter*, Hemel Hempstead: Harvester Wheatsheaf.

Boyle, J. (1996) *Shamans, Software and Spleens: Law and the Construction of the Information Society*, Cambridge (MA) and London: Harvard University Press.

Chakrabortty, A. (2012) 'Economics has failed us, but where are the fresh voices?', *The Guardian*, 16 April.

Dosi, G. (1982) 'Technological paradigms and technological trajectories', *Research Policy*, 11: 147–162, reprinted in C. Freeman (ed.) (1983), *Long Waves in the World Economy*, London and Dover (NH): Pinter.

Dosi, G. (1988) 'The nature of the innovative process', in G. Dosi, C. Freeman, R. Nelson, G. Silverberg and L. Soete (eds), *Technical Change and Economic Theory*, London: Pinter.

The Economist (2010) 'Schools of hard knocks', Vol. 396, Issue 8699, 9 September.

The Economist (2011) 'Marginal revolutionaries: heterodox economics', Vol. 401, Issue 8765, 31 December.

Etzkowitz, H., Webster, A., Gebhardt, C. and Terra, B. (2000) 'The future of the university and the university of the future: evolution of ivory tower to entrepreneurial paradigm', *Research Policy*, 29: 313–330.

Fagerberg, J. (2006) 'Innovation: a guide to the literature', in J. Fagerberg, D. Mowery and R. Nelson (eds), *Oxford Handbook of Innovation*, Oxford: Oxford University Press.

Fine, B. (2010) 'Zombieconomics: the living death of the dismal science', in K. Birch and V. Mykhnenko (eds), *The Rise and Fall of Neoliberalism*, London: Zed Books.

Fine, B. and Saad-Filho, A. (2004) *Marx's 'Capital'* (4th edition), London and Sterling (VA): Pluto Press.

Freeman, C. (1994) 'The economics of technical change', *Cambridge Journal of Economics*, 18: 463–514.

Freeman, C. (2001) 'A hard landing for the "new economy"? Information technology and the United States national system of innovation', *Structural Change and Economic Dynamics*, 12(2): 115–139.

Freeman, C. and Louça, F. (2002) *As Time Goes By: From the Industrial Revolutions to the Information Revolution*, Oxford: Oxford University Press.

Freeman, C. and Perez, C. (1988) 'Structural crises of adjustment, business cycles and investment behaviour', in G. Dosi, C. Freeman, R. Nelson, G. Silverberg and L. Soete (eds), *Technical Change and Economic Theory*, London: Pinter Publishers Ltd.

Freeman, C. and Soete, L. (1997) *The Economics of Industrial Innovation* (3rd edition), London and Washington (DC): Pinter.

Godin, B. (2006) 'The knowledge-based economy: conceptual framework or buzzword?', *Journal of Technology Transfer*, 31: 17–30.

Jasanoff, S. (ed.) (2004) *States of Knowledge: The Co-Production of Science and Social Order*, London: Routledge.

Keen, S. (2011) *Debunking Economics* (2nd edition), London and New York: Zed Books.

Kleinman, D.L. (2010) 'The commercialization of academic culture and the future of the university', in H. Radder (ed.), *The Commodification of Academic Research: Science and the Modern University*, Pittsburgh, PA: University of Pittsburgh Press.

Kline, S. and Rosenberg, N. (1986) 'An overview of innovation', in R. Landau and N. Rosenberg (eds), *The Positive Sum Strategy: Harnessing Technology for Economic Growth*, Washington, DC: National Academy Press.

Krimsky, S. (2003) *Science in the Private Interest: Has the Lure of Profits Corrupted Biomedical Research?*, Lanham, MD: Rowman & Littlefield.

Kuhn, T. (1970) *The Structure of Scientific Revolutions* (2nd edition), Chicago, IL: Chicago University Press.

Lawson, T. (1997) *Economics & Reality*, London and New York: Routledge.

Lawson, T. (2003) *Reorienting Economics*, London and New York: Routledge.

May, C. and Sell, S. (2006) *Intellectual Property Rights: A Critical History*, Boulder, CO and London: Lynne Rienner Publishers.

Mirowski, P. (2009) 'Why there is (as yet) no such thing as an economics of knowledge', in H. Kincaid and D. Ross (eds), *Oxford Handbook of Philosophy of Economics*, Oxford: Oxford University Press.

Mirowski, P. and Sent, E.-M. (2008) 'The commercialization of science and the response of STS', in E. Hackett, J. Wacjman, O. Amsterdamska and M. Lynch (eds), *New Handbook of STS*, Cambridge, MA: MIT Press.

Mirowski, P. and Van Horn, R. (2005) 'The contract research organization and the commercialization of scientific research', *Social Studies of Science*, 35(4): 503–548.

Mowery, D. and Sampat, B. (2006) 'Universities in national innovation systems', in J. Fagerberg, D. Mowery and R. Nelson (eds), *Oxford Handbook of Innovation*, Oxford: Oxford University Press.

Mowery, D., Nelson, R., Sampat, B. and Ziedonis, A. (2004) *Ivory Tower and Industrial Innovation*, Stanford, CA: Stanford University Press.

National Science Foundation (2010) *National Patterns of R&D Resources: 2008 Data Update*. NSF 10–314. Arlington, VA.

Nelson, R. and Winter, S. (1982) *An Evolutionary Theory of Economic Change*, Cambridge, MA: Harvard University Press.

Orsenigo, L. (1989) *The Emergence of Biotechnology – Institutions and Markets in Industrial Innovation*, London: Pinter Publishers.

Pagano, U. and Rossi, M.A. (2009) 'The crash of the knowledge economy', *Cambridge Journal of Economics*, 33: 665–683.

Perez, C. (1983) 'Structural change and assimilation of new technologies in the economic and social systems', *Futures*, 15: 357–374.

Perez, C. (2002) *Technological Revolutions and Financial Capital – The Dynamics of Bubbles and Golden Ages*, Cheltenham and Northampton, MA: Edward Elgar.

Perez, C. (2009) 'After crisis: creative construction', *OpenDemocracy*, 5 March, available at: opendemocracy.net/article/economics/email/how-to-make-economic-crisis-creative.

Radder, H. (2010) 'The commodification of academic research', in H. Radder (ed.), *The Commodification of Academic Research: Science and the Modern University*, Pittsburgh, PA: University of Pittsburgh Press.

Rosenberg, N. (1982) *Inside the Black Box*, Cambridge: Cambridge University Press.

Rosenberg, N. (1994) *Exploring the Black Box: Technology, Economics and History*, Cambridge: Cambridge University Press.

Sell, S. (2003) *Private Power, Public Law: The Globalization of Intellectual Property Rights*, Cambridge: Cambridge University Press.

Sent, E.-M. (1999) 'Economics of science: survey and suggestions', *Journal of Economic Methodology*, 6: 95–124.

Shapin, S. (2008) *The Scientific Life: A Moral History of a Late Modern Vocation*, Chicago, IL: University of Chicago Press.

Shore, C. (2008) 'Audit culture and illiberal governance: universities and the politics of accountability', *Anthropological Theory*, 8(3): 278–298.

Slaughter, S. and Rhoades, G. (2004) *Academic Capitalism and the New Economy*, Baltimore, MD and London: John Hopkins University Press.

Swedberg, R. (1987) 'Economic sociology: past and present', *Current Sociology*, 35:1–144.

Tyfield, D. (2012a) *The Economics of Science: A Critical Realist Overview* (Volume 1), Abingdon & New York: Routledge.

Tyfield, D. (2012b) *The Economics of Science: A Critical Realist Overview* (Volume 2), Abingdon & New York: Routledge.

Tyfield, D., Lave, R., Randalls, S. and Thorpe, C. (eds) (forthcoming) *The Routledge Handbook of the Political Economy of Science*, London and New York: Routledge.

Verspagen, B (2006) 'Innovation and economic growth', in J. Fagerberg, D. Mowery and R. Nelson (eds), *Oxford Handbook of Innovation*, Oxford: Oxford University Press.

4

INACCURATE AND BIASED

Cost–benefit analyses of transport infrastructure projects

Petter Næss

Introduction

Along with the increasing influence of neoclassical economics on public-sector decision-making, there has been increasing pressure in a number of countries to employ cost–benefit analyses to decide whether or not to implement governmental initiatives. Examples of projects subjected to cost–benefit analysis include waste-incineration plants, hydro-electrical development, training programs, health care systems, and, not least, transportation infrastructure investments.

This chapter critically discusses the use of cost–benefit analyses of transportation infrastructure investment projects. The transportation sector is interesting because national governmental goals in many countries have been changed since the 1990s from facilitating projected growth in road traffic to channeling needs for transportation into more environmentally friendly modes of travel than the private car, combined with land-use planning aiming to reduce the need for transport. However, due to the use of individual willingness-to-pay as a criterion for impact valuation, cost–benefit analyses tend to legitimate a market-based development, although the adopted political goals within the transportation sector imply that the hitherto dominating "predict and provide" approach should be replaced by strategies meeting accessibility needs in other ways than through facilitating more traffic.

The main points of criticism leveled in this chapter are the following:

- Cost–benefit analyses rely on unrealistic assumptions about social value, human nature, and the natural environment.
- The method's reliance on exact, quantified predictions of future situations ignores measurement problems and inevitable forecasting uncertainty.
- The traffic forecasts are often not only inaccurate but also biased.
- The valuation of many impact categories is arbitrary, including the monetizing of time savings and environmental impacts.

- The discounting rules conjure away long-term negative environmental impacts.
- The willingness-to-pay principle implies an ethical bias against the poor.
- The method tends to undermine political objectives of changing current trends of traffic growth.

Cost–benefit analysis of large-scale public works projects is no exact science – it includes considerable subjective elements and scope for bias. For example, according to a 2005 study of practices of cost–benefit analysis among 25 EU countries, the valuation of time savings for journeys to work varied by a factor of 10 between two neighboring countries, Austria and Hungary. The valuation of a "statistical life" varied by a factor of 10 between Finland and Slovakia, and by a factor of 2 between Norway and Denmark. Moreover, the valuation of CO_2 emissions varied by a factor of 5 between Sweden and Finland. There was also large variation between EU countries in discounting rate levels – in four countries it was below 4 percent, in three countries it was above 7 percent, and there was no regional pattern in the variations in discounting rate levels (Odgaard *et al.*, 2005).

Before addressing the above-mentioned points of criticism, the main purpose, techniques, and areas of use of cost–benefit analyses will be reiterated briefly.

Cost–benefit analysis: purpose, techniques, and areas of use

The purpose of cost–benefit analyses (CBA) is to estimate and aggregate a monetary value equivalent to the benefits and costs to society of proposed projects in order to assess whether or not they are worthwhile to implement. If the calculated aggregated value of all impacts of a project is positive, the project is considered profitable for society. The main valuation principle on which cost–benefit analyses are usually based is that the monetary value of a positive impact is defined as equal to the amount of money that the population is willing to pay to obtain it. When analyzing a project, it will be necessary to compare costs and benefits appearing at different times. This is dealt with by discounting future economic benefits and costs to a reference date (normally the time of decision to implement the project), applying a given annual discounting rate.

For transportation investment projects, the main impacts on the benefit side are normally time savings and any safety and local environment improvements, whereas construction costs (notably materials and labor power) and operational costs are obvious items on the cost side. However, depending on the actual context and the type of project, the safety and environmental impacts can also be negative, for example encroachments into landscapes, demolition of houses, or increase in accidents due to additional traffic. Such impacts will then occur on the cost side in the calculation. This also applies to long-term and global impacts such as greenhouse gas emissions, where some types of projects, for example road-pricing schemes and improved public transport in cities, may contribute to reduced emissions, while other types of projects, for example road-capacity increases, typically lead to greater emissions.

Following the general principle of discounting, benefits as well as costs of transportation projects occurring in the future are discounted to their present value using a stated discounting rate. This rate varies somewhat across nations. In Sweden, for example, it is 3.5 percent annually, while in Denmark it is 6 percent. In the UK, the discounting rate is 3.5 percent for impacts occurring during the first 30 years, 3 percent for impacts occurring between 30 and 75 years after project implementation, and thereafter it is gradually reduced to 1 percent for impacts occurring more than 300 years after implementation. In Norway, discounting rates similar to those of the UK have recently been adopted, with 4 percent for impacts within 40 years, 3 percent for impacts occurring between 40 and 75 years, and 2 percent for later impacts (Ministry of Finance, Norway, 2012, 2014).

The discounting rates also apply to environmental impacts, positive as well as negative. In the literature, there is some debate about the reasonableness in using the stated discounting rates for very long-term environmental impacts, for example the contribution of the projects to global warming. The recommendations of national governments on how to deal with such impacts in cost–benefit analyses also vary, as does the treatment of such impacts in actual project evaluations. In the European countries where cost–benefit analyses in decision-making processes are most prominent (for example, the Netherlands and Denmark), greenhouse gas emissions, noise, and local/regional air pollution are monetized and discounted with the normal discounting rates.

As mentioned above, time savings are an important item on the benefit side of cost–benefit analyses of transportation infrastructure investments, and in many cases they are the main positive economic value, making up 80–90 percent of the calculated economic benefits. In order to estimate this value, the value of each time unit saved must be assessed, as well as the number of travelers affected and the average number of minutes (or seconds) saved by each traveler. The two latter components are usually estimated using transport model computations, whereas the value of each time unit saved is most often based on willingness-to-pay investigations. Normally, different values per saved minute are used for different transport modes and travel purposes, reflecting differences in perceived inconvenience when making the trip, differences in average income levels, and whether trips are carried out during the working hours or in leisure time.

Transport model computations also make up important inputs to the assessments of safety and environmental impacts. For example, based on transport model calculations, estimates are made of the total amount of traffic, its distribution on the road network and between different hours of the day, as well as the average speed levels. From these estimates, assessments are made of, among others, energy use and greenhouse gas emissions, local air pollution, noise, and the number of traffic accidents. A translation of the estimates measured in physical entities into monetary terms is then carried out, using some willingness-to-pay-based assumptions. This also applies to the social value of non-traffic impacts such as encroachments and fragmentation of natural and outdoor recreation areas, cultural heritage, and so forth.

Assumptions about social value, human nature, and the natural environment

Cost–benefit analyses are based on a certain set of ontological assumptions that is far from uncontested. As mentioned above, the social value of a project's impact is assumed to be equal to the population's willingness-to-pay for obtaining or avoiding this impact. In other words, social values are considered to be the aggregate of individuals' willingness-to-pay (which in its turn is a combination of the preferences of these individuals and their ability to pay). This is an extremely individualist assumption that disregards that much of what is of value to society are things that a separate individual does not necessarily perceive as immediately useful and is willing to pay a price for that reflects its real value for society. Although economists involved in such investigations may hold that they are able to uncover willingness-to-pay for several common goods for which no market price exists, it is a leap of faith to believe that what is measured this way is a good indicator of the importance of the value of the good in question. More fundamentally, individuals and society make up different strata of reality (Bhaskar, 2008). According to critical realism, reality is stratified and differentiated, consisting of different "layers" where new causal powers and properties that are irreducible to lower layers emerge when moving from a lower to a higher layer. The value of something for society is thus not reducible to the aggregate preferences of individuals, let alone their willingness (or acceptance) to pay for it.

Furthermore, for cost–benefit analyses to yield accurate results, conditions of perfect market competition must exist. These conditions include, among other things, the requirement that humans act as fully informed, utility-maximizing consumers. Actual human behavior hardly conforms to this requirement. Besides instrumental rationality, human actions are guided by social as well as communicative rationality and influenced by traditions and habits (Diesing, 1962; Habermas, 1984; Bourdieu, 1984). They are also guided by ethical considerations which may well differ from the principle of individual utility maximizing. The method is thus based on a reductionist and flawed assumption about human nature. Neither is the presupposition of fully informed individuals met in real life. In particular, this applies to the ramifications of the various environmental impacts of the alternatives. For example, very few, if any, individuals are likely to be fully informed about the environmental changes and related impacts on societies and individuals resulting from greenhouse gas emissions. The assumption of neoclassic economics (and willingness-to-pay investigations in cost–benefit analyses) that human agents are all fully informed market agents implies an extreme, individual-level degree of cognitive triumphalism (Hartwig, 2007), entailing that reality is necessarily knowable to us.

Moreover, the method neglects the fact that decisions about the future contribute to shape future preferences. This reflects the generally static conceptualizing of the economy in neoclassical welfare economics despite its dynamic character. For example, the Norwegian ban on smoking in public spaces had little popular support before it was enacted, but after implementation opinion quickly changed to overwhelmingly positive attitudes. An ex-ante cost–benefit analysis of the ban would likely have found costs to exceed benefits, whereas an ex-post analysis of the act would obviously have found it to be profitable.

As mentioned above, environmental impacts are main items of the cost side of transportation investment projects (apart from the mere construction costs). A final, highly problematic ontological assumption of cost–benefit analyses of such projects is the belief that nature is fully, or at least to a very high extent, substitutable with human-made capital, with an unlimited capacity to bear growth in consumption and production. Without this assumption, the discounting of long-term negative environmental consequences down to negative present values much smaller than the originally calculated negative values would not have been possible (see below).

Measurement problems and forecasting uncertainty

Many of the impacts dealt with in cost–benefit analyses of transportation investment projects are ramifications of changes in human behavioral patterns resulting from the projects. This applies, for example, to time savings and changes in traffic accidents, emission levels, and noise. Economic valuation of these effects presupposes that it is possible to predict each of these outcomes with a high degree of accuracy. However, for several reasons, such precise predictions will hardly be possible. Even if the usually highly imperfect transport modeling tools currently in use were replaced by models representing state-of-the-art knowledge about relevant mechanisms influencing travel behavior, precise prediction about the future amount of traffic and its distribution between modes of conveyance would not be possible.

Several studies have shown substantial lack of correspondence between forecasted and actual traffic (see Nicolaisen and Driscoll, 2014 for an overview). Based on a study of transport infrastructure projects in Scandinavia and the UK, Figure 4.1 shows the distribution of forecasts overestimating (negative inaccuracy) and underestimating (positive inaccuracy) the actual traffic volumes for built road projects, the "zero alternatives" (i.e. alternatives where the proposed new infrastructure is not built) to which the built projects were compared, and for built rail projects (Nicolaisen and Driscoll, 2014; Nicolaisen and Næss, 2015). Inaccuracies are measured as the percentage that the actual traffic volume exceeded or was below the forecasted traffic volume. As can be seen, forecasts are highly inaccurate, with standard deviations of 33–35 percent inaccuracy for the completed road and rail projects. In addition, there are tendencies of bias (see "Biased forecasts," below).

The knowledge relevant for assessments of travel behavioral impacts of transportation infrastructure projects is seldom context-independent. If such knowledge is to be used in impact assessments, it must therefore be adapted and modified according to the actual context. Both for this reason and because society is constantly changing, any predictions about the impacts of transport investment projects on travel behavior will always be crude. Society is not a closed system but a system where many different causal mechanisms are at work, combined in a more or less contingent way. Therefore, any generalization to other geographical contexts or to the future must include careful, qualitative assessments of possible differences between the original space/time context and the context to which we want to generalize the research results (Næss and Strand, 2012). Regarding the generalization across time, this implies a discussion of possible traits of development that may reproduce, weaken, or strengthen existing relationships (Næss, 2004).

The predictions that are possible to make on the basis of social science studies (such as studies of the relationships between urban land use, transport infrastructure, and travel) are therefore of the crude "rule of thumb" type. They are limited to aggregate-level predictions of the impacts of the causal factor, not of future events or states (the latter being much more difficult and uncertain due to the impossibility of knowing the future combination and development of a multitude of other causal mechanisms influencing travel behavior). They are also necessarily non-exact, i.e. limited to the direction and order of magnitude of the impact (Næss, 2004).

Because cost–benefit analyses require precise, quantitative input data about, for example, traffic volumes and travel speed levels, the cost–benefit analysis regime in transport planning and decision-making arguably transforms transport modeling into a truth-producing technology (Henman, 2002) rather than a tool for planners to explore possible impacts of different combinations of infrastructure solutions and other policy measures during the process of plan-making. For example, the requirements of cost–benefit analyses direct modeling resources toward forecasting the general, "background" traffic growth (which is necessary to predict future traffic volumes on the pieces of infrastructure investigated), although such forecasting is virtually impossible to carry out accurately (Næss and Strand, 2012). At the same time, most traffic models are still very poor at estimating the additional traffic induced when infrastructure is being built, if they take induced traffic into consideration at all (MOTOS, 2007; Næss *et al.*, 2014). Moreover, the purported exactness of cost–benefit analyses probably makes up a disincentive against communicating the great uncertainties of the traffic forecasts on which the cost–benefit analyses are made. In a study of how uncertainty was communicated in decision-support documents for a sample of Scandinavian and British road projects, Nicolaisen (2012) found that uncertainty was ignored or suppressed in more than 80 percent of the cases.

Biased forecasts

The traffic forecasts on which the calculation of time savings, traffic safety, and environmental impacts are based are not only frequently inaccurate, they also tend to be biased. The traffic-generating effect of increased road capacity in situations with congestion on the road network is often ignored, or at least underestimated. The forecasts of the investigated road projects shown in Figure 4.1 underestimated the actual traffic volumes by 11 percent on average. At the same time, the forecasts for the "do nothing" alternative overestimated traffic on existing roads in the case

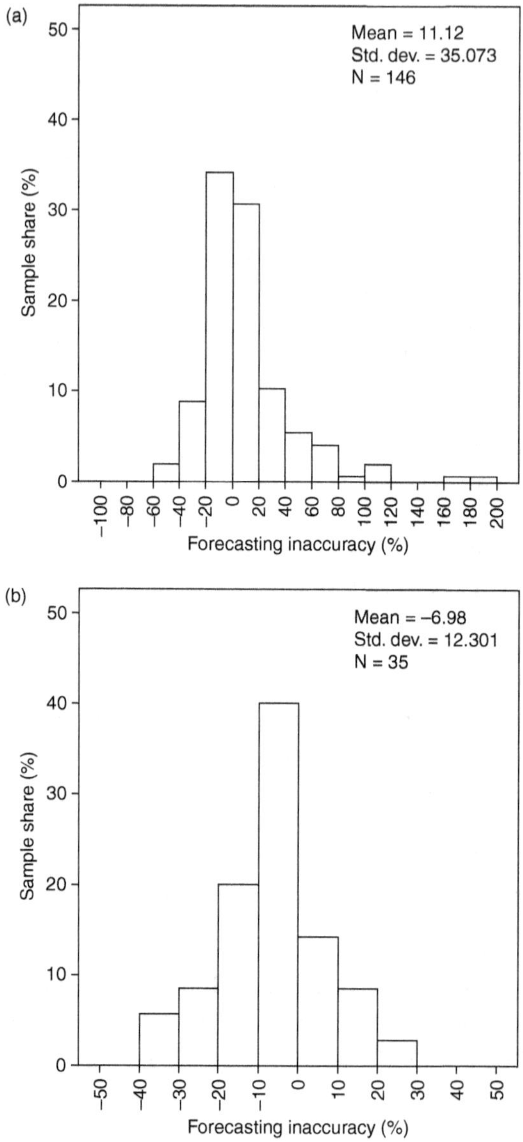

FIGURE 4.1 Forecasting inaccuracies for traffic on constructed roads (upper left), road traffic in the "zero" alternatives (upper right), number of passengers on built rail projects (lower left), and construction costs for rail projects (lower right). Inaccuracies are defined as the percentage that the actual traffic volumes or costs exceeded or was below those forecasted

Sources: Nicolaisen and Driscoll (2014); Nicolaisen and Næss (2015)

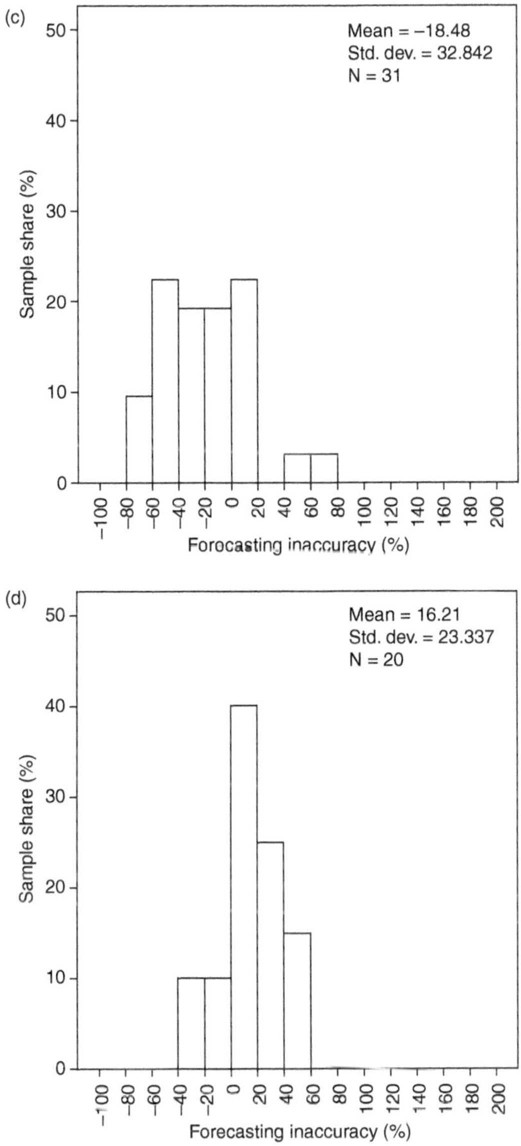

FIGURE 4.1 *(continued)*

of non-implementation of the projects by 7 percent on average. Together, this represents a bias of 15–20 percent, most likely reflecting neglect or underestimation of the traffic-increasing effects of road-capacity increases. There is ample evidence of the existence of such effects, which include longer trip distances, new trips, as well as a shift from public and non-motorized modes of travel to car driving (Noland and Lem, 2002; Litman, 2014). Furthermore, traffic forecasts for rail projects tend to overestimate the future number of passengers, thus depicting the projects in a more favorable light than if the forecasts had been accurate (Flyvbjerg *et al.*, 2005; Nicolaisen and Driscoll, 2014).

Studies indicate that there are several explanations of forecasting errors: ontological explanations (the inevitable uncertainty about how the future will be), optimism bias, technical problems, but also "strategic misrepresentation" (Flyvbjerg *et al.*, 2005; Næss *et al.*, 2015). The forecasts are worked out by experts who belong to a particular professional "culture." In modern society, different sectors represent different "cultures" with varying values, attitudes, and perceptions of the situation. Forecasters may also be under pressure to produce forecasts that agree with their clients' or superiors' visions, or they may be influenced by attitude-based preferences for certain modes of transport. Moreover, if forecasters are primarily interested in comparing different designs of a proposed project rather than comparing implementation with non-implementation, they may accept traffic models ignoring the traffic-increasing effect of road-capacity expansion (Næss *et al.*, 2014).

Neglect of the latter effect (often referred to as "induced traffic") can, however, render the cost–benefit analysis highly misleading, especially in an urban context with congestion on the road network. For example, using a traffic model ignoring induced traffic, the net present value of a planned new urban highway in Copenhagen (Nordhavnsvej) was calculated to be DKK2.16 billion, compared with only DKK0.40 billion if induced traffic was taken into consideration. In the latter case, the initial congestion relief, and hence travel time savings, would be substantially reduced as the new road was filled up with additional cars. The environmental impacts were also severely underestimated in the model omitting induced traffic (Næss *et al.*, 2012). The tendency to overestimate travel time savings and underestimate negative environmental impacts serves to legitimize higher spending on road construction in congested urban contexts than would otherwise be the case, and arguably increases the possibility for lobbyists in favor of capacity expansions to set the political agenda.

Arbitrary valuation of key impact categories

Not only will the assessment of travel behavioral impacts necessarily be crude, but the economic valuation of these impacts is also inevitably uncertain and contested (Atkins, 1984; Metz, 2008). Traditionally, the valuation of time savings has been based on a comparison with the most profitable alternative use of the time. Here, the value of travel time has usually been set as zero, whereas the alternative time use has been the value of working hours. An underlying assumption for this way of assessment is that the seconds or minutes saved when new transportation infrastructure is introduced will by and large translate into a higher number of working hours at an aggregate level. Obviously, several objections may be raised against this assumption, for example in situations with unemployment. People may also choose to utilize their time saving for leisure purposes instead of using the time to earn more money.

Another question is whether it is at all meaningful to add up tiny increments of time savings to an aggregate economic value for society. Tiny time savings can hardly be utilized in any meaningful way for either work or leisure purposes. British studies indicate an average time saving of road projects of 1–3 minutes per traveler (Welsh and Williams, 1997). Experience from the Danish National Travel Surveys indicates that people value time savings twice as high per minute if the saving is 20 minutes than if it is only 3 minutes. Still, Danish cost–benefit analyses operate with a fixed value per minute. Furthermore, the option to work while traveling, for example on a train journey, may strongly influence whether or not travel time saving equates to increases in productivity.

During recent years, this method has been supplemented by an alternative approach based on willingness-to-pay studies. However, here too considerable uncertainty is involved. For example, the time value of different parts of a trip (for instance, walking to public transport stops, waiting time, in-vehicle time, and so forth) has been found to vary significantly, as has the value of time spent on car driving under different driving conditions. A more fundamental issue is that people tend to expand their radius of action rather than use travel time savings from higher travel speed for non-travel purposes (Metz, 2008). In the short term, this may give accessibility benefits (but also negative environmental and safety impacts due to increased traffic volumes, cf. "Biased forecasts," above). In the longer term, shorter travel times within a region tend to contribute to urban sprawl, and the increased access to distant jobs that local residents may experience is counterweighed by higher competition for locally available jobs from non-local residents. Increased travel speeds thus tend to make it not only possible but also necessary for people to transport themselves longer distances to reach daily and weekly activities.

The economic valuation of environmental consequences of transport investment projects is possibly even more problematic. Apart from the difficulties associated with the discounting of long term effects (see "Discounting of long-term environmental impacts," below), willingness-to-pay-based valuation of environmental impacts is encumbered with several validity problems. First, people often do not have sufficient knowledge about the impact of a project to be able to state in a meaningful way how much they are willing to pay in order to make a contribution to avoid an impact. Willingness-to-pay investigations are hardly able to account for the multi-faceted social value of (changes in) environmental qualities such as climatic conditions, clean air, or the combined function of a particular area as a beautiful landscape, an outdoor recreation area, a rich ecosystem, and the habitat of particular species (some of which may be rare or threatened by extinction). In particular, most people (and scientists, too!) have far too little knowledge of the various direct and indirect impacts of global warming to make meaningful economic statements. Maybe for this reason, the monetizing of greenhouse gas emissions is often arbitrary and at a low value. In Norway, the price per ton of CO_2 emissions was on average set to US$35 in the cost–benefit analyses of 111 large public works projects performed in the period 2005–2013 (Volden, 2013). With this low value, it is highly unlikely that a project's contribution to global warming will influence the results of the cost–benefit analysis to any extent worth mentioning. In some cases, the carbon price is based on the even lower price of $5 per ton of CO_2, as set in 2015 by the malfunctioning carbon credit market.

Second, for several reasons, individuals' statements about their willingness-to-pay do not necessarily reflect their actual valuation of an environmental good. Some people, for example, may consider the protection of an outdoor recreation area to be something that should be subject to political decision-making, for which they, on grounds of principle, should not pay. Such a person may perhaps tick "zero" as her answer to the question of how much she is willing to pay in order to maintain the opportunity of experiencing the area with the same landscape qualities as today – even if the person is an outdoor life enthusiast and strongly opposed to technical encroachments in the area. In the cost–benefit analysis, however, the answer would be interpreted as if the person were little concerned about protecting the area.

Third, if the establishment or protection of collective goods such as a publicly accessible outdoor recreational area or clean air is to be left to the willingness-to-pay of individuals, each individual is free to under-communicate her/his real preferences regarding these goods in the hope that others will pay for them. Furthermore, since there is no expectation for people to actually pay what they state they would be willing to pay, it also seems plausible that they might over-state the value. This is because there would be nothing to stop them reporting a higher value than they would accept in a real-life situation, and this might seem like a good strategy if they are in favor of attaching high importance to the collective good in question.

Fourth, in a willingness-to-pay investigation, affluent people are more likely to show higher willingness-to-pay than those who can afford less (provided that the answers about willingness-to-pay are honest, cf. above). It is a fallacy to believe that the sum of the amounts of money that individuals are willing to pay is a good measure of society's total valuation of a good. If $1 more or less is of greater importance to some people than to others, aggregated willingness-to-pay is, according to mainstream economic theory, not a precise measure of aggregated utility (Nyborg, 2002).

Discounting of long-term environmental impacts

The justification for discounting future consequences is based on expectations of continuous economic growth: if we will be ten times richer in the future, paying a cost of $1,000 then will affect our welfare much less than paying the same amount of money today. This justification thus depends upon the assumption that growth can go on continually without running into environmental limits. This way of thinking has several serious flaws. From a moral perspective, discounting rates can logically apply only when the people benefiting from a development are the same as the people suffering the costs. A motorway built today may give (short-term) benefits to contemporary car travelers, while the negative impacts of its contribution to global warming will mainly affect future generations, no matter how rich they might have become.

Among the negative impacts of transport infrastructure projects, greenhouse gas emissions is one of the most important. In a cost–benefit analysis of strategies concerning greenhouse gas emissions, the renowned American economist Nordhaus (1994) applied a discounting rate of 3 percent annually. According to this study, a 3°C rise in the global average temperature by the end of the twenty-first century would result in only a 1.33 percent loss in world output. Nordhaus therefore claimed that the costs of trying to reduce greenhouse gas emissions are much higher than the benefits resulting from such policies. In a report for the British government, Stern (2006) applied a lower discount rate (1.4 percent). Distinct from Nordhaus, Stern concluded that mitigation policies would be clearly economically beneficial. But even Stern's discount rate of 1.4 percent annually presupposes a global economy in 2100 more than three and a half times bigger than in 2008.

Applying the considerably higher discount rates that were common in Europe as well as in the US a decade or two ago, the diminishing factor would be substantially higher. For example, with the discount rate of 7 percent used by the US Office of Management and Budget in the 1990s, the present value of a climate disaster occurring in 150 years would be 26,000 times smaller than if it occurred next week (Small, 1999). Even with the reduced discounting rate of 2 percent recently proposed in Norway for impacts occurring after more than 75 years, a climate disaster occurring in 150 years has a discounted cost today 20 times smaller than if it occurred next week. In the Nordhavnsvej case in Denmark (cf. "Biased forecasts," above), the additional CO_2 emissions resulting from the project were calculated to reduce the net present value by only 0.05 percent.

Needless to say, the discounting of future impacts of global warming places alternatives generating high greenhouse gas emissions in a much more favorable light than would otherwise be the case, and may lead to the preference for such solutions rather than lower-emission alternatives. In principle, similar bias will also occur in relation to other long-term environmental consequences, such as loss of biodiversity and biological productivity due to local pollution, and the fragmentation of natural areas represented by transportation infrastructure construction. The continual economic growth on which the discounting is based disregards that exponential economic growth at a rate corresponding to the discounting rates of cost–benefit analyses is highly unlikely in a century perspective (see other chapters in this book). The discounting of long-term and irreversible environmental impacts indicates that the negative value attributed to such impacts is very small. This reveals a fundamental ignorance about the functions of the various ecosystems as life support systems for human and non-human life, reflecting a discipline that has been characterized as being immune to any insight from other sciences (Fullbrook, 2004).

Discounting long-term and irreversible environmental impacts implies a "short termism" where consequences to future generations are considered insignificant. Such discounting represents serious bias against future generations, playing hazard with their basic life conditions.

In critical realist terms, the neoclassical assumptions about discounting and economic growth disregard the dependence of the economic processes on the natural environment, which consists of strata below the strata of individual actions and social structures. While social life cannot be reduced to the powers and mechanisms of lower strata, it still by necessity involves the powers and mechanisms of, among others, physics, chemistry, and biology. The neoclassical assumptions about infinite economic growth represent a particular sort of "downward conflation" (Archer, 2000) where the powers and mechanisms of the natural world are considered totally controllable by humans as if they were mere epiphenomena of the human world (Næss, 2006a).

Bias against the poor

The blindness to issues of intergenerational equity pointed at in the previous section is just one example of the general neglect in cost–benefit analysis of issues concerning a just distribution of burdens and benefits between different affected parties. Unfortunately, those who benefit and those carrying the burdens are usually not identical. If the cost is borne by a different group from the one that benefits, the cost–benefit analysis is morally on thin ice. By neglecting issues of fair distribution, cost–benefit analysis legitimizes a practice where costs are passed on to others (for example, other generations, less privileged classes, or disadvantaged ethnic groups).

The principle of willingness-to-pay gives the highest influence on decisions to those whose ability to pay is highest. While democratic majority decisions are based on the principle of one vote per person, the number of "votes" available for each person to influence which alternative will obtain the highest willingness-to-pay are determined by his/her level of affluence. If a majority prefers alternative A to alternative B, but the minority has a high willingness-to-pay for alternative B, the latter project may well be the one that obtains the highest total willingness-to-pay. Negative impacts on, and needs among, population groups with a low ability to pay are considered insignificant. Considering the sum of the individuals' willingness-to-pay as an adequate indicator of the need among the population thus implies an underestimation of the needs among low-income groups.

Failure to distinguish between human needs on the one hand and wants and market demand on the other hand (Assiter and Noonan, 2007; Dean, 2007) legitimizes a utilitarian focus only on the total amount of demand satisfaction. This disregards the question as to whether this actually leads to the satisfaction of real needs, as well as the distribution of need satisfaction between different groups and individuals in society.

Generally, market mechanisms are not able to secure a socially acceptable distribution of burdens and benefits. If, for example, there is a high extent of agreement in society that the inhabitants in all parts of a region – including those without a car and on a low income – should be secured basic transport opportunities, a public transportation service with affordable fares will be required, even in the local communities where pure market considerations would conclude that the population base was too low. Such a service would typically be justified on the ground that a *need* for public transport existed among the affected population groups. If the need for such a service had been defined as identical to the willingness-to-pay, this need would not have been recorded and acknowledged.

Ackerman and Heinzerling (2004) show a grotesque example of this from a cost–benefit analysis of proposed restrictions on the use of cell phones while driving in California. Researchers had found that people talking on cellular phones while driving were four times more likely to get into car accidents than drivers who did not. However, some of the US's most influential economists concluded that restrictions on the use of cell phones while driving would be a bad idea, because those who were talking while driving were willing to pay a lot to talk on the phone – more than those facing the highest risk of such accidents (such as poor immigrants walking along the roadside) were willing to pay to avoid the risk of being killed. The proposed restrictions were therefore withdrawn.

Undermining of political objectives

Within the transportation sector, cost–benefit analysis serves to legitimate a market-based development, although the adopted political goals of the sector imply that the hitherto dominating, demand-led "predict and provide" approach should be replaced – or a least supplemented to a greater extent than currently – by strategies meeting accessibility needs in ways other than facilitating more traffic. Several researchers have pointed out that transportation is a sector where deviations between official goals and implemented measures are particularly high. Neglect of the difference between demand and societal needs may be part of the reason why "decisions on transport policy is a field where a substantial gap between intentions and realities is common both at national and local level" (Ministry of the Environment, Norway, 2001). The political consequence of this is that increasing mobility, in particular by car and airplane, is given priority at the cost of environmental concerns.

Cost–benefit analysis, with its reliance on willingness-to-pay (be it in the form of "stated" or "revealed" preferences) as a measure of social value, is based on the assumption that being a customer is the same as being a citizen. However, as stated by Atkins (1984), it is logically consistent for an individual to choose a particular course of action under current circumstances while preferring and even advocating structural changes that would change those circumstances in ways that would make their current choice less attractive. For example, in the absence of improved public transport, a car commuter might support road-capacity increases to relieve congestion although she would have preferred to travel by transit if the buses departed more frequently and were running on separate lanes unaffected by the congestion caused by private cars.

Admittedly, cost–benefit analyses of transport infrastructure projects do not influence decisions about project implementation in a one-to-one manner (Odeck, 2010; Eliasson and Lundberg, 2012). However, systematic overestimation of travel time savings resulting from infrastructure construction (especially in urban areas), combined with a tendency to underestimate construction costs and adverse environmental effects, generally tends to legitimize high spending of society's resources on infrastructure construction. It also tends to delegitimize environmental opposition against road-capacity expansion and disarm environmentalists.

Concluding remarks

Above, I have argued that cost–benefit analysis as practiced in the transportation sector is based on a number of untenable ontological and epistemological assumptions. In line with the point made by Tony Lawson in Chapter 2, I consider the quantitative estimates of costs and benefits to be inevitably inaccurate for ontological reasons, despite the purported higher exactness of cost–benefit analysis than other evaluation methods. Unlike Lawson, however, I find cost–benefit analyses to be not only inaccurate but also biased. Some of these biases could be reduced without letting go of the method of cost–benefit analysis itself (for example, by using traffic models taking into consideration induced traffic, or using zero or negative interest rate for greenhouse gas emissions), although such reforms would probably meet considerable resistance and inertia among cost–benefit analysis practitioners. However, other biases pertain to the method itself, carrying an ideological slant that cannot be reformed away within the framework of the method (for example, the substitution of votes with purchasing power implicit in the willingness-to-pay principle).

The biases of cost–benefit analyses have social and environmental effects that involve ethical and political values. Accepting the ontological and epistemological assumptions of cost–benefit analysis involves an implicit acceptance of the ethical and political values favored by these assumptions. Uncovering the ethical and political values served by the method may help in understanding why cost–benefit analyses are used to such a great extent despite their considerable validity problems. According to Ackerman and Heinzerling (2004), the method of cost–benefit analysis generally promotes a deregulatory agenda under the cover of scientific objectivity. The method sits well with neoliberal growth policies while depicting policies prioritizing environmental protection or measures to promote a higher degree of equality in society above growth as being economically irrational.

Due to its complexity and lack of transparency, the calculations of cost–benefit analyses will often be impossible to penetrate for people other than a narrow group of experts. The lack of transparency refers to the assumptions inherent in the valuation of different types of impacts, the way of discounting, and (especially) the forecasts of traffic consequences of projects. For politicians, the public at large, and experts within other fields, the lack of transparency makes it difficult or impossible to evaluate the results and find a basis for critique and development of alternative solutions. This is aggravated by the widespread practice of presenting conclusions at a highly aggregated level, concentrating on only a few main indicators such as the benefit–cost ratio or the net present value while omitting the more nuanced and detailed information collected, let alone the uncertainty associated with the various estimates (Nicolaisen, 2012).

Above, a number of problems associated with the quantification and economic valuation of important impact categories of transportation investment projects were discussed. Among cost–benefit analysts, two different ways of reacting to this are common: reducing the analysis to the impact categories that most easily lend themselves to economic valuation, or refining the assessment and valuation methods in order to measure the "intangible" impacts in a better way. However, since the low validity and reliability of the present ways of trying to put price tags on these impacts are rooted in ontological misconceptions (Næss, 2006b), improving the surveying methods, for example in willingness-to-pay investigations, can hardly lead to more than marginal improvements. Reducing the analysis to the ontologically and epistemologically least problematic categories therefore seems a better option. But what will then be left of the analysis? As mentioned above, time savings often make up the main benefit category in cost–benefit analyses of transport infrastructure projects. However, the assessment of the magnitude of these savings as well as the valuation of these savings in monetary terms is highly uncertain and controversial. The same applies to environmental impacts. The mere construction costs should, in principle, be possible to estimate relatively accurately (although what happens in practice is often serious underestimation of costs – see Flyvbjerg *et al.*, 2003). However, since the economic valuation of nearly all the other items of the analysis, on both the benefit and the cost side, is encumbered with uncertainty and contestation, it is difficult to avoid the conclusion that the entire method of cost–benefit analysis is inappropriate for the assessment of transportation investment projects.

Cost–benefit analysis appears particularly inadequate for assessing whether or not to build a proposed project of a particular category (for example, a road project) in a specific geographic context. It may be less inappropriate if the task is to compare different alternative ways of designing this project (for example, layout A, layout B, or layout C for a proposed new road). However, due to the uncertainty mentioned above, the cost–benefit analysis should then be used only to assess the marginal differences between variants of the project, not its absolute economic value.

Suggestions to ameliorate the situation

When presented with one or more of the issues of criticism raised in this chapter, proponents of cost–benefit analysis often point to the necessity of having some sort of criteria for choosing between alternatives of action and deciding whether or not to implement a proposed project. I agree in this, and also in the claim of defenders of the method that the criteria should be made explicit to as high an extent as possible instead of being concealed in the minds of the individual planners and decision-makers. However, cost–benefit analysis is not the only way to systematically evaluate and rank projects.

Instead, an impact analysis should be carried out, with assessment of all relevant impacts of the project that might be anticipated (including intended, non-intended, direct, and indirect effects). According to Bhaskar (1993), every social event must be understood in terms of [a] material transactions with nature, [b] social interaction between agents, [c] social structure proper, and [d] the stratification of embodied personalities of agents. The stratification of embodied personality connotes psychological aspects that may come into play, whereas the notion of material transactions with nature connotes ecological aspects. The impact analysis should cover all these categories of impacts [a–d]. This means that the analysis should encompass environmental, social, and psychological effects as well as impacts of the proposed project on the direction in which society at large develops.

Interestingly, such a non-reductionist view need not be in conflict with the thoughts of Adam Smith on which cost–benefit analyses are purportedly based. In his major works *The Theory of Moral Sentiments* and *The Wealth of Nations*, Smith arguably addressed two different levels of reality (Wilson and Dixon, 2006). Or, in the words of Price (2007: 251):

> If we are part of the world, then to take care of oneself is to take care of the world, but to sacrifice oneself in certain circumstances to ensure the well-being of others is still to take care of oneself, since the self is part of that totality. Whether or not the balance falls on using resources for protecting the "self singularity", or using resources for protecting the whole, out of which the self is an unfolded singularity, is entirely dependent on the empirical circumstances of each different situation.

Deciding whether to act according to principles of immediate self-interest or in a more "altruistic" way (which in the long term might be beneficial also from an individual point of view) requires the kind of "practical wisdom" that Aristotle refers to as *phronesis* (Price, ibid.).

The impact categories of the analysis should correspond to a goal hierarchy reflecting the multitude of needs affected by the project (including both "project-triggering" needs and needs related to side effects of the project, and needs among different population groups) (Næss, 2009). The relevant consequence categories should be identified on the basis of a broad hearing among experts from different disciplines and representatives of different stakeholder and population groups. The scope of the impact analysis must not be reduced to the most easily measurable effects or those impacts that may most readily be valorized in economic terms. The documentation material of the impact analysis should in an easily accessible way give an account of the criteria, assumptions, weighting, and uncertainties on which the conclusions are based.

Due to the inherent and substantial uncertainty of forecasts of the general (background) traffic growth, and the context-dependency of each particular planning situation, traffic forecasting at the so-called strategic, tactical, and operational levels (Brems *et al.*, 2007) should be separated into three distinct methodological approaches reflecting the different degrees of openness/closure of the systems at hand: scenario analyses at the strategic level where the general, nation-scale traffic development is assessed; theory-informed, mainly qualitative analyses supplemented with simple calculations at the tactical level where the difference between building or not building a project is assessed; while more traditional micro-simulations should be applied only at a detailed operational level, for instance for comparison between different layouts of a proposed project (Næss and Strand, 2012).

Direct economic expenses (including costs for land purchases, materials, construction work, financing costs, compensation for demolished buildings, and so forth) should, of course, be estimated as exactly as possible in monetary terms. The economic valorizing may also include benefit effects that may reasonably be expressed in monetary terms (but, as mentioned above, in the case of transportation projects, key effect types such as time savings may not belong to this category). Some other effects (for example, the conversion of different types of natural areas, or the size of noise zones and number of dwellings within these areas) may be quantified without monetization. Effects that are difficult to measure should be made subject to more qualitative descriptions, or be assessed from a combination of qualitative and quantitative indicators, possibly by placing the effect on a certain level of a goal-achievement scale.

Proponents of cost–benefit analysis may argue that the approach proposed above does not provide decision-makers with the answer about whether or not a project should be implemented, or which among several implementation-worthy projects should be given priority. However, the belief that it is possible to give a technical answer to these questions is trying to do the impossible: to reconcile incommensurable values in one quantitative objective figure.

Some analytical tools for helping stakeholders in their process of synthesizing disaggregated information to an overall assessment of each alternative, and a ranking of alternatives, may still exist, for example the so-called Multi-Attribute Utility Technology (MAUT) (Edwards and Newman, 1982). However, because of the considerable disagreement in society over the importance of different normative values, such techniques are suitable only for consensus-building within relatively homogeneous groups (such as an environmentalist group, an organization of local residents, or the chamber of commerce), and not for arriving at conclusions about the "optimal" solution for society as a whole. Separate processes of evaluation and discussion of the alternatives could be carried out among each group of stakeholders, based on the importance each group attaches to different impact categories. The total, weighted score of each alternative for non-monetized dimensions could then be compared to each alternative's economic score (construction costs and possible other items that may be valorized in an appropriate way). This could make up a basis for an interactive discussion within each stakeholder group of the mutual ranking of the alternatives. Whether or not a synthesizing method like the one outlined above is used, uncertainty analyses and sensitivity analyses should be conducted in order to give indications about the ways the project alternatives will perform under different conditions and for different affected groups.

Acknowledgment

The author would like to thank Bent Arne Sæther for valuable comments on an earlier draft of this chapter.

References

Ackerman, F. and Heinzerling, L. (2004): *Priceless: On Knowing the Price of Everything and the Value of Nothing*. New York: New Press.

Archer, M. S. (2000). *Being Human. The Problem of Agency*. Cambridge: Cambridge University Press.

Assiter, A. and Noonan, J. (2007). Human needs: a realist perspective. *Journal of Critical Realism*, 6(2), 173–198.

Atkins, S. T. (1984). Why value travel time? The case against. *Highways & Transportation*, 31(7), 2–7.

Bhaskar, R. (1993). *Dialectic – The Pulse of Freedom*. London: Routledge.

Bhaskar, R. (2008). *A Realist Theory of Science – With a New Introduction*. London: Routledge. (First published 1975.)

Bourdieu, P. (1984). *Distinction: Critique of the Judgment of Taste*. Cambridge, MA: Harvard University Press.

Brems, C., Fosgerau, M., Hansen, C. O. and Nielsen, O. A. (2007). *Trafikmodeller. Arbejdsnotat til Infrastrukturkommissionen* [Traffic models. Working paper for the Danish National Infrastructure Commission]. Kgs. Lyngby: Denmark's Technical University.

Dean, K. (2007). Needs. In Hartwig, M. (ed.) *Dictionary of Critical Realism*, pp. 323–324. London/New York: Routledge.

Diesing, P. (1962). *Reason in Society: Five Types of Decisions and Their Social Conditions*. Urbana, IL: University of Illinois Press.

Edwards, W. and Newman, J. R. (1982). *Multiattribute Evaluation*. Thousand Oaks, CA: Sage Publications.

Eliasson, J. and Lundberg, M. (2012). Do cost–benefit analyses influence transport investment decisions? Experiences from the Swedish Transport Investment Plan 2010–21. *Transport Reviews*, 32, 29–48.

Flyvbjerg, B., Holm, M. S. and Buhl, S. (2003). How common and how large are cost overruns in transport infrastructure projects? *Transport Reviews*, 23, 71–88.

Flyvbjerg, B., Holm, M. S. and Buhl, S. (2005). How (in)accurate are demand forecasts in public works projects? The case of transportation. *Journal of the American Planning Association*, 71(2), 131–146.

Fullbrook, E. (2004). Broadband versus narrowband economics. Introductory chapter in Fullbrook, E. (ed.) *A Guide to What's Wrong With Economics*. London: Anthem Press.

Habermas, J. (1984). *The Theory of Communicative Action. Volume 1: Reason and the Rationalization of Society*. London: Heinemann.

Hartwig, M. (2007). Cognitivism or cognitive triumphalism. In Hartwig, M. (ed.) *Dictionary of Critical Realism*, p. 68. London/New York: Routledge.

Henman, P. (2002). Computer modelling and the politics of greenhouse gas policy in Australia. *Social Science Computer Review*, 20, 161–173.

Litman, T. (2014). *Generated Traffic and Induced Travel. Implications for Transport Planning.* Victoria: Victoria Transport Policy Institute, www.vtpi.org/gentraf.pdf.

Metz, D. (2008). The myth of travel time saving. *Transport Reviews*, 28, 321 – 336.

Ministry of Finance, Norway (2012). *NOU 2012:16 Samfunnsøkonomiske analyser. [Social cost–benefit analyses.]* Oslo: Ministry of Finance.

Ministry of Finance, Norway (2014). *Prinsipper og krav ved utarbeidelse av samfunnsøkonomiske analyser mv. [Principles and requirements pertaining to the preparation of social cost-benefit analyses etc.]* Oslo: Ministry of Finance.

Ministry of the Environment (Norway) (2001): *Miljøbyrapport. Vedlegg A.* [Report from the Sustainable Cities program, appendix A.] Oslo: Ministry of the Environment.

MOTOS (2007). *Transport Modelling: Towards Operational Standards in Europe.* MOTOS Project EU. Handbook. www.motosproject.eu/?po_id=handbook (accessed 18 December 2009).

Næss, P. (2004). Prediction, regressions and critical realism. *Journal of Critical Realism*, 3(1), 133–164.

Næss, P. (2006a). Unsustainable growth, unsustainable capitalism. *Journal of Critical Realism*, 5(2), 197–227.

Næss, P. (2006b). Cost–benefit analyses of transportation investments: neither critical nor realistic. *Journal of Critical Realism*, 5(1), 32–60.

Næss, P. (2009). Up-front assessment of needs. In Samset, K., Sunnevåg, K. and Williams, T. (eds) *Making Essential Choices with Scant Information. Front-end Decision-making in Major Projects*, pp. 85–105. London: Palgrave Macmillan.

Næss, P. and Strand, A. (2012). What kinds of traffic forecasts are possible? *Journal of Critical Realism*, 11(3), 277–295.

Næss, P., Andersen, J, Nicolaisen, M. S. and Strand, A. (2014). Transport modelling in the context of the "predict and provide" paradigm. *European Journal of Transport and Infrastructure Research*, 14(2), 102–121.

Nicolaisen, M. S. (2012). *Forecasts: Fact or Fiction? Uncertainty and Inaccuracy in Transport Project Evaluation* (Ph.D.thesis). Aalborg: Aalborg University.

Nicolaisen, M. S. and Driscoll, P. (2014). Ex-post evaluations of demand forecast accuracy: a literature review. *Transport Reviews*, 34, 540–557.

Nicolaisen, M. S. and Næss, P. (2015). Roads to nowhere: the accuracy of travel demand forecasts for do-nothing alternatives. *Transport Policy*, 37, 57–63.

Noland, R. B. and Lem, L. L. (2002). A review of the evidence for induced travel and changes in transportation and environmental policy in the US and the UK. *Transportation Research Part D*, 7(1), 1–26.

Nordhaus, W. D. (1994). *Managing the Global Commons: The Economics of Climate Change.* Cambridge, MA: MIT Press.

Nyborg, M. (2002: *Miljø og nytte-kostnadsanalyse. Noen prinsipielle vurderinger.* [Environment and cost–benefit analysis. Some fundamental considerations.] Rapport 5/2002. Oslo: Frisch senteret.

Næss, P., Andersen, J., Nicolaisen, M. S. and Strand, A. (2015). Forecasting inaccuracies: a result of unexpected events, optimism bias, technical problems, or strategic misrepresentation? *Journal of Transport and Land Use*, 8(3), 39–55.

Odeck, J. (2010). What determines decision-makers' preferences for road investments? Evidence from the Norwegian road sector. *Transport Reviews*, 30, 473–494.

Odgaard, T., Kelly, C. and Laird, J. (2005). *Current Practice in Project Appraisals in Europe.* Paper for the conference Trafikdage på Aalborg Universitet, Aalborg, August 2005.

Price, L. (2007). *A Transdisciplinary Explanatory Critique of Environmental Education. Volume 1: Business and Industry.* PhD thesis. Grahamstown: Rhodes University.

Small, K. (1999). Project evaluation. In Gómez-Ibanez, J. A., Tye, W. B. and Winston, C. (eds) *Essays in Transportation Economics and Policy: A Handbook in Honor of John R. Meyer*. Washington, DC: Brookings Press.

Stern, N. (ed.) (2006). *The Economics of Climate Change*. London: HM Treasury, Cambridge University Press.

Volden, G. H. (2013). *Use of Carbon Prices in Cost–Benefit Analysis Practices in Project Appraisals of Major Public Investment Projects under the Norwegian State Project Model*. Concept report no. 37. Trondheim: Norwegian University of Science and Technology.

Welsh, M. and Williams, H. (1997). The sensitivity of transport investment benefits to the evaluation of small travel-time savings. *Journal of Transport Economics and Policy*, 31(3), 231–254.

Wilson, D. and Dixon, W. (2006). Das Adam Smith problem: a critical realist perspective. *Journal of Critical Realism*, 5(2), 251–272.

5

ARGUMENTS FOR AND AGAINST ECONOMIC GROWTH

Jin Xue

Introduction

The ideology of economic growth can be traced back at least to the second half of the eighteenth century, when Adam Smith published his *Wealth of Nations*. Still, it is only fairly recently, in the latest six decades, that the pursuit of growth has become the dominant ideology across the world. During this period, the global economy has increased almost tenfold (Maddison, 2010). In the 1960s and 1970s, a critical discussion on growth began to emerge, culminating in the publication of the famous report from the Club of Rome, *The Limits to Growth* (Meadows *et al.*, 1972). The growth debate was further strengthened by the economic crisis in the 1970s, triggered by two times trebling of oil prices. During the 1980s, however, the acknowledgment of the negative effect on the environment of the growth ideology resulted in the idea that we can "decouple" economic growth from environmental deterioration. This "decoupling" view was emphasized, for instance, by the World Commission on Environment and Development (WCED) as a key strategy of sustainable development in its report *Our Common Future* (1987), as well as in a number of books and reports focusing on "ecological modernization" (Huber, 1985; Spaargaren and Mol, 1992; Hajer, 1995).

More recently, however, the possibility of maintaining economic growth through decoupling has been increasingly questioned by critics who propose a steady-state economy or even de-growth instead (Jackson, 2009; Schneider *et al.*, 2010). Faced with multiple crises characterized by ecological deterioration, social injustice, and economic recession, it is urgent for humans to make decisions on their future and the path to this future. The dominant position taken by politicians, media, and business for a future scenario has been reviving growth. However, limits to growth and the social and environmental downsides of growth have gained increasing attention, leading to the emerging de-growth debates calling for a democratically led redistributive downscaling of production and consumption in industrialized countries as a means to achieve environmental sustainability, social justice, and well-being.

The purpose of this chapter is to critically scrutinize arguments for and against economic growth as a strategy to deal with the multiple crises. Four lines of arguments are identified. The following four sections discuss the arguments originating from economic, social, environmental, and underlying ethical perspectives, respectively. Each section will present the arguments both for and against economic growth, explore the grounds for their propositions, and discuss the limitations or implications of these arguments. The conclusion makes a short discussion on the growth imperative.

Arguments from an economic perspective

Economic growth has been a major concern of the discipline of economy right from the beginning. The period of classical political economy from the mid eighteenth century to the late nineteenth century coincided with the dawn of the industrial revolution, where wealth was created on a larger scale than ever before. The unprecedented rapid economic growth due to economic liberty and an increasing division of labor were welcomed by the new group of political economists (Zweig, 1979). Although they generally believed that economic growth as a process of accumulating wealth is desirable, they also expressed concerns about the unintended consequences of economic growth. David Ricardo, for instance, realized that the introduction of machinery seemed likely to result in unemployment. Interestingly, the "old school" of political economists from Adam Smith to David Ricardo assumed that it was impossible to avoid a stationary state of capital and wealth. For them, this was an unpleasant, disheartening, yet inevitable, prospect. For John Stuart Mill, however, the establishment of a stationary state would be a considerable improvement. For him, it would be sad if humanity continued to spread all over the world until no areas were left to experience solitude.

The stationary state may not be easy to achieve. Karl Marx was possibly the first person to state that capitalists are subject to an inescapable growth imperative. He used the simple formula M-C-M' to illustrate how the capitalist economy tends to entail limitless accumulation. By producing commodities (C) that can be sold at a higher price than the money needed to produce them, the original amount of money (M) can be converted into a greater amount (M'). Then M' becomes capital in turn and is the new point of departure to make more money (Marx, 1858/1993). At an individual level, each capitalist accumulates his wealth in this manner. Even if a capitalist is capable of rejecting the temptation of money fetishism, he or she is still forced to grow. A company that considers its present level of profit as sufficient and does not attempt to increase it will soon lose market share because its competitors are increasing their productivity and are able to lower their prices. The competition among capitalists thus drives each individual capitalist to increase his profit to avoid losing out in the capitalist market. At an aggregate level, the profit maximization of each capitalist tends to result in economic growth. Zero growth would imply that some capitalists lose profits and face the threat of bankruptcy.

In capitalists' attempts to maximize profits and accumulate capital, technological innovation plays an important role. Through developing and adopting advanced technologies, capitalists are able to increase efficiency of the production so as to reduce the costs of products and gain excess profits compared with their competitors. Market competition cannot result in economic growth without a continual expansion of consumer demand for new products. Material goods play a role that goes way beyond their material functionality. They are also tightly connected to status, identity, and social affiliation. Conspicuous consumption is an important way to demonstrate and maintain social status (Veblen, 1899/1994). Only this social dynamic can explain why people in affluent countries continue to strive for more goods (Jackson, 2009).

The rapid global financialization since the 1990s appears to be another factor driving economic growth. Deregulation of the financial sector makes it possible for banks to issue loans with few restrictions. The money supply from banks can theoretically increase infinitely. This has led to an imbalance between the claims on wealth in the form of debt and the real wealth in terms of material goods and services. Debt-based claims on wealth have become increasingly detached from the real economy (Dietz and O'Neill, 2013). Therefore, there is always an imperative to produce more and more products in order to keep pace with growth in the debts. The financial system will risk collapse if growth in the real economy fails. For individual consumers, the more one borrows from banks, the more money one has to earn by engaging in economic activities in order to repay the loans (ibid.), constituting another driver of economic growth.

The existence of the growth mechanisms implies a growth tendency in capitalism, regardless of whether the economy is actually growing or not. Historically, capitalist societies have experienced periods of downturns and even crises, suggesting a stagnation tendency in capitalism. The mechanisms for a declining trend of growth rates emanate from both the production and the consumption sides (Nielsen and Næss, 2011). On the production side, exponential growth undermines its very conditions by depleting natural resources and degrading the environment (O'Connor, 1998). It therefore becomes increasingly difficult to increase profitability when the costs of overcoming the limits of nature increase. Apart from that, Marx identified a tendency of falling profit rates as more and more labor-saving devices are applied in the production processes. On the consumption side, consumer demands tend to stagnate after basic material needs are satisfied. As mentioned earlier, rising consumption level beyond basic goods is about luxury and positional goods. People have to work more and harder in order to consume more, but there are physiological, mental, and social limits to people's working life. In addition, the tendency of individual entrepreneurs and corporations to replace labor with automation in order to increase profitability will result in large segments of people being considered redundant and disposable (Harvey, 2014). The aggregate demand for an increasing output of goods and services will decline as jobs and incomes shrink.

A number of attempts have been employed to counteract this tendency of a decreasing growth rate. These include a rising rate of exploitation on both labor forces employed and nature, increasing market demand by advertising, expansion of credit system to facilitate debt-based consumption, and globalization to convert non-capitalist countries into the capitalist economy. However, as these strategies are fully utilized, the sufficiency of these countervailing forces to stave off falling growth rates in the long run is questionable.

Serious doubts about economic growth began to occur in the late 1960s. Nicholas Georgescu-Roegen and Herman Daly were some of the first prominent scholars since Mill to recommend a "steady-state economy," "zero-growth," and even "de-growth." They argued that the larger the economic subsystem becomes, the more it will have to conform to the steady-state mode of the Earth as a whole (Daly, 2008). In a steady-state economy, the capital stock tends to be constant, due to a low goods production rate equal to the rate of depreciation. According to Daly, this does not imply a break with the capitalist system. The market is still the most efficient way to allocate resources, but vital decisions, first of all concerning the total volume of the economy, should be kept outside the market (Daly, 1993). The market mechanisms' urge to grow continually may be offset by strong state intervention in terms of raising prices on scarce resources. In order for this to happen, moral growth will be required.

However, there are serious challenges to this line of argument. In order to install a steady-state economy, robust and powerful interventions from public authorities are needed. So far policies in virtually every nation have been officially structured for economic growth, and it seems difficult for governments to change their role in favour of non-growth. Unlike previous radical political changes, there is no easily identifiable group of people currently who clearly benefit from the shift to a steady-state economy. This change will depend on moral engagement from people, who feel committed to care for the well-being of future people.

Second, even if a moral awakening is strong enough to design a stable economy in certain countries or regions, it may be difficult to keep it stable if capitalist mechanisms are expected to continue the way Daly assumes. Although there are plenty of green initiatives in the most developed countries, one should not ignore arguments such as Kovel's (2002), showing how the relentless competition in a transnational capitalist environment favours the most self-seeking and ruthless managers, particularly when they act in poor countries with weak or corrupt states. The more corporations fulfil their quest for expansion, the more grandiose these managers' way of thinking seems to become, and the more they are able to remove themselves from environmental constraints and from the life conditions of the less privileged.

The difficulty of achieving a moral shift to stability is true for consumers as well. Highly durable goods may not satisfy consumers' desire for new products, especially not if consumption continues to play a key role in showing social status. With a low throughput in a steady-state economy, people have to inhibit their aspiration for more and newer goods. It would be tempting for a minority of producers or governments to satisfy this demand, and their competitive advantage could easily inspire or force others to do likewise.

Arguments from a social perspective

A number of the arguments for and against economic growth that emerged in the 1960s focused on the role that economic growth has in improving quality of life by, for example, alleviating poverty, reducing unemployment, and enhancing social equity. This convention, of associating social benefits with economic growth, has been adopted by developing countries seeking to advance living standards. Many scholars continue to argue that it ought to be the supreme goal of national policy (Ravallion, 1997).

However, since the 1970s, this traditional view has been criticized by a number of social scientists. They doubt that economic growth inevitably contributes to human progress and prosperity, no matter how high the achieved affluence level. This doubt was supported in particular by Easterlin's studies (1973, 1974). Subsequent empirical findings by other researchers have confirmed Easterlin's conclusion that life satisfaction is not proportional to economic growth in the most advanced economies (Duncan, 1975; Shin, 1978; Easterlin, 1995, 2005).

Empirical data comparing countries with different per capita income levels show that in poor countries, a small increase in GDP per capita leads to a large rise in happiness. However, after reaching a certain affluence level, economic growth does not bring proportional increase in happiness (Jackson, 2009). Instead, countries with lower income levels, such as Iceland, the Netherlands, Denmark, and Sweden, have higher happiness levels than the US. When observing the historical relationship between economic growth and happiness in the US, it was found that the percentage of people who reported being very happy had stabilized at around 30 percent during the years 1945–2005, although GDP per capita had more than tripled (Dietz and O'Neill, 2013).

The lack of proportionality between economic growth and happiness is what we observe and experience in the empirical domain. The underlying mechanisms producing this phenomenon may be elucidated by the difference between absolute utility theory and relative preference theory. Absolute utility theory argues that people living at a low economic level are in great need of supplies of material goods; greater income can fill more needs and raise the level of happiness. When people's basic needs for materials are satisfied, the gains from any further increase in material wealth decrease gradually. At this stage, the mechanisms of relative preference theory begin to play the main role. According to this theory, an individual's utility of income is relative to other people (reference groups) or the individual's own previous income stream (adaptive expectations) (Hagerty and Veenhoven, 2003). The individual does not gain much from an additional income as long as other people's income increases similarly. The individual's expectations adjust so quickly to the increased income level that it brings no additional satisfaction.

Another possible explanation for the lack of proportionality between happiness and growth is that people tend to make choices that make them unhappier when income level is high, for instance long commutes and working hours (Oswald, 2006). Delhey (2009) argues that when basic needs are met, a shift in value priorities takes place away from materialist scarcity values focusing on income toward post-materialist self-expression values giving priority to personal autonomy and job creativity.

Arguments are not limited to the relationship between growth and happiness. Other aspects of our social life, such as life expectancy, health, and educational participation, display a similar pattern as happiness in their relationship with economic growth. Some low-income countries are not performing any worse than those with high income as regards these three concerns (Jackson, 2009). Particularly, income growth seems insignificant in relation to health. Studies suggest that, compared with GDP per person, economic inequality contributes more in reducing public health (Wilkinson and Pickett, 2009). What matters instead are the institutional factors and the spread of inexpensive health and sanitation technologies (Kenny, 2009).

Economic growth is often argued to be the best solution to eliminate poverty. A famous metaphor for this argument can be found in the slogan "a rising tide lifts all boats." Others talk about a "trickle-down effect," according to which economic growth sooner or later will benefit even the worst off. Being used both within and across countries, these metaphors assume that the improvement of the general economy should be pursued first and foremost in order to expand the beneficiaries from the rich to the poor. The World Bank, for instance, holds the view that the economy of rich countries should continue to grow as rapidly as possible to provide markets for the poor and to accumulate capital to invest in poor countries (Daly, 2008). Instead of redistributing the cake from the rich to the poor, economic growth becomes an attractive and convenient solution simply because it tries to make the cake bigger so that everyone will have their amounts increased.

Economic growth during the latest decades has clearly helped a large number of people out of extreme poverty. According to the World Bank estimate, the poverty rate (living below $1.25 a day) fell by about 25 percent between 1981 and 2005 (Chen and Ravallion, 2008). However, the economic growth seems to have benefited the rich considerably more than the poor. An OECD study on income distribution and poverty (2008) shows that the gap between rich and poor has grown in more than three-quarters of rich countries since the mid-1980s. Relative poverty has thus become more pronounced during the decades of economic growth. This seems to suggest that all boats are not lifted equally and that economic growth helps to concentrate the fruits of growth in the hands of the wealthiest. Between 1990 and 2001, for every $100 increase in the world's average per capita income, only $0.60 contributed to the UN Millennium Development Goal of reducing poverty among those who earn less than $1 a day (Woodward *et al.*, 2006).

"Raising the tide" is not an efficient way of eliminating poverty, though, compared with policies focusing directly on the poor. If economic growth enlarges income inequality, it underpins rich people's social status, power, and influence, but undermines those of poor people. This is particularly the case if access to the basic prerequisites of capabilities, education for instance, is dependent on ability to pay. If people with high income can send their children to private schools of significantly higher quality than public schools, they further their future career opportunities considerably, leading to positions with higher income and influence (Talbott, 2008). This way the capabilities of rich people are reinforced, whereas poor people gradually become marginalized. In addition, high inequality leads to status competition in which the poor, mostly in vain, strive to reach the consumption level of the wealthiest group. This results in a greater consumption of resources than is necessary to meet basic needs for a quality of life.

The growth debate in affluent countries has also been closely linked to a social discourse on unemployment (Spangenberg, 2008). Without growth, increasing levels of productivity per capita are assumed to reduce the size of the workforce. However, this is true only if working hours remain constant or increase. If the number of working hours decreases more quickly than productivity grows, increased productivity will not result in higher unemployment. Several ecologically oriented scholars have therefore proposed to harvest the gains from productivity improvements by reducing working hours instead of increasing production and consumption (Jespersen, 2004; Spangenberg, 2008). Reducing the number of working hours implies maintaining or reducing income levels and thus the levels of consumption. There seems to be popular support for this idea. In Denmark, since 1964 a growing proportion of the population has stated that they would prefer reduced working time rather than more income, reaching 73 percent in 2007 (Nørgaard, 2009). Reducing working time not only has the social benefit of preventing unemployment, it also contributes to enhancing well-being by giving people more free time to devote to social and physical activities outside of work, such as spending time with friends and family, developing hobbies, and participating in community activities. In a series of surveys of residents of the state of Oregon, a strong majority supported reducing consumption and believed doing so would improve societal and individual well-being (Markowitz and Bowerman, 2012). In addition, work-time reduction has the potential to benefit the environment, as constant or reduced income stabilizes or declines consumption levels.

A growth-based society does not necessarily lead to reduced unemployment. Increasing production and productivity through technological innovations involves a general "acceleration of society" (Rosa, 2003). Adaptability to changing conditions is increasingly becoming a requirement. As a result, vulnerable groups have been expelled from the workforce (Nielsen and Næss, 2011). Information technology blurs the borders between leisure and work, but work tends to colonize leisure time rather than the opposite. This has disruptive effects on family life and other social relations, and is likely to have negative psychological impacts.

To sum up, when examined critically, the social arguments in favor of growth become shaky when affluence reaches a certain level. The diminishing happiness returns from increases in income imply that economic growth concentrating on material goals is not a decisive and essential element in making people in affluent nations happier. In addition, enlarged inequality triggered by economic growth may lead to unexpected and undesired effects. Economic growth does not guarantee full employment.

Arguments from an environmental perspective

Many modern arguments for and against growth originated in the 1960s in response to widespread environmental pollution and ecological deterioration. The debates became fierce particularly during two waves of public and political interest in the environment. The first wave started in the late 1960s, reaching its high point with the Stockholm conference in 1972, and was backed up by a number of publications such as *The Limits to Growth* (Meadows *et al.*, 1972); the second wave began with the Brundtland Report (WCED, 1987), and culminated in the Rio Summit in 1992.

When it comes to environmental sustainability, proponents of economic growth based their arguments on a strong belief that economic growth can be decoupled from negative environmental impacts. In light of the "decoupling" view, economic growth can go on forever without limits imposed by the natural environment. Rather, environmental problems can be dealt with by continual growth. This later position is supported by the Environmental Kuznets Curve (EKC) hypothesis (Barry and Paterson, 2003). According to this hypothesis, economic growth in poor countries usually entails environmental degradation; when countries get wealthier, more money can be spent on the development of environmentally friendly technologies. As such, continual economic growth is considered to be a prerequisite for successfully dealing with environmental problems.

Advocated by environmental economists, one way to decouple environmental impacts from economic growth is to incorporate environmental degradation into economic accounting. The price on environmental goods is determined by people's willingness-to-pay. A so-called Pigovian tax should be put on products, equal to the marginal value of the damages they cause (James *et al.*, 1978; Pearce, 1993). Charging emission fees and assigning ownership rights to environmental resources are also traditional methods proposed by economists to tackle environmental problems (Cropper and Oates, 1992). Implicit in these arguments is the point that even though growth leads to environmental problems, these are only externalities due to market failures, and need to be internalized. If this happens, sound growth will emerge.

The environmental economists' points are somewhat associated with the idea of ecological modernization that was developed in the early 1980s (Mol and Sonnenfeld, 2000). In this discourse, dematerialization emerged as a basic political goal. "Eco-efficiency," "substitution," and "qualitative improvement" are usually advocated as decoupling strategies to dematerialize economic growth. The Factor 4 and Factor 10 concepts are widely used specifications of the goals of eco-efficiency improvement (von Weizsäcker *et al.*, 1997). Factor 4 means a fourfold increase in resource productivity, thus "doubling wealth while halving resource use." Substitution refers to changing the composition of economic growth from resource-demanding sectors to sectors that are less material and energy intensive. Daly (1996) distinguishes between "growth" as quantitative increase and "development" as qualitative improvement. He claims that it is possible to dematerialize the economy through qualitative improvement, which implies that economic development does not entail any increase in material input.

The arguments recommended by environmental economists are subject to important limitations. The inverted U-shaped curve of the EKC hypothesis has mainly been found for specific pollutants at a local scale. There is no indication that it is valid for total resource throughput (Spangenberg, 2001), and certain pollutants, such as CO_2 emissions, have not been reduced with higher GDP (Galeotti *et al.*, 2006). Even N-shaped and linear-shaped relationships have been found for some pollutants. Observed inverted U curves can be partly attributable to changes in international trade: pollution-intensive goods are imported at the expense of environmental quality in foreign nations (Suri and Chapman, 1998; Agras and Chapman, 1999).

The arguments of willingness-to-pay for environmental pollution are problematic in dealing with a broad range of environmental problems. Consequences that are invisible or non-sensible for those whose willingness-to-pay is requested tend to be ignored or underestimated. Often only "tangible" environmental consequences, which can be felt immediately by current people, are included. Even for those tangible environmental consequences, there are huge difficulties in assigning an accurate monetary value due to the impossibility of quantifying and monetizing their real effects (Goodland and Ledec, 1993). This is particularly the case with border-crossing and long-term environmental effects. Nor is it obvious whose willingness is represented in the shadow price. If people influenced are living beyond the region where pollution is caused, or not yet alive, the taxes or fees charged through willingness-to-pay are likely to be unfair. Apart from this, some environmental consequences remain irreversible no matter how much people would like to pay to get rid of them (Ackerman and Heinzerling, 2004).

Although the idea of decoupling through improving eco-efficiency may be a theoretically viable short-term strategy, it has not been substantiated by a broad range of empirical evidence. At the aggregate economy level, the total emissions of CO_2 in OECD countries showed relative decoupling from economic growth during 1990–1999, which means the absolute emissions have been increasing but at a lower rate compared with GDP growth (OECD, 2002). At the sector level, studies on the transport sector find that only indications of a slight, relative decoupling between GDP, traffic volume, and CO_2 can be identified in the European Union (Tapio, 2005). The same applies to the housing sector. In studies on the extent of decoupling between housing sector growth and environmental consequences in the Copenhagen Metropolitan Area in Denmark and Hangzhou in China, it was found that residential energy consumption and land consumption for residential purposes had increased since the 1990s, despite tightened building energy standards and compact urban development policies (Xue, 2013). In addition, eco-efficiency improvements are likely to generate rebound effects, since reduced resource consumption due to higher efficiency will release purchasing power that can be spent on other items, offsetting the expected environmental benefits or even making the efficiency strategy counterproductive (Alcott, 2005). The general picture for the trend of decoupling seems to be that the drop in environmental impacts per unit of product is canceled out by the rising scale of the economy.

Moreover, even if ample and pollution-free energy is made easily accessible, endless economic growth in such a "solar energy paradise" would still be environmentally problematic. As long as energy is used to produce products that are material-consumptive and environmentally negative, the environmental effect will not be neutral (Næss and Høyer, 2009). Furthermore, the ratio of energy return on energy invested is much lower for exploiting renewables than fossil fuels, indicating that using renewable energy to sustain economic growth needs more energy input than non-renewable energy sources (Dietz and O'Neill, 2013).

Substituting growth in manufacturing industries with service industries is often assumed to impose less environmental load. Some rich countries have experienced a shift to a service-based economy or "knowledge economy." The environmental benefits from this shift are in fact partly due to the outsourcing of heavy-polluting industries to developing countries. On a global scale, the total environmental load posed by human activities does not decrease. This shift to a service-based economy is short-sighted and problematic in the long run since the dirty industries will be unable to find suitable locations if poor countries stop importing them from rich countries.

The decoupling idea reflects an "econocentric" view on the relationship between nature and economy. This view falsely assumes that the economy interacts with the environment in a closed self-relying system (Venkatachalam, 2007), where atomistic and mechanistic economic models are seen as universal laws that can be applied everywhere, including the ecological system (Nørgaard, 1985; Ramos-Martin, 2003). Ecological economists, however, consider the economy, society, and nature to be mutually influencing and structured in a hierarchical way where the economic system is treated as a sub-system of the global ecosystem (Venkatachalam, 2007). Thus human society and its economic system are emergent from the Earth's ecosphere. Human economy takes up more or less "space" in relation to the closed system of a planet with a finite natural capacity. The larger the scale of the economy becomes, the greater the risk of destroying the conditions for human life on Earth in the long term. Human economic growth should not exceed the "carrying capacity" or "biocapacity" that represents the theoretical maximum supply of natural resources and ecological services that can be provided by an area (Daly *et al.*, 1989; Røpke, 2004, 2005). Numerous studies, such as those that consider our ecological footprint, suggest that the scale of our economic activity has grown too large to be sustainable. The human ecological footprint has overshot the planet's biocapacity by 50 percent (WWF, 2014). To avoid further environmental degradation and ecological catastrophe, reducing the economic scale to be within the limit of the ecosystem's biocapacity is a necessity for long-term human prosperity.

Arguments from a moral perspective

The most disquieting argument against continuous economic growth rests in the emphasis on external limits. The presence of such limits accentuates issues of distributional ethics moving far beyond the confines of our local environments and contemporary situation. People and other living creatures distant from us in more than one dimension are affected, leaving us with a fairly complex pattern of potential obligations. The discussion from an ethical point of view makes these arguments against growth even more justifiable. Figure 5.1 illustrates potential moral obligations in the three dimensions: time, space, and species (Arler, 2001, 2006).

Intergenerational equity is a main moral concern when judging the plausibility of the arguments against growth. From an environmental perspective, intergenerational equity is simply our obligation to leave future generations living conditions comparable to those we inherited ourselves (Arler, 2006; Weiss, 1990). This obligation to preserve the quality of our planet will constrain the present generation's actions in exploiting and using resources. Continuing current levels of growth will result in higher risks of undermining the capacity of succeeding generations to create well-being. Even though depletion of natural resources may lead to a number of the substitutions that defenders of weak sustainability rely on (Solow, 1993), substitution opportunities are not without limits. Some fundamental functionalities of nature are critical in the sense that they are impossible to live without and may be irreversibly lost once destroyed (Ekins, 2003). Other goods – the diversity of biological organisms, for instance – may not be impossible to live without, but are unique in the sense that we would think of life without them as degraded (Arler, 2001).

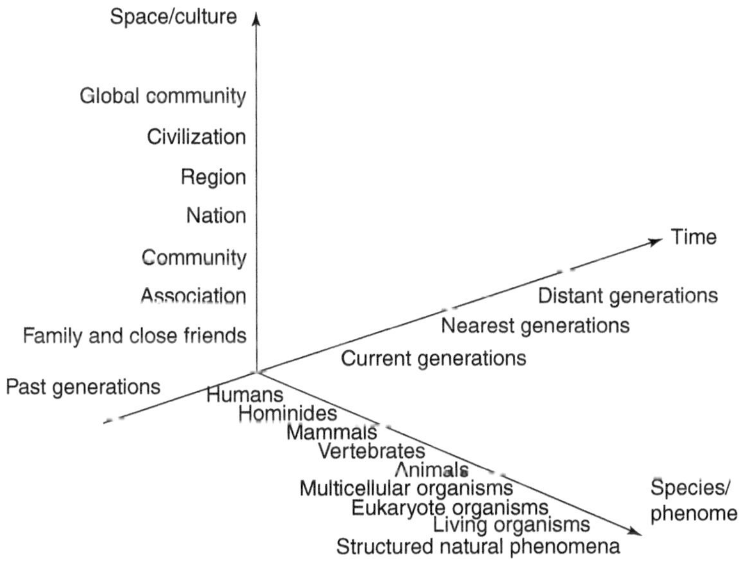

FIGURE 5.1 Three dimensions where obligations may become relevant
Source: Arler (2006)

The spatial or cultural dimension of human moral obligation extends the traditional scope of ethical concerns by including moral responsibility toward population groups beyond one's specific community or nation. This is referred to as intragenerational equity. In terms of environmental justice, some populations or regions may face greater risks from exposure to environmental hazards or lack of resources than others. It would be unfair to let certain groups of people suffer significant environmental hazards simply because they live far away from the polluters. In addition, there is an uneven use of the Earth's biocapacity. According to the *Living Planet Report 2014* (WWF, 2014), the ecological footprint per capita of high-income countries is about five times greater than that of low-income countries, and high-income countries often rely on the biocapacity of other nations or the global commons to meet their consumption demands. As mentioned before, humanity's ecological footprint was assessed to exceed the Earth's total biocapacity by 50 percent in 2010. Greater use of the limited biocapacity to meet the demand of the affluent nations means less biocapacity available to meet the demand of the impoverished nations. With a non-growing biocapacity, substantial cuts in resource consumption and waste generation in rich countries are required if more ecological space should be left for the poor to increase welfare. Out of the consideration of equity in sharing the world's ecological space, affluent countries have to assume more obligations to control their unlimited growth.

In a society without growth, it is even more important to emphasize distributional justice, as the potential for conflicts over distribution of resources is higher in a world of finite resources than in a world without limits. If overall production and consumption are kept within ecological limits, there will be no rising tide to lift all boats, or the cake cannot be baked bigger. Getting a bigger slice of the cake by some people means reducing the size of the rest of the cake available to others. Poor people are likely to be losers in these conflicts since they are often vulnerable and less powerful than the rich (Martinez-Alier, 2002). However, attempts to redistribute wealth from the rich to the poor may encourage national-chauvinistic attitudes and policies in rich countries, if increased welfare in poor countries is seen as a threat against their own lifestyles and privileges (Hardin, 1974). Needless to say, such a development will not be conducive to peace between nations.

The overload of ecological footprints burdening the Earth's biocapacity not only brings conflicts within the human species across regions, cultures, and classes, but also means that less ecological space is left for other organisms. It thus raises concern in the third dimension of human moral obligation: the respect we owe to organisms from other species, i.e. cross-species equity.

Much ethical reflection uses the general categories "anthropocentrism" and "biocentrism." Anthropocentrism is often seen as a position placing inherent worth on humans flourishing, whereas the rest of nature has only instrumental value in satisfying human desires. However, we should at least separate this strong anthropocentrism from a weaker kind that allows the use of non-human organisms only as means of human desires and needs, if these are consistent with rational worldviews including scientific theories, aesthetic values, and moral ideals (Norton, 1993). Strong anthropocentrism tends to legitimate human behaviors that wantonly conquer, dominate, and exploit non-human nature. However, weak anthropocentrism considers ruthless exploitation to be an irrational option if this results in destroying beautiful or interesting species that have no narrowly defined utility value for humans.

This weak anthropocentric perspective is challenged by various kinds of biocentrism, based on the assumption that not only humans but other organisms or species as well have some kind of inherent worth or intrinsic value. So-called "biospherical egalitarianism" even considers all kinds of life to have equal value, arguing that they should have an equal possibility to live and blossom (Næss, 1973, 1993). Killing, exploiting, and suppressing organisms violates this principle. Even killing of bacteria to prevent human illness seems difficult to allow, as long as the illness is not serious. The intense interference made by economic activities would be difficult to accept. However, in any realistic praxis, this absolute egalitarianism cannot take place. There is a principle of ecological balance that some damage to other species is necessary for most species to survive. This is the physical law of nature to which both humans and non-humans submit. An absolute egalitarianism, therefore, entrenches a view of the moral superiority of humans who are capable of perceiving killing other species or organisms for survival as wrong.

If humans and other species do not have equal value, there must be a ranking of values. Then one cannot avoid asking how much more valuable human projects and activities are compared to those of other species. Applying this to the question of economic growth, one could ask to what extent human economic activities should be allowed to displace or interfere with other organisms' lives. In the ecological footprint debate this is presented as a spatial conflict over potentially arable land left in a state of wilderness. Some say we should leave 20 percent for wildlife, others opt for more. Conflicts also occur within the territories occupied by humans, for instance as conflicts about the use of pesticides and fertilizers in agriculture.

The questioning of strong anthropocentrism, or human chauvinism, from the various kinds of weak anthropocentrism and biocentrism can be seen as vaccinations against hubris. They converge in their insistence on conservation of various natural features, for example richness and biodiversity of ecosystems, even though they diverge in some of the underlying assumptions for this position. Weak anthropocentrists argue that we should not forget that humans benefit from the continuous presence of other species, even when they are not useful in a narrow sense. Biocentric ethicists argue that humans have responsibilities not to overexploit non-human resources because the flourishing of other organisms and species continues to be important even in the absence of humans to enjoy it.

Concluding remarks

We have examined a variety of arguments for and against unlimited economic growth from different perspectives. Table 5.1 summarizes these arguments. The

TABLE 5.1 Arguments for and against perpetual economic growth

	For	*Against*
Economic system	- A growth imperative in the capitalist economic system - Technological innovation is an important driver of economic growth - Debt-based money creation drives economic growth - A continual consumer demand for new products supports growth	- Economic growth collides with the inescapable need for a steady state in biophysical terms - There is a stagnation tendency in capitalism emanating from human and social domains which makes perpetual economic growth impossible
Society	- Growth brings human progress - Growth solves the problem of unemployment - Growth reduces poverty - Non-growth in a competitive society aggravates social conflicts over the distribution of goods	- Social benefits do not increase proportionally with growth - Growth tends to increase inequality - Growth is not essential for human prosperity - Growth does not guarantee full employment
Environment	- Environmental problems can be internalized into the current economic system - Economic growth makes it possible to develop better solutions to solve environmental problems - Growth can be decoupled from environmental impacts	- Current economic growth has exceeded a sustainable scale - There is an ecological limit to growth - Decoupling strategies are not sufficient to reduce economic scale to be within the limit of the ecosystem's biocapacity
Ethics	- Growth furthers happiness, preference satisfaction, freedom of choices, and promotes virtues such as autonomy, self-command and self-reliance, prudence, accuracy, diligence, frugality, innovation, and industry - Growth in affluent countries is necessary to provide markets for the poor and to ease investments in poor countries. Rejecting growth in affluent countries will cause increased hardship for the world's poor	- The moral premise of intergenerational equality suggests that present generations have an obligation not to ruin future people's opportunities to lead lives of a quality comparable with their own - The moral premise of intragenerational equity suggests affluent nations have an obligation to reduce their use of ecological space to save space for poor countries to increase their welfare on a planet with finite resources - The moral premise of cross-species equity suggests that humans have a duty to conserve and protect non-human nature

diversity of the arguments shows that economic growth cannot be considered a default goal to be pursued without reservation.

Continual economic growth in affluent countries is neither desirable nor possible

In affluent countries, growth is not necessary in order to achieve human flourishing. Growth is beneficial to humankind only up to a point, beyond which it seems to fail to be of much help. Future economic growth in rich countries is likely to primarily benefit those who already live on top of the social pyramid. Economic growth should not be regarded as the end itself, but rather as a means to the end. However, reducing human progress to economic growth is a widely held misconception. This point is partly embedded in an alternative measure of human progress, the Human Development Index (HDI), which captures longevity, knowledge, and economic prosperity as essential elements of human progress (UNDP, 1990). Country rankings by the HDI do not match income rankings (UNDP, 1996), indicating that human well-being cannot be judged by income alone, and that economic growth is only one of the factors leading to human flourishing. Another alternative measure of human prosperity is the Happy Planet Index (HPI) proposed by the New Economics Foundation. The HPI is a measure of sustainable well-being using data on experienced well-being, life expectancy, and ecological footprint to reveal the ecological efficiency of producing long, happy lives (Abdallah *et al.*, 2012).

Endless economic growth seems impossible due to limits set by the environment. The degree of dematerialization that would be required in order to combine long-term growth with environmental sustainability would presuppose an unrealistically high degree of eco-technological efficiency increase. The human economy has expanded to a level that justifies using the term "uneconomic growth" (Daly, 1999) where environmental (for example, climate change), social (such as income inequality), and human (for instance, mental and psychological health) costs have exceeded the perceived benefits (such as increased purchasing power to consume more products) of economic growth. Since it seems both unessential and impossible to sustain economic growth forever, the crucial question is for how long it should continue. Moral arguments of distributive justice within and across generations, along with responsibilities for non-human nature, suggest that economic growth in affluent countries should be replaced by de-growth within the next few decades. For those countries that are in desperate need of basic subsistence materials such as food, shelter, and hygiene, economic growth still makes sense for their material improvement. However, even poor countries should not seek growth at any price, and the growth ought not to continue once it reaches a certain point.

The structural necessity of growth

Why do growth policies still have a hegemonic status in public debates and politics when there is convincing evidence that economic growth is no longer essential for human well-being in wealthy countries? For example, economic growth fails to reduce unemployment, poverty, and income inequality, and it is limited by finite resources. The contemporary hegemonic status of growth policies is well illustrated in the book *Enough is Enough* by Dietz and O'Neill (2013). They describe a "growth imperative" constituted by profit motives, a debt-based monetary and financial system, population growth, the use of GDP as a measure of progress, the fear of unemployment, and the culture of consumerism.

Several authors have pointed out that the growth imperative is intrinsic to the market-dominated socio-economic system (Gordon and Rosenthal, 2003; Griethuysen, 2010; Harvey, 2010). This proposition supports Marx's position as described in "Arguments from an economic perspective," above. Fierce competition in the market economy sets the "growth or die" dynamic in motion and forms the profit-driven economy. The widely prevailing neoliberalism since the 1980s has further propelled the development of this market-oriented competitive economy at the global level.

Not only does the capitalist economic structure generate a growth compulsion, it also reacts back to the social domain by generating new social relations, behaviors, and ideologies that sustain and reinforce the growth imperative. As Bonaiuti (2012) points out, the spread of the capitalist market economy leads to the spread of individualistic behaviors and positional competition. When people's basic needs are satisfied, continual economic growth will enable them to shift their consumption to positional goods. Positional goods are characterized as relative scarcity, and the satisfaction of consuming this kind of good is not from their use value but the fact that other people are not able to own or consume them (Hirsch, 1976). Along with economic growth, the number of people who can afford a certain positional good increases, leading to greater positional competition and hence the diminishing of satisfaction. People therefore begin to seek other positional goods. Such consumption behavior, emerged from continuous economic growth, in turn propels further growth. Distinct from the consumption of basic goods, there is theoretically no limit to pursue positional goods (Bonaiuti, 2012).

The current economic system has let the benefits of growth accrue to the rich and powerful while the costs fall on the poor and disempowered. I argue that the dominant discourse of economic growth reflects the intention of the elite to maintain and strengthen their economic, political, and social power. This discourse tendency, where the dominant ideology maintains the deception that what is best for the elite is also what is best for everyone, is well acknowledged by discourse analysts such as Kress and Hodge (1988: 3–5). Despite the fact that strong arguments from natural sciences, social sciences, and moral philosophy speak against a continuous pursuit of economic growth as the primary goal for societal development in affluent countries, these arguments do not gain a dominant position in public debates and politics. It seems that the assumption that there is no alternative to economic growth is backed up by so much power emanating from vested interests and entrenched politics that it hardly needs to be supported by rational arguments (Flyvbjerg, 1998).

References

Abdallah, S., Michaelson, J., Shah S., Stoll, L., Marks, N., 2012. *The Happy Planet Index: 2012 Report*. London: New Economics Foundation.

Ackerman, F., Heinzerling, L., 2004. *Priceless: On Knowing the Price of Everything and the Value of Nothing*. New York: New Press.

Agras, J., Chapman, D., 1999. A dynamic approach to the Environmental Kuznets Curve hypothesis. *Ecological Economics*, 28: 267–277.

Alcott, B., 2005. Jevons' paradox. *Ecological Economics*, 54(1): 9–21.

Arler, F., 2001. Distributive justice and sustainable development, in: Tolba, M. K. (Ed.), *Our Fragile World: Challenges and Opportunities for Sustainable Development*. Oxford: EOLSS/ UNESCO.

Arler, F., 2006. Ethics of large-scale change. Geografisk Tidsskrift, *Danish Journal of Geography*, 106: 131–144.

Barry, J., Paterson, M., 2003. The British state and the environment: New Labour's ecological modernisation strategy. *International Journal of Environment and Sustainable Development*, 2: 237–249.

Bhaskar, R., 1979/1998. *The Possibility of Naturalism*. London: Routledge.

Bonaiuti, M., 2012. Degrowth: Tools for a complex analysis of the multidimensional crisis. *Capitalism Nature Socialism*, 23(1): 30–50.

Chen, S., Ravallion, M., 2008. The developing world is poorer than we thought, but no less successful in the fight against poverty. Policy research working paper of the World Bank.

Cropper, M. L., Oates, W. E., 1992. Environmental economics: A survey. *Journal of Economic Literature*, 30: 675–740.

Daly, H. E., 1993. The steady-state economy: Toward a political economy of biophysical equilibrium and moral growth, in: Daly, H. E., Townsend, K. N. (Eds.), *Valuing the Earth: Economics, Ecology, Ethics*, Cambridge: The MIT Press.

Daly, H. E., 1999. Uneconomic growth in theory and in fact. FEASTA review 1 – The First Annual Feasta Lecture. Trinity College, Dublin, 26 April. Downloaded September 2015 from www.feasta.org/documents/feastareview/daly1.pdf.

Daly, H. E., 2008. A steady-state economy: A failed growth economy and a steady-state economy are not the same thing; they are the very different alternatives we face. Report to Sustainable Development Commission.

Daly, H. E., Cobb, J. B., Cobb, C.W., 1989. *For the Common Good*. Boston, MA: Beacon Press.

Delhey, J., 2009. From materialist to postmaterialist happiness? National affluence and determinants of life satisfaction in cross-national perspective. *World Values Research*, 2: 30–54.

Dietz, R., O'Neill, D., 2013. *Enough is Enough. Building a Sustainable Economy in a World of Finite Resources*. Oxford: Routledge.

Duncan, O. D., 1975. Does money buy satisfaction? *Social Indicators Research*, 2: 267–274.

Easterlin, R. A., 1973. Does money buy happiness? *The Public Interest*, 30: 3–10.

Easterlin, R. A., 1974. Does economic growth improve the human lot? Some empirical evidence, in: M. Abramovitz, P. A. David, and M. W. Reder (Eds.), *Nations and Households in Economic Growth: Essays in Honour of Moses Abramovitz*. New York: Academic Press, Inc.

Easterlin, R. A., 1995. Will raising the incomes of all increase the happiness of all? *Journal of Economic Behavior and Organization*, 27: 35–47.

Easterlin, R. A., 2005. Feeding the illusion of growth and happiness: A reply to Hagerty and Veenhoven. *Social Indicators Research*, 75: 429–443.
Ekins, P., 2003. Identifying critical natural capital. Conclusions about critical natural capital. *Ecological Economics*, 44: 277–292.
Flyvbjerg, B., 1998. *Rationality and Power*. Cambridge: Cambridge University Press.
Galeotti, M., Lanza, A., Pauli, F., 2006. Reassessing the environmental Kuznets curve for CO_2 emissions: A robustness exercise. *Ecological Economics*, 57(1): 152–163.
Goodland, R., Ledec, G., 1993. Neoclassical economics and principles of sustainable development. In: Armstrong, S. J., Botzler, R. G. (Eds.), *Environmental Ethics: Divergence and Convergence*. New York: McGraw-Hill.
Gordon, M. J., Rosenthal, J. S., 2003. Capitalism's growth imperative. *Cambridge Journal of Economics*, 27(1): 25–48.
Griethuysen, P., 2010. Why are we growth-addicted? The hard way towards de-growth in the involutionary western development path. *Journal of Cleaner Production*, 18(6): 590–595.
Hagerty, M. R., Veenhoven, R., 2003. Wealth and happiness revisited – growing national income does go with greater happiness. *Social Indicators Research*, 64: 1–27.
Hajer, M. A., 1995. *The Politics of Environmental Discourse: Ecological Modernization and the Policy Process*. Oxford: Clarendon Press.
Hardin, G., 1974. Living on a lifeboat. *BioScience*, 24: 561–568. Republished in *The Social Contract*, Fall 2001 issue.
Harvey, D., 2010. *The Enigma of Capital and the Crises of Capitalism*. London: Profile Books.
Harvey, D., 2014. *Seventeen Contradictions and the End of Capitalism*. London: Profile Books.
Hirsch, R., 1976. *Social Limits to Growth*. London: Routledge.
Huber, J., 1985. *Die Regenbogengesellschaft: Ökologie und Sozialpolitik*. Frankfurt am Main: S. Fischer.
Jackson, T., 2009. Prosperity without growth? Sustainable Development Commission.
James, D. E., *et al.*, 1978. *Economic Approaches to Environmental Problems: Techniques and Results of Empirical Analysis*. Elsevier.
Jespersen, J., 2004. Sustainable development and macroeconomic stability, in Reich, L., Røpke, I. (Eds.), *The Ecological Economics of Consumption*. Cheltenham: Edward Elgar.
Kenny, C., 2009. There's more to life than money: Exploring the levels/growth paradox in income and health. *Journal of International Development*, 21: 24–41.
Kovel, J., 2002. *The Enemy of Nature: The End of Capitalism or the End of the World?* New York: Zed Books.
Kress, G., Hodge, R., 1988. *Social Semiotics*. New York: Cornell University Press.
Maddison, A., 2010. *Historical Statistics of the World Economy: 1–2008 AD*. Groningen: University of Groningen.
Markowitz, E. M., Bowerman, T., 2012. How much is enough? Examining the public's beliefs about consumption. *Analyses of Social Issues and Public Policy*, 12(1): 167–189.
Martinez-Alier, J., 2002. *The Environmentalism of the Poor*. Cheltenham, Northampton, MA: Edward Elgar Publishing.
Marx, K., 1858/1993. *Grundrisse: Foundations of the Critique of Political Economy*. Harmondsworth: Penguin.
Meadows, D. H., Meadows, D. L., *et al.*, 1972. *The Limits to Growth: A Report for the Club of Rome's Project on the Predicament of Mankind*. New York: Universe Books.
Mol, P. J., Sonnenfeld, D. A., 2000. Ecological modernisation around the world: An introduction. *Environmental Politics*, 9: 1–14.
Næss, A., 1993. The deep ecological movement: Some philosophical aspects. In: Armstrong, S. J., Botzler, R. G. (Eds.), *Environmental Ethics: Divergence and Convergence*. New York: McGraw-Hill.

Næss, A., 1973. The shallow and the deep, *Long-Range Ecology Movement. Inquiry*, 16.

Næss, P., Høyer, K. G. 2009. Shadows in Schwartzman's Sunny Society. *Capitalism, Nature, Socialism*, 20(4): 98–102.

Nielsen, P., Næss, P., 2011. Der er intet naturgivent ved vækst. In: Holten-Andersen, J., Christensen, T. H., Holten-Andersen, K., Hansen, S. F. (Eds.), *Modvækst: Omstilling til fremtiden*. Århus: Hovedland, pp. 205–221.

Nørgaard, R. B., 1985. Environmental economics: An evolutionary critique and a plea for pluralism. *Journal of Environmental Economics and Management*, 12(4): 382–394.

Nørgaard, J. S., 2009. Avoiding rebound through a steady-state economy. In: Herring, H., Sorrell, S. (Eds), *Energy Efficiency and Sustainable Consumption*. London: Palgrave Macmillan.

Norton, B. G., 1993. Environmental ethics and weak anthropocentrism. In: Armstrong, S. J., Botzler, R. G., (Eds.), *Environmental Ethics: Divergence and Convergence*. New York: McGraw-Hill.

O'Connor, J., 1998. On capitalist accumulation and economic and ecological crisis. In: J. O'Connor (Ed.), *Natural Causes: Essays on Ecological Marxism*. New York: Guilford Press.

OECD, 2002. *Indicators to Measure Decoupling of Environmental Pressure from Economic Growth*. Paris: OECD.

OECD, 2008. *Growing Unequal? Income Distribution and Poverty in OECD Countries*. Paris: OECD.

Oswald, A., 2006. The Hippies were right all along about happiness. *Financial Times*, 19 January

Pearce, D., 1993. *Environmental Values and the Natural World*. London: Earthscan.

Ramos-Martin, J., 2003. Empiricism in ecological economics: A perspective from complex systems theory. *Ecological Economics*, 46(3): 387–398.

Ravallion, M., 1997. Good and bad growth: The Human Development Reports. *World Development*, 25: 631–638.

Røpke, I., 2004. The early history of modern ecological economics. *Ecological Economics*, 50: 293–314.

Røpke, I., 2005. Trends in the development of ecological economics from the late 1980s to the early 2000s. *Ecological Economics*, 55: 262–290.

Rosa, H., 2003. Social acceleration: Ethical and political consequences of a desynchronized high-speed society. *Constellations*, 10: 3–33.

Schneider, F., Kallis, G., Martinez-Alier, J., 2010. Crisis or opportunity? Economic degrowth for social equity and ecological sustainability. Introduction to this special issue. *Journal of Cleaner Production*, 18: 511–518.

Shin, D. C., 1978. Does rapid economic growth improve the human lot? *Empirical evidence. Social Indicators Research*, 8: 199–221.

Solow, R. M., 1993. Sustainability: An economist's perspective. In: Dorfman, R., Dorfman, N. S., (Eds.), *Economics of the Environment: Selected Readings*. New York: W.W. Norton & Co.

Spaargaren, G., Mol, A. P. J., 1992. Sociology, environment, and modernity: Ecological modernization as a theory of social change. *Society and Natural Resources*, 5: 323–344.

Spangenberg, J. H., 2001. The environmental Kuznets curve: A methodological artifact? *Population and Environment*, 23: 175–191.

Spangenberg, J. H., 2008. Growth and sustainable development. In Filipo, F., Schneider, F. (Eds.), *Proceedings of the First International Conference on Economic De-Growth for Ecological Sustainability and Social Equity*. Paris: INT, pp. 119–123.

Statistics Denmark, 2009. *Statistisk Tiårsoversigt 2009* (Statistical ten-year review, 2009). Copenhagen: Statistics Denmark.

Suri, V., Chapman, D., 1998. Economic growth, trade and energy: Implications for the environmental Kuznets curve. *Ecological Economics*, 25: 195–208.

Talbott, J. R., 2008. *Obamanomics: How Bottom-up Economic Prosperity Will Replace Trickle-down Economics*. New York: Seven Stories Press.

Tapio, P., 2005. Towards a theory of decoupling: Degrees of decoupling in the EU and the case of road traffic in Finland between 1970 and 2001. *Transport Policy*, 12(2): 137–151.

Trainer, T., 2001. The "de-materialisation" myth. *Technology in Society*, 23: 505–514.

United Nations Development Program (UNDP), 1990. *Human Development Report*. New York: Oxford University Press.

United Nations Development Program (UNDP), 1996. *Human Development Report*. New York: Oxford University Press.

Veblen, T., 1899/1994. *The Theory of the Leisure Class*. Bremen: Kessinger Publishing.

Venkatachalam, L., 2007. Environmental economics and ecological economics: Where they can converge? *Ecological Economics*, 61: 550–558.

von Weizsäcker, E., Lovins, A. B., Lovins, H., 1998. *Factor Four: Doubling Wealth, Halving Resource Use – A Report to the Club of Rome*. London: Earthscan.

Weiss, E. B., 1990. Our rights and obligations to future generations for the environment. *The American Journal of International Law*, 84: 198–207.

Wilkinson, R., Pickett, K., 2009. *The Spirit Level: Why More Equal Societies Almost Always Do Better*. London: Penguin Books.

Woodward, D., Simms, A., Murphy, M., 2006. *Growth Isn't Working: The Unbalanced Distribution of Benefits and Costs from Economic Growth*. London: New Economics Foundation.

World Commission on Environment and Development, 1987. *Our Common Future*. Oxford: Oxford University Press.

WWF, 2014. *Living Planet Report 2014*. Gland: WWF.

Xue, J., 2013. *Economic Growth and Sustainable Housing: An Uneasy Relationship*. London: Routledge.

Zweig, K., 1979. Smith, Malthus, Ricardo, and Mill – the forerunners of limits to growth. *Futures*, 11: 510–523.

6

THE SYMPTOMATOLOGY OF CRISES

Some critical realist reflections

Bob Jessop

Introduction

This chapter interrogates the ontologically stratified nature of crises from a general critical realist perspective. Reflecting the hackneyed but still useful observation that the Chinese ideogram for crisis combines the characters for danger and opportunity, it highlights the objectively overdetermined, subjectively indeterminate character of crises as events and/or processes (cf. Debray 1973). It also considers the resulting challenges for social agents to understand the *real* causes of *actual* crisis symptoms as a basis for crisis management intended to restore the status quo ante and/or to decide on possible courses of transformative action in response to crisis. This requires moving beyond a strictly scientific program to consider the emancipatory potentials present in a given crisis conjuncture, which involves thinking of crisis in counterfactual terms. A general critical realist perspective can also illuminate issues such as crisis management, crises of crisis management, and lesson drawing. The analysis then turns to the abstract possibility of crisis in the capitalist mode of production and the concrete forms of crisis. Key issues here include money as capital and, in particular, capitalist credit money and the interaction of economic and political mechanisms in explaining the duration of the crisis. The chapter ends with general remarks on the potential of crisis as an analytical entry point into the contradictory nature of social structures.

Critical realism in general

Critical realism is not a general theory – it provides a distinctive philosophical standpoint with strong ontological commitments that have major meta-theoretical implications for theory construction, theory confirmation, and theory application (Bhaskar 1998: 132). Its depth ontology posits that the world is stratified into layers and regions that require different concepts, assumptions, and explanatory principles corresponding to their emergent properties. In particular it distinguishes real mechanisms, actual events and processes, and empirical observations.

The deepest layer comprises the generative structures or causal mechanisms and related properties of a given set of relations. These relations include tendencies, counter-tendencies, capacities, affordances (i.e. the possibilities of action afforded, of offered by, a given material object or social network), liabilities, and vulnerabilities. These properties may be contingently actualized in specific conjunctures but, because of diverse factors or actors, may remain latent. Regarded as tendencies, real mechanisms are doubly tendential, that is, they themselves exist only to the extent that the sets of relations that generate them are reproduced. In other words, the existence of particular naturally necessary powers is contingent rather than necessary and their actualization is therefore "contingently necessary" as well as "necessarily contingent" (Jessop 1982: 228–35; also Sayer 1992: 117; Danermark *et al.* 2002: 56; Manicas 2006: 31–43). Second, the actual comprises patterns of events or processes that result from the interaction of a plurality of mechanisms, tendencies, and counter-tendencies, in specific conditions. Third, the empirical concerns evidence about the actual – that is, those potentials that are actualized (observations concerning the actual and/or the real, lived experience, observations, measurements of actual pattern of events). Together the empirical and the actual provoke questions about the nature of the real.

The existence of the real world is a crucial "regulative idea" in critical realism, but its adherents do not claim direct access thereto. Instead they rely on retroduction. This method asks: What must the world be like for "x" to happen? Theory building and testing are never final and complete but always "under construction."[1] Critical realist knowledge advances – fallibly – via continuing confrontation between retroductive theoretical hypotheses about intransitive objects and socially produced evidential statements generated by transitive inquiry that are never a direct reflection of real or actual phenomena (cf. Bhaskar 1998: 14; Bhaskar 2008: 328; also Jessop 1982; Sayer 1992: 87; Danermark *et al.* 2002: 51, 116–17, 144–46). This open process switches among concept building, retroductive moments, empirical inquiries, conceptual refinement, further retroduction, and so on. How to resolve inconsistency between hypotheses and evidence is determined within the rules of a given scientific program. Critical realist inquiry also combines analytical and dialectical reasoning (Bhaskar 2008: 348; cf. Aglietta 1979: 15–16).

Our knowledge of and/or about the real world is never theoretically innocent but starts from a pre-interpreted analytical object. The movement occurs from a research problem defined in more or less simple and, perhaps, one-sided, superficial or, worse, chaotic, terms to an account that is more complex and has greater ontological depth. This does not mean that the complexities of the external world can ever be fully grasped in real time; on the contrary, all accounts, however concrete-complex, remain partial. Nonetheless, as the spiral of scientific inquiry continues, the explanandum is defined with increasing complexity and concreteness (Danermark *et al.* 2002). In general, this involves (1) forming concepts by combining categories from different analytical planes to produce "hybrid" concepts that are more or less concrete-complex in character; and (2) explanations that focus on the contingent interactions among causal mechanisms, tendencies and counter-tendencies, agential forces, and so forth, to produce a given explanandum. This often poses serious forensic problems of causal attribution in the face of complex-concrete objects and many competing explanations. This is a major issue for the symptomatological interpretation of crises.

Critical realism relates (scientific) knowledge production to the distinction between the intransitive and transitive moments of scientific inquiry. The former denotes the external world as the object of observation and, in many cases, intervention; the latter denotes the practices of science and scientific communities as a set (or sets) of observers and, perhaps, interveners. This said, science is embedded in other practices and its practitioners may have mixed motives in undertaking scientific investigation. Other modes of knowledge production and knowledge claims also affect scientific practices just as they do other kinds of social practice. A useful entry point here is Foucault's concept of "truth regimes," which recognizes various sources of truth effects linked to diverse discursive practices and dispositifs (Foucault 2000).

Critical realism in particular

Critical realism (CR) has an important "underlabouring" role in the natural and social sciences (Bhaskar 1998 18; Collier 1989; Lawson 1999; Cruickshank 2003). It examines, critiques, refines, and reflects on the ontological, epistemological, methodological, and substantive presuppositions of different philosophical and theoretical traditions, disciplines, schools, and so forth. It also provides meta-theoretical grounds for preferring some approaches, notably critical realism, over others by establishing rigorous criteria of "judgemental rationality" for choosing among them (cf. Archer *et al.* 1998: xi). This implies that, while philosophical argument can justify a "critical realist ontology and epistemology in general" on the basis of a negative or diacritical underlabouring role,[2] thereby excluding alternative philosophical positions (such as empiricism, rationalism, or idealism), it cannot validate, let alone elaborate, a "critical realist ontology and epistemology in particular." For example, in the social sciences, critical realism clarifies the relation of social structure and agency through its transformational model of social action (Bhaskar 1998). But this is consistent with various specific critical realist accounts of this relation (for example, Archer *et al.* 1998; Danermark *et al.* 2002; Lawson 1999, 2009; Cruickshank 2003: 6, 36ff; Elder-Vass 2007: 227). I suggest that this holds especially for particular CR ontological arguments rather than general CR arguments. To paraphrase Marx's comments on production in his 1857 Introduction to *Contribution to the Critique of Political Economy* (1973: 85), there is no such thing as critical realism in general or general critical realism, only particular critical realisms and the sum of CR arguments.[3] This holds for its philosophical underlabouring role and, even more acutely, for specific research applications. By definition, such underlabouring cannot supply the substantive concepts and methods needed for particular research investigations.

This poses the challenge of how to translate general meta-theoretical work into relevant research questions, strategies, studies, and conclusions regarding particular analytical objects, generative structures, actual events, and processes (Danermark *et al.* 2002; cf. Collier 1994: 208–9). Benton and Craib (2001: 5) call these regional ontologies, Bhaskar calls them scientific ontologies (1986: 36; see also Lawson 2009: 71–75),[4] and Cruickshank calls them "domain-specific meta-theories" that serve an underlabouring role for particular social ontologies or substantive research problems (2003: 144–5). These ontologies must be developed through means adequate to the specific object of inquiry (cf. Bhaskar 1998: 54). This does not occur in a vacuum (remember the transitive dimension of science) and is also subject to the above-noted spiral movement of continuing and reflexive critical realist inquiry.

A further complication is that disputes occur within regional or scientific ontologies. As Nielsen notes, citing Bhaskar in general and Lawson for economics, philosophy and science are different disciplines, and the former cannot do the latter's work (Nielsen 2002: 730; on Lawson, see also Brown *et al.* 2002: 776–78; Callinicos 2008: 583–4; Dean *et al.* 2006: 28; and, on Marxism specifically, Joseph 2002: 23–4; Joseph 2006: 116; Roberts 2006: 71f). Specifically, Nielsen argues that critical realism in economics is too concerned with the philosophy of political economy and not enough with its practice (Nielsen 2002: 732; see also Fine 2004; Davidsen 2009).[5] Kemp further proposes that, for critical realism to be persuasive, it must address the explanatory problems entailed in a particular research topic rather than engage in general philosophical argument (2005: 16). Likewise, Bhaskar insists that, whatever the source of scientific ontologies, "they should be embedded in a practical research programme yielding hypotheses, subject to empirical test, of greater explanatory power (and *ceteris paribus* emancipatory potential)" (1998: 195). In short, the challenge is to move from abstract, philosophical, and meta-theoretical reflections on critical realism in general to specific, practical, and theoretically grounded research programs.

Crises, what crises?

A topic that is little explored in critical realism is crisis. It mostly figures in the guise of epistemological inadequacies or disorientation as an aspect of philosophical and social scientific inquiry. Beyond these concerns, it is astonishing to note how little substantive (let alone substantial) discussion there is in self-described critical realist work[6] concerning crisis events and processes, their underlying crisis tendencies, or the causal complexes that produce crises or overdetermine their timing, forms of appearance, and so on (on overdetermination, see below). In general, crisis seems to figure largely as an actual event or state of affairs that is treated as a nodal point or critical juncture and/or serves as the context for another kind of analysis. In other words, there is far less interest than one might expect from critical realist work in the relation between their interrelated empirical, actual, and real aspects.

This seems to be a major lost opportunity. For, as several critical realists have commented (see below), crisis is an important potential source of retroductive insight and hypothesis generation. Thus Bhaskar conjectured that "in periods of transition or crisis, generative structures, previously opaque, become more visible to agents" (1998: 52; 2008: 152). He suggested that crisis could be construed as a partial analogue to experimentation in the nature sciences – even though it lacks the requisite closure of a controlled laboratory investigation (Bhaskar 1998: 52; cf. Lawson 1998: 153; on the role of extreme situations, such as pathologies, crises, and "pure" cases, see also Collier 1994: 164–5; and Danermark *et al.* 2002: 104ff). In general, one might argue that, because crises are never purely objective, extra-semiotic events or processes that automatically produce a particular response or outcome, they offer a real-time laboratory to study the dialectic of semiosis and materiality, which is a key aspect of critical realist inquiries in the social sciences. It is also relevant to the structure–agency relation, to the critique of domination, and to reflection on human flourishing and emancipation. Accordingly, a serious account of crisis must not only be critical realist in its ontological, epistemological, and methodological underpinnings but must also develop appropriate substantive concepts, mechanisms, tendencies and counter-tendencies, and conjunctural analyses for crises in question.

Accordingly, this section explores crisis from a meta-theoretical (or underlabouring) critical realist perspective. It asks how one might distinguish between the phenomenal forms of crisis and underlying causes and causal connections, contingent trigger events – often external – that reveal crisis, and the more internal, structural factors that make the crisis necessary. The disjunction between objective and subjective aspects of crisis also has implications about the *longue durée*, secular crisis tendencies, and the immediacy of crisis "events." For it encourages a tendency to focus on immediate local symptoms rather than on longer-term and broader causal factors. These are often entangled and require correspondingly complex periodizations in terms of interwoven temporalities and/or complex socio-spatial analyses reflecting the substantive causal mechanisms at play. Noting these complexities involves a concern with overdetermination in two senses. One is the general analytical notion of the "multi-mechanistic" nature of causation in open systems, whether understood in sequential, path-dependent, and/or additive, synchronic terms (Næss 2004).[7] The other is the specific, dialectical sense, proposed by Althusser, of more or less profound modifications in individual causal mechanisms, including particular contradictions, crisis-tendencies, and conflicts, working within and across different social spheres in an emerging social whole, where these modifications result from reciprocal causal interactions that develop unevenly in time–space in specific historical contexts and thereby make each crisis distinctive, if not unique (Althusser 1977: 99–102, 200–18). Overdetermination indicates the Janus face of crises – that is, the need to interpret their objective overdetermination for retroductive, diagnostic purposes, and, regarding subjective indeterminacy, to assess them for prospective, prognostic purposes concerned with evaluating current possibilities of intervention in open systems to make potentially decisive intervention to change (and not just predict) the future.

Crisis is a polysemic word and a problematic concept and denotes multi-faceted phenomena that invite approaches from different entry points and standpoints. Its meaning depends on its articulation into a broader set of concepts and on the meta-theoretical framework in which "crisis" is embedded (for example, idealist, empiricist, actualist, realist). It is also an inherently temporal concept with spatial connotations. The concept implies that time unfolds unevenly, with continuities and discontinuities, transition points and ruptures, with scope for irreversible change rather than simple iteration, hence scope for path-shaping alongside path-dependence. "[T]ime moves faster in periods of crisis, and stagnates in times of regression" (Debray 1973: 90). This indicates an important uncertainty in the crisis concept: is it a single event (and, if so, how would one identify its beginning and its conclusion?), a contingent series of events distributed in time and space that is connected, if at all, because of earlier crisis responses that could have taken a different turn with different effects, or a series of events with an underlying tendential logic that therefore unfolds as a relatively predictable process (if only from the perspective of informed observers)?[8]

The Chinese ideogram for crisis highlights its duality and suggests several important issues for crisis theory. First, it signifies that crises have objective and subjective aspects corresponding to danger and opportunity respectively. Following Debray, we can say that, objectively, crises occur when a set of social relations (including their ties to the natural world) cannot be reproduced (cannot "go on") in the old way. Subjectively, crises tend to disrupt (even "shock") accepted views of the world and how to "go on" in it. They threaten established views, practices, institutions, and social relations, calling into question theoretical and policy paradigms as well as everyday routines. Without the objective aspect, we have, at worst, deliberately manufactured "crises," at best, unwarranted panic. Without the subjective aspect, while observers may perceive a crisis developing either in real time or after the "event," the crisis will lack the resonance to stir decisive action by actual participants. In short, for Debray, crises are complex, objectively overdetermined moments of subjective indeterminacy, where decisive action can make a major difference to the future (1973: 113; also 99–100, 104–5).

It is useful in critical realist terms to classify crises on two dimensions. The first concerns their aetiology. On the one hand, some crises appear "accidental," that is, they are readily (if sometimes inappropriately) attributable to natural or "external" forces (for example, a volcanic eruption, tsunami, crop failure, invasion). When these have significant effects, they may be termed "disasters" (Quarantelli 1988). This serves to distinguish them from the other kind of crisis. These are form-determined, that is, rooted in crisis tendencies or antagonisms grounded in specific structural forms (for example, profit-oriented, market-mediated capitalism). In other words, they result from the inherent crisis potentials and crisis tendencies of a given social form and, as we shall see below, may have corresponding patterns of crisis management. This may require attention to systemic contradictions, structurally grounded antagonisms, and social conflicts without assuming that every crisis derives therefrom. This category of crises is more interesting for critical realism as it is more readily analyzed, at least in principle, in terms of one or more sets of real mechanisms, their overdetermined actualization in specific conjunctures, and their empirical manifestations (Bhaskar 1998: 47; for an example, Bhaskar 2008: 258, 327; cf. Manicas 2006). This distinction does not imply that accidental crises lack causes – just that the latter are so varied and overdetermined (in its analytical, rather than dialectical sense) that they are less suited to critical realist retroduction and investigation. This said, external, coincidental, incidental causes may trigger structural or systemic crises by working "through the intermediary of the internal, structural, essential causes which constitute the determining element in society's crises" (Debray 1973: 101–2).

The second dimension concerns the significance of crises in terms of its potential impact on the simple or expanded reproduction of the relevant "order" or "system," including its typical modes of reproduction, its conditions of existence, and its relative embedding in a wider social formation. Such reproduction in the social world depends on the reproduction of the social relations that support the relevant "order" or "system" – relations that can be contradictory, conflictual, or antagonistic (the capitalist mode of production is an obvious example). Crises "in" are normal (expected). They occur within the parameters of a given natural environment and/or set of social arrangements. There are also well-developed routines for dealing with accidental crises, reducing subjective indeterminacy. These are reflected and systematized in a large literature on how to respond to accidents and emergencies, whether these be natural disasters, large-scale accidents, or reputational damage to companies, organizations, and governments (Farazmand 2001; Gottschalk 2002). Indeed, repeated observation of "normal" disasters, accidents, and crises, learning about and from recurrent crises may encourage monitoring, risk management, disaster education and preparedness, rehabilitation, and the sharing of best practice (Kirschenbaum 2004; Pinkowski 2008) such that subjective indeterminacy is reduced. This could mean that crisis management has become so routinized that a "crisis" no longer exists even when objective crisis symptoms are present because its subjective moment is lacking and the basic features of disturbed arrangements are routinely restored through internal adjustments and/or shift crisis effects into the future, elsewhere, or onto marginal and vulnerable groups. This is exemplified in alternating phases of unemployment and inflation in the post-war advanced capitalist economies and their treatment through countercyclical economic policies – although it was often badly executed, was often pro-cyclical, and, over time, led to stagflation.

Conversely, crises "of" are less common. They occur when there is a crisis of crisis management (that is, normal responses no longer work) and efforts to defer or displace crises encounter growing resistance (Offe 1984; on the use of "in/of," see below). Offe relates this to potential second-order effects of crisis-management routines, which may displace crisis tendencies into extra-economic spheres (for example, fiscal crisis, administrative crisis). Similar ideas are found in Habermas (1976) regarding rationality, legitimation, and motivational crises. This displacement implies that crisis tendencies remain incompressible but have different forms of appearance linked to different institutional and spatio-temporal fixes and to different crisis-management routines. Shifts in the balance of forces may also intensify crisis tendencies by weakening or resisting established modes of crisis management. One reason why crises of crisis management occur is that crises are overdetermined, that is, they result from the interaction of different crisis tendencies in complex conjunctures, so that no crisis in all its complex overdetermination is ever self-identical with previous actualizations of the same crisis tendency (see above). Thus, whatever the universal features of crisis tendencies in any given system (such as the capitalist mode of production), the particular features of any particular set of crisis tendencies associated with a particular type of crisis (for example, overproduction, underconsumption, disproportions, tendency of the rate of profit to fall, credit crisis, fiscal crisis, sovereign debt crisis), mean that no algorithm, even if based on learning in, about, and from crisis, would be cognitively adequate in the face of the singularity of the crisis, which therefore remains subjectively indeterminate.

Crises of crisis management are more disorienting than crises "in" specific structures or systems, indicating the breakdown of previous regularities and an inability to "go on managing crises in the old way." In certain regards, one might consider these as crises in/of crisis management. The prepositional ambivalence of "in/of" reflects the prospective aspects of crisis construal. Whereas the retroductive explanation of a crisis involves scientific analysis, prospective analysis depends more on speculative bets about the future. *A fortiori*, this concerns whether crisis-management routines are irretrievably broken or open to piecemeal reform. This reflects the open nature of social systems and the scope for human agency (as well as the non-linear interaction of non-agential causal mechanisms) to make a difference to the future. This creates space for strategic interventions to significantly redirect the course of events rather than "muddling through" until the crisis is eventually resolved or hoping that "business as usual" can be restored through emergency measures. This poses a whole series of counterfactual epistemological problems about crisis construal and the asymmetry, emphasized in critical realism, between explanation and prediction. For example, the crisis of crisis management in the Fordist regime prepared the ground for a neoliberal regime shift and transition to a finance-dominated mode of growth in some cases and, in others, led at most to neoliberal policy adjustments intended to stabilize the inherited growth model (cf. Jessop 2012). More generally, such crises can cause social stasis or regression, attempts to restore the old system by *force majeure*, fraud, or corruption; efforts at more radical social innovation for good or ill, leading in some cases to temporary states of emergency or more enduring exceptional regimes (for example, military dictatorship, fascism), or to efforts to break the power of such regimes.

This classification could be misleading if it one-sidedly highlights the objective aspect of crisis. A crisis is never a purely objective, extra-semiotic event or process that automatically produces a definite response or outcome. This objective moment becomes socially and historically relevant by virtue of subjective indeterminacy. This refers to the lack of an algorithm that unambiguously identifies the correct response to the crisis on the basis of its objective features, i.e. the absence of a self-evident way to restore simple or expanded reproduction or to move smoothly to another stable "order" or "system." The subjectively indeterminate response set includes non-decision or non-intervention – which, given the objective nature of crisis in itself, also has system-relevant effects and is therefore a mode of decision and intervention. Without subjective indeterminacy, there is no crisis – merely chaos, disaster, or catastrophe, and, perhaps, fatalism or stoicism. Ideas and imaginaries[9] shape the interpretation.

The importance of subjective indeterminacy also poses the question of the resonance of crisis construals and responses, on the one hand, and material adequacy of these construals and responses to the crisis in itself, on the other hand. This is a source of massive theoretical and practical problems in analyzing and managing crises. A crisis is also a moment for contestation and struggle to construe it and inform individual and collective responses. Interpretations can range from denial (business as usual) through claims of a major break (tipping or turning points) to a more radical rupture (revolutionary moment). This said, we must beware of manufactured crises, i.e. creating crises where none exists (or exaggerating the nature, degree, and import of a crisis) for "political" motives.

Crisis construals may also address a more or less broad range of questions. This involves, among other issues, delimiting the origins of a crisis in space–time and its uneven spatio-temporal incidence and development; identifying rightly or wrongly purported causes (agential, structural, discursive, and technical) at different scales, over different time horizons, in different fields of social practice, and at different levels of social organization from nameless or named individuals through social networks, formal organizations, institutional arrangements, specific social forms, or even the dynamic of a global society; determining its scope and effects, assessing in broad terms whether it is a crisis "in" or "of" the relevant arrangements; reducing its complexities to identifiable causes that could be targeted to find solutions; charting alternative futures; and promoting specific lines of action for socially identified forces over differently constructed spatio–temporal horizons.

Often, wider ideational and institutional innovation going beyond the economy narrowly conceived is needed, promoted, and supported by political, intellectual, and moral leadership. Indeed, as Milton Friedman put it hyperbolically but tellingly: "[O]nly a crisis produces real change. When that crisis occurs, the actions that are taken depend on the ideas that are lying around" (1962: 32). Thus, preparing the ground for crisis-induced strategic interventions helps to shape the modes and outcome of crisis management and crisis responses. Further, with hindsight, the crisis diagnosis may prove misleading, manufactured, or plain wrong. Inadequate preparation (for whatever cause) makes it harder to influence struggles over crisis construal and crisis management – a factor that made it harder for left-wing forces to exploit the recent North Atlantic financial crisis as compared with neoliberal forces.

As Friedman notes, those affected by crisis typically disagree on both their objective and subjective aspects because of their different entry points, standpoints, and capacities to read the crisis. The system-specific and conjunctural aspects of crises have many spatio-temporal complexities and affect social forces in quite varied ways. The lived experience of crisis is necessarily partial, limited to particular social segments of time–space. So it is hard to read crises. Indeed, if spatio–temporal boundaries are uncertain, if causes and effects are contested, can we speak of *the crisis*? As Gramsci remarked about the Great Depression:

> Whoever wants to give one sole definition of these events, or what is the same thing, find a single cause or origin, must be rebutted. We are addressing a process that shows itself in many ways, and in which causes and effects become intertwined and mutually entangled. To simplify means to misrepresent and falsify. ... When did the crisis begin? This question is bound up with the first since we are dealing with a process and not an event ... It is hard in real terms to separate the economic crisis from the political and ideological ones, etc.
>
> *(Gramsci 1995: 219; cf. 1975: Q15, §5)*[10]

Resolving a crisis into one essential crisis, let alone one with one main cause, involves at best strategic essentialism[11] rather than rigorous scientific practice. But such simplifications may facilitate learning lessons and taking effective action. This is why we must examine processes of learning in, about, and from crisis from the viewpoint of different actors or social forces – these aspects or processes may not coincide across all actors or forces (in part because crises will affect them differently in space–time as well as in relation to their different identities, interests, and values).

Symptomatology

One way to develop a critical realist analysis of crises is to appropriate (and transform) St Augustine's distinction in *De Doctrina Christiana* (Augustine of Hippo 389 AD), between *signa data* and *signa naturalia*. He writes that "a sign is something which, offering itself to the senses, conveys something other to the intellect." *Signa data* largely comprise words, that is, the conventional linguistic explored by Saussureans. They link *signum* (sign) and *signans* (signifier); they are used intentionally to convey a particular meaning. *Signa naturalia* are natural, indexical signs that can be interpreted as symptoms of something beyond the *signum–signans* relation. "Natural signs are those which, apart from any intention or desire of using them as signs, do yet lead to the knowledge of something else, as, for example, smoke when it indicates fire" (389 AD, Book 2, Chapter 1). His other examples include animal tracks and an angry or sorrowful countenance that is an unintended expression of inner feelings. They are symptoms of an underlying reality, outward manifestations of some other fact, internal condition, quality, or overall state of affairs. We can add symptoms of disease (linked to the medical notion of crisis) and of economic crisis (and the challenge of interpreting their connection to economic crisis tendencies).

The objective causal nexus that connects an invisible entity and its visible signs is not immediately transparent or self-evident but requires interpretation because there is no one-to-one relation between event and symptom; it is underdetermined. There is no algorithm that can establish *the* cause (though expert systems with fuzzy logic may attempt to narrow down possible causes). Thus, if we read symptoms as signifiers, we can ask: what is being signified and what is its referent (cf. Bhaskar on the semiotic triangle, 2008: 207–9; also Collier 1994: 5)? This fits the critical realist "depth ontology," which distinguishes the real (the invisible entity), the actual (an event), and the empirical (the visible sign). In these terms, crises can be seen as stratified. They are generated by real mechanisms, they are actual events or processes, and they have evidential symptoms. This poses the well-known CR retroductive question. Here this takes the form: what must the real world be like for this event to have occurred and/or these symptoms to exist? Thus the challenge is to relate the empirical symptoms, actual crisis, and underlying mechanisms as a basis for possible decisive interventions. This is the field of "symptomatology." It is based on trial-and-error observation and construal that draws on past experience but may also require forgetting as a basis for "correct" intervention.

The validity of a scientific explanation of the objective overdetermination of a crisis depends on scientific procedures and rules of evaluation according to specific scientific programs and paradigms. Provided that they have some basis in the objectively overdetermined nature of the crisis, different scientific readings may reduce its complexity in different ways by selectively construing some aspects of its objective features as important, while others are marginalized, ignored, or remain invisible. However, besides cognitive limits related to the scientific legibility of a crisis for differently situated observers, construals may also reflect their ideal and material interests as revealed through *Ideologiekritik* and/or *Herrschaftskritik* (critique of domination). Such influences are a common criticism of efforts by orthodox economists to explain the recurrence of economic crises. We should also note that a crisis can be instrumentalized (even rhetorically manufactured) to enable, justify, legitimate intervention not immediately related to the crisis itself (cf. Rahm Emanuel's comment, made in November 2008 in his capacity as transition manager for President-elect Barack Obama, that "you never want a serious crisis to go to waste"). In this context, crisis can become a central category of system or societal self-description and medium of self-transformation. This brings us to another aspect of crisis construal: the moment of subjective indeterminacy rather than objective overdetermination.

Symptoms can be assessed in two ways: in terms of scientific validity and in terms of pragmatic correctness. This distinction partly overlaps with that in critical realism between the explanation of past and present events, processes, or conjunctures and the prediction of the future of more or less open systems. However, these pragmatic predictions are not predictions of future situations (let alone mere extrapolations from past trends); nor do they concern plausible impacts of a specific course of action in a specific policy field (Næss and Strand 2012: 286–8). The latter can be assimilated to the critical realist scientific method if this is not defined in "scientistic" terms (Fleetwood and Hesketh 2006). In contrast, what is at stake in the cases of interest here are strategic calculations and judgements based on agents' capacities to read what may exist in *potentia* in a concrete situation with a specific balance of social forces and to intervene in this conjuncture to realize one of these possibilities even in the face of competing strategies pursued by opposing forces.

This suggests that construals can also be judged in terms of their correctness, i.e. their ability to read a conjuncture, discern potential futures, and guide action that transforms the conjuncture. This is mediated through language as well as through social practices and institutions beyond language. Indeed, since the development of print media at least, crisis construal is heavily mediatized, depending on specific forms of visualization and media representations, which nowadays typically vary across popular, serious, and specialist media. Correctness depends on (1) the limits set by the objectively overdetermined form of a crisis conjuncture; (2) the interpretive and mobilizing power of crisis construals and strategic perspectives – notably its ready communicability to relevant audiences; and (3) the balance of forces associated with different construals or, at least, the ability of some forces to impose their preferred construals, crisis-management options, and exit solutions (Lecercle 2006: 40–1; Debray 1973: 106–7; and, on the analysis of the first limit, Patomäki 2008: passim).[12]

Considered in these terms, to paraphrase Gramsci, "there is a world of difference between conjunctural analyses [he writes of ideologies] that are arbitrary, rationalistic, and willed and those that are organic" (1971: 376–7; cf. 1975: Q7§19, 868). The former analyses misconstrue the crisis – minimizing or exaggerating its scale and scope and potential impact – and misidentify necessary or feasible solutions. An organic analysis is at least minimally adequate to the objective dimensions of the crisis and its manageability or transformability through attenuation of crisis symptoms, muddling through, displacement, or deferral, and so forth, and in terms of the correlation of forces and the strategic horizons of action of the social forces whose ideal and material interests it represents. This raises the key issue of the (always limited and provisional) fit between imaginaries and real, or potentially realizable, sets of material interdependencies in the real world. Proposed crisis strategies and policies must be (or seen to be) effective within the spatio–temporal horizons of relevant social forces in a given social order.

In both cases, how a crisis is managed has path-shaping effects and responses affect the nature of subsequent crises. This corresponds to the idea that crises are moments where a decisive intervention can mark a turning point in the progress of a disease or other critical conjuncture. Furthermore, even scientifically invalid and/or conjuncturally incorrect construals, when translated into responses, will have constitutive or constructive effects. As moments of profound disorientation, crises often generate a wide range of initial construals of crisis symptoms (variation). Getting consensus on interpretations about which of many crises matters is to have framed the problem as a basis for action (selection). Nonetheless this consensus must be translated into coherent, coordinated policy approach and solutions that match objective dimensions of the crisis. Effective policies adapt crisis-management routines and/or discover new routines through trial and error and can be consolidated as the basis of new forms of governance, meta-governance, and institutionalized compromise (retention). Only crisis construals that grasp key emergent extra-semiotic features of the social world as well as mind-independent features of the natural world are likely to be retained. In other words, effective construals have constructive force and produce changes in the extra-semiotic features of the world and in related (always) tendential real mechanisms and social logics.

Crisis: abstract-simple possibilities and concrete-complex actualities

Following these general ontological and epistemological remarks on crisis, I now offer a critical realist reading of Marx's account of crisis. This is because (1) Marx is widely regarded as a pioneer and, sometimes, as a supreme exemplar of critical realism; (2) he identified the abstract forms of crisis (the abstract potential of crisis) in commodity circulation and, especially, the circulation of capitalist commodities; (3) he studied the basic crisis tendencies of capitalist production and some of their concrete manifestations; (4) he extended this analysis to basic crisis tendencies in the money and credit forms and their role in expressing the crisis tendencies of capitalist production, mediating these crisis tendencies, and in generating their own crisis tendencies rooted in the specific qualities of different forms of money and credit; (5) he recognized the potential for the autonomization of finance, especially in the form of interest-bearing capital, as a powerful independent crisis-generating factor; and (6) much recent Marxist work on crisis ignores these achievements and attempts to develop economics without Marx (on the defects of such efforts, see Freeman 2010). In short, Marx moved from abstract-simple to concrete-complex analyses of crisis.

In developing this approach, Marx provides his own answer to the question of whether crises are natural, inevitable, normal, endogenous processes rooted in basic crisis tendencies in capitalism, or unnatural, accidental, exceptional events triggered by exogenous events, actions, or processes. Whereas business cycle theorists tend to see crises as accidental or manageable, restoring the rhythms of accumulation, Marx saw them as structural and inevitable. Indeed, rather than being improbable or atypical events in capitalism, they are perfectly normal. This response also answers the question sometimes posed as to whether it is necessary to develop a specialized crisis theory separate from the general Marxist critique of political economy. This is not required if we start from the improbability of accumulation and its expanded reproduction. Instead the question becomes what general and/or particular counter-tendencies and fixes are at work that help to prevent crisis tendencies being actualized (Freeman 2014). Interestingly, critical realist comments tend to focus on reproduction rather than its improbability, on morphostasis rather than metamorphosis.[13] This may occur because critical realist analyses in this regard generally abstract from specific cases characterized by particular contradictions, antagonisms, and forms of conflicts. In contrast, Marx's critical realist analyses were specifically concerned with developing such a theory and establishing the internal connections between capitalism and crisis (cf. Roberts 2001: 554–9; 2006: 84–7). Indeed, he saw crises both as contingently necessary products of the inherent structural contradictions and strategic dilemmas of the capitalist mode of production, and as the means whereby capitalism partially, provisionally, and temporarily resolves its recurrent crisis tendencies.

Let me begin with two quotations from *Theories of Surplus Value, Volume 2*:

> The general abstract possibility of crisis denotes no more than the most abstract form of crisis, without content, without a compelling motivating factor. Sale and purchase may fall apart. They thus represent potential crisis and their coincidence always remains a critical factor for the commodity. The transition from one to the other may, however, proceed smoothly. The most abstract form of crisis (and therefore the form of possibility of crisis) is thus the metamorphosis of the commodity itself; the contradiction of exchange-value and use-value, and furthermore of money and commodity, comprised within the unity of the commodity, exists in metamorphosis only as an involved movement. The factors which turn this possibility of crisis into [an actual] crisis are not contained in this form itself; it only implies that the framework for a crisis exists.
>
> *(Marx 1969: 509)*

> The general possibility of crisis is the formal metamorphosis of capital itself, the separation in time and space, of purchase and sale. But this is never the cause of the crisis. For it is nothing but the most general form of crisis, i.e. the crisis in its most generalized expression. But it cannot be said that the abstract form of crisis is the cause of crisis. If one asks what its cause is, one wants to know why its abstract form, the form of its possibility, turns from possibility to actuality.
>
> *(Marx 1969: 515)*

Thus, before we develop an explanation for specific crises, we must consider the conditions that create the abstract possibility of crisis (cf. Kenway 1980; for a critical realist recognition of this abstract possibility based on Marx's analysis, see Dean *et al.* 2006: 26). The first quotation provides a crucial entry point for the analysis of crises. For it implies that crisis is an abstract possibility, that concrete crisis tendencies may exist, and that the specific actualization of a crisis may lead to its overdetermination. Nonetheless, as Marx intriguingly and ambiguously notes:

> These factors which explain the possibility of crises, by no means explain their actual occurrence. They do not explain *why* the phases of the process come into such a conflict that their inner unity can only assert itself through a crisis, a violent process.
>
> *(Marx, 1969: 502)*

Marx approaches this question through his analysis of the causal powers and liabilities implicated in capital as a social relation. He typically analyzed these in terms of the tendencies and counter-tendencies that together constitute its "laws of motion."

These "laws" operate as causal mechanisms whose outcome depends on specific initial conditions. Thus, in addition to retroducing and explaining real mechanisms, Marx described their actual results in specific conjunctures and often gave empirical indicators of events and processes. The tendency of the rate of profit to fall and its counter-tendencies are the best known (and certainly the most contentious) of these real mechanisms – and also provide the default position for those who insist on a common underlying mechanism of capitalist crises, regardless of their forms of appearance. Moreover, whether or not the profit rate actually falls (and by how much) depends on the conditions in which the tendency and counter-tendencies operate. This realist ontology implies that the social world comprises a complex synthesis of multiple determinations (1973 [1857]: 101).

The abstract possibility of breakdown is given by the anarchy of production in simple commodity production exemplified in the separation of the production of commodities from the sale of commodities. This involves the C-M-C circuit.[14] The abstract possibility is reinforced (becomes more likely) through the development of capitalist commodity production, which adds the role of *money as capital* to the role of *money as money*. The emergence of money as capital reflects the transformation of a simple exchange economy into a capitalist monetary economy together with a reorientation of the end and aim of social production, i.e. the accumulation of money in the form of capital. The distinction between money as money and money as capital is one of Marx's critical contributions to the critique of political economy and the analysis of crises. For, while money, credit, usury, and debt pre-date capitalism, the capitalist mode of production radically alters their place in economic relations, their relation to class powers, and their role in exploitation and social domination. This distinction enables him to analyze the M-C-M' circuit (and its elaborations). Transformed into capital, money mediates the most fundamental social relation in capitalism: that of wage labour to capital. Money-capital expresses the capitalists' domination of the process of production and their power to organize and control labour-power. Further, the transformation of money into capital lays the foundation for the modern system of financial markets and institutions (Marx 1976: 156–76, 579–712). It also entails that Marx's theory of crisis is inevitably a monetary (and credit) theory – it cannot be anchored solely in simple market exchange or the immediate organization of production. This is a major source of problems in orthodox Marxist readings of the crisis – they focus one-sidedly on production, value relations, and price formation on the basis of value relations.

The abstract possibility of crisis does not imply, as Carchedi (2010) and Roberts (2014) claim, that crises can all be traced back to the same cause – in the case of these two authors, the tendency of the rate of profit to fall. This treats the tendency of the rate of profit to fall as *the* ontological foundation of crisis tendencies in capitalism. Even if we ignored other crisis-generating mechanisms identified by Marx himself, there is a further complication to be addressed. This is the incompleteness of Marx's critique of political economy. One aspect of this is his pointed but unsystematized critique of political ecology, that is, the critique of the effects of capital accumulation on first and second nature (for summaries, see, for example, Burkett

1999; Foster 2000; Moore 2015). In addition, although never realized (and possibly soon abandoned), his so-called "six-book plan" points beyond the three[15] volumes of *Capital*. The last three books were to have studied, respectively, the state, foreign trade, and the world market and crises. This implies that a complete analysis of differential accumulation and its crisis tendencies on a world scale must extend beyond the capital–labour relation and the circuits of capitalist production to include at least the following themes, all of which Marx explored in one context or another and that correspond to the six-book plan. They comprise the concentration of bourgeois society in the form of the state; the role of taxes (and tax competition); the relation between national monies, international currencies, and an emergent world money; public debt and state credit; colonies; international relations, diplomacy, and war; and the international division of labour, foreign trade, and exchange rates. These would all have been related to the integration and development of the world market and the playing out of capital's contradictions and crisis tendencies on a world scale. Many of these factors bear directly on the explanation of crisis tendencies and would have been integrated into an eventual concrete-complex analysis of the laws of motion and crisis tendencies of capital on a world scale (for further comments, see Jessop 2015).

Conclusions

Crises are potentially path-shaping moments that provoke responses that are mediated through semiotic-cum-material processes of variation, selection, and retention. A critical realist approach to crises that takes seriously their duality – objectively overdetermined, subjectively indeterminate – must combine structural and semiotic analyses. It would examine (1) how crises emerge when established patterns of dealing with structural contradictions, their crisis-tendencies, and strategic dilemmas no longer work as expected and, indeed, when continued reliance thereon may even aggravate matters; (2) how contestation over the meaning of the crisis shapes responses through processes of variation, selection, and retention that are mediated through a changing mix of semiotic and extra-semiotic mechanisms. This approach opens space for studying the variation, selection, and retention of crisis construals and policy lessons as crises develop. Crisis construals establish "truth effects," i.e. the hegemonic or dominant meanings of crisis result from power relations. They are not the outcome of a cooperative language game with fixed rules but of a political struggle with variable rules and contested stakes (Lecercle 2006: 98). In this sense, construals are not simple linguistic (re-)descriptions of a conjuncture but, when backed by powerful social forces, involve strategic interventions into that conjuncture. In this regard, the interaction of semiotic, structural, technological, and agential selectivities and their mediation through the evolutionary mechanisms of variation, selection, and retention produces particular "modes of crisis management" that are not dictated solely by the objective overdetermination of the crisis nor by "arbitrary, rationalistic, and willed" construals of this, that, or another social force. At stake here is the production of "truth effects" that are not so much scientifically valid as conjuncturally correct, i.e. offer a sound objective analysis in terms of the correlation of forces as well as underlying causes, and can gauge and guide the strategic horizons of action, organizing effective action and disorganizing opposition.

Acknowledgments

Thanks are due to Andrew Brown, Norman Fairclough, and Andrew Sayer for comments on earlier thoughts; participants in the IACR Conference in London, July 2014, for stimulating questions at the plenary from which this article stems; and Mervyn Hartwig, Petter Næss, and David Tyfield for excellent suggestions on the original article in the *Journal of Critical Realism* or its present abbreviated version. The usual disclaimers apply. I dedicate this chapter to the memory of Roy Bhaskar, whose work has accompanied and influenced my intellectual career from the 1980s, including this example, and who commented at the plenary from which it is drawn.

Notes

1 One can also study science as a set of social practices. Here, scientists remain "located" in the intransitive world (which varies across the natural and social sciences), and observers act as if they operate outside it, at least for observational purposes.

2 On negative vs positive underlabouring, see Cruickshank 2003: 6, 103; Collier (1994: 208) makes a similar argument on the diacritical vs positive roles of underlabouring.

3 Cf. on the impossibility of "sociology-in-general" Bhaskar (1998: 48); and, on the impossibility of the method of critical realism as opposed to the utility of methodological guidelines, Danermark *et al.* (2002: 73–4, 110–11).

4 Cited in Elder-Vass (2007: 231).

5 "[C]ritical realist ontological theories are primarily, and perhaps only, suited for the one purpose that critical realists within economics seem to eschew – for establishing a basis for the development of critical realist-inspired analyses of substantive economic questions and issues" (Davidsen 2009: 40).

6 If one includes analysis of crises by Marx and diverse later Marxists as implicitly rather than avowedly critical realist, this observation would need to be modified. But with rare exceptions, few critical realists explicitly identify with Marx or Marxism; and, in economics, critical realist scholarship is far more concerned with engaging in dialogue within economics rather than developing the critique of political economy.

7 I owe this point to Petter Næss (personal communication).

8 For a less complex, but still important (and widely cited), discussion of crisis as event vs crisis as process, see Forgues and Roux-Dufort (1998).

9 Imaginary refers here to sets of cultural elements common to a given social group (or groups) that shape "lived experience" and help to reproduce social relations.

10 The whole note is interesting from a critical realist as well as a Marxist perspective because it distinguishes empirical features, the crisis as event and process, and its underlying causes considered as crisis tendencies and counter-tendencies.

11 This notion comes from Spivak (1987), for whom it denotes the discursive construction of an "essential unity" among heterogeneous groups as a basis for strategic political action in relation to nationalities, ethnic groups, gender politics, and other movements. It can be generalized to other strategic interventions.

12 "The study of possible futures must be grounded on the analysis of causally efficacious geo-historical layers of reality – agency, structures, and mechanisms" (Patomäki 2008: xiii).
13 For an important, explicit, and elaborate exception, see Tyfield (2012: 67–70, 79–84, 127 and passim).
14 In the conventional Marxist notation, C = commodity, M = money, C' = commodities embodying surplus value, and M' = money augmented by realized surplus value in the form of profits of enterprise. Matters become more complicated when capitalist credit money, other fractions of capital, and fictitious capital are introduced.
15 While the publication of the Marx–Engels *Gesamtausgabe* has complicated the analysis of Marx's intentions, it also reveals far more about his method of research and the spiral nature of a critical realist critique of political economy.

References

Aglietta, M. (1979) *A Theory of Capitalist Regulation. The US Experience*, London: New Left Books.

Althusser, L. (1977) *For Marx*, London: Verso.

Archer, M., Bhaskar, R., Collier, A., Lawson, T., and Norris, A. (eds) (1998) *Critical Realism: Essential Readings*, London: Routledge.

Augustine of Hippo (389 AD) *De Doctrina Christiana*, Oxford: Oxford University Press <1995>.

Benton, T. (1998) 'Realism and social science: Some comments on Roy Bhaskar's "The Possibility of Naturalism"', in Archer *et al.* (1998), pp. 297–312.

Benton, T. and Craib, I. (2001) *Philosophy of Social Science*, Basingstoke: Palgrave.

Bhaskar, R. (1986) *Scientific Realism and Human Emancipation*, London: Verso.

——(1998) *The Possibility of Naturalism*, 3rd edn, London: Routledge.

——(2008) *Dialectic. The Pulse of Freedom*, London: Routledge.

Brown, A., Slater, G., and Spencer, D.A. (2002) 'Driven to abstraction: Critical realism and the search for the "inner connection" of social phenomena', *Cambridge Journal of Economics*, 26(4): 773–88.

Burkett, P. (1999) *Marx and Nature: A Red and Green Perspective*, New York: St Martin's Press.

Callinicos, A. (2008) 'Roy Bhaskar and critical realism'. In J. Bidet and S. Kouvelakis (eds) *Critical Companion to Contemporary Marxism*, Leiden: Brill, pp. 567–85.

Carchedi, G. (2010) 'Zombie capitalism and the origin of crises', *International Socialist Journal*, 125, www.isj.org.uk/?id=614.

Collier, A. (1989) *Scientific Realism and Socialist Thought*, Hemel Hempstead: Harvester Wheatsheaf.

——(1994) *Critical Realism: An Introduction to Roy Bhaskar's Philosophy*, London: Verso.

Cruickshank, J. (2003) *Realism and Sociology. Anti-Foundationalism, Ontology, and Social Research*, London: Routledge.

Danermark, B., Ekström, M., Jakobsen, L., and Karlsson, J.C. (2002) *Explaining Society. Critical Realism in the Social Sciences*, London: Routledge.

Davidsen, B.-I. (2009) 'Critical realism in economics: A different view', In E. Fullbrook (ed.) *Ontology and Economics: Tony Lawson and his Critics*, London: Routledge, pp. 40–57.

Dean, K., Joseph, J., Roberts, J.M., and Wight, C. (eds) (2006) *Realism, Philosophy and Social Science*, Basingstoke: Palgrave.

Debray, R. (1973) *Prison Writings*, London: Allen Lane.

Elder-Vass, D. (2007) 'A method for social ontology: iterating ontology and social research', *Journal of Critical Realism*, 6(2): 226–40.

Farazmand, A. (2001) *Handbook of Crisis and Emergency Management*, New York: Marcel Dekker.

Fine, B. (2004) 'Addressing the critical and the real in critical realism'. In P. Lewis (ed.) *Transforming Economics: Perspectives on the Critical Realist Project*. London: Routledge, pp. 202–26.

Fleetwood, S. and Hesketh, A. (2006) 'Beyond measuring the human resources management–organizational performance link: applying critical realist meta-theory', *Organization*, 13(5): 677–99.

Forgues, B. and Roux-Dufort, C. (1998) '*Crises: events or processes?' Paper presented at Hazards and Sustainability Conference*, Durham, 26–27 May.

Foster, J.B. (2000) *Marx's Ecology: Materialism and Nature*, New York: Monthly Review Press.

Foucault, M. (2000) *Essential Works of Foucault 1954–1984*, New York: The New Press.

Freeman, A. (2010) 'Marxism without Marx: a note towards a critique', *Capital & Class*, 34(1): 84–97.

——(2014) 'What causes booms?' In A.K. Bagchi and A. Chatterjee (eds) *Marxism: With and Beyond Marx*, London: Routledge, 92–114.

Friedman, M. (1962) *Capitalism and Freedom*, Chicago, IL: University of Chicago Press.

Gottschalk, J. (2002) *Crisis Management*, Oxford: Capstone Publishing.

Gramsci, A. (1971) *Selections from the Prison Notebooks*, London: Lawrence & Wishart.

——(1975) *Quaderni del Carcere. Edizione Critica dell'Istituto Gramsci*, 4 volumes, ed. V. Gerratana, Rome: Einaudi.

——(1995) *Further Selections from the Prison Notebooks*, London: Lawrence & Wishart.

Habermas, J. (1976) *Legitimation Crisis*, London: Hutchinson.

Jessop, B. (1982) *The Capitalist State: Marxist Theories and Methods*, Oxford: Martin Robertson.

——(2012) 'Neo-Liberalism'. In G. Ritzer (ed.) *The Wiley-Blackwell Encyclopedia of Globalization, Vol. 3*, Chichester: Wiley-Blackwell, pp. 1513–21.

——(2015) 'Variegated capitalism and the political economy of austerity'. In R. Westra, R. Albritton, and D. Badeen (eds) *The Future of Capitalism After the Financial Crisis*, London: Routledge, pp. 19–38.

Joseph, J. (2002) 'Five ways in which critical realism can help Marxism'. In A. Brown, S. Fleetwood, and J.M. Roberts (eds) *Marxism and Critical Realism*, London: Routledge, pp. 22–44.

——(2006) 'Marxism, the dialectic of freedom and emancipation'. In K. Dean, J. Joseph, J.M. Roberts, and C. Wight (eds) *Realism, Philosophy and Social Science*, Basingstoke: Palgrave, pp. 99–122.

Kemp, S. (2005) 'Critical realism and the limits of philosophy', *European Journal of Social Theory*, 9(2): 171–91.

Kenway, P. (1980) 'Marx, Keynes and the possibility of crisis', *Cambridge Journal of Economics*, 4(1): 23–46.

Kirschenbaum, A. (2004) *Chaos Organization and Disaster Management*, New York: Marcel Dekker.

Lawson, T. (1998) 'Economic science without experimentation'. In M. Archer *et al.* (eds) *Critical Realism: Essential Readings*, London: Routledge, pp. 144–69.

——(1999) 'Critical issues in economics as realist social theory'. In S. Fleetwood (ed.) *Critical Realism in Economics: Development and Debate*, London: Routledge, pp. 209–57.

——(2009) 'Underlabouring for substantive theorising: reply to Davidsen'. In E. Fullbrook (ed.) *Ontology and Economics: Tony Lawson and his Critics*, London: Routledge, pp. 58–82.

Lecercle, J.J. (2006) *A Marxist Philosophy of Language*, Leiden/Boston, MA: Brill.

Manicas, P.T. (2006) *A Realist Philosophy of Social Science: Explanation and Understanding*, Cambridge: Cambridge University Press.

Marx, K. (1969) *Theories of Surplus Value, Volume 2*, London: Lawrence & Wishart.
——(1973 [1857]) 'Introduction'. In idem, *Grundrisse*, Harmondsworth: Penguin, pp. 83–111.
——(1976) *Capital, Volume 1*, London: Lawrence & Wishart.
Moore, J.W. (2015) *Capitalism in the Web of Life*, London: Verso.
Næss, P. (2004) 'Predictions, regressions and critical realism', *Journal of Critical Realism*, 3(1): 133–64.
Næss, P. and Strand, A. (2012) 'What kinds of traffic forecasts are possible?', *Journal of Critical Realism*, 11(3): 277–95.
Nielsen, P. (2002) 'Reflections on critical realism in political economy', *Cambridge Journal of Economics*, 26(4): 727–38.
Offe, C. (1984) *Contradictions of the Welfare State*, London: Hutchinson.
Patomäki, H. (2008) *The Political Economy of Global Security: War, Future Crises and Changes in Global Governance*, London: Routledge.
Pinkowski, J. (ed.) (2008) *Disaster Management*, New York: CRC Press.
Quarantelli, E.I. (1988) 'Disaster crisis management: A summary of research findings', *Journal of Management Studies*, 25(4): 373–85.
Roberts, J.M. (2001) 'Realistic spatial abstraction? Marxist observations of a claim within critical realist geography', *Progress in Human Geography*, 25(4): 544–67.
——(2006) 'Method, Marxism and critical realism'. In K. Dean, J. Joseph, J.M. Roberts, and C. Wight (eds) *Realism, Philosophy and Social Science*, 65–98. Basingstoke: Palgrave.
Roberts, M. (2014) 'Marx's law of the tendency of the rate of profit to fall and theory of crises: does it fit the facts?' Presentation to *Critique* Conference, April 11.
Sayer, A. (1992) *Method in Social Science: A Realist Approach*, 2nd edn, London: Routledge.
Spivak, G.C. (1987) *In Other Worlds: Essays in Cultural Politics*, London: Routledge.
Tyfield, D. (2012) *The Economics of Science: A Critical Realist Overview. Volume 2: Towards a Synthesis of Political Economy and Science and Technology Studies*, London: Routledge.

7

USING RETRODUCTION TO ADDRESS WICKED PROBLEMS

Leigh Price

Introduction

Complex bio/socio/economic problems were first described as *wicked* in 1973 by Horst Rittel and Melvin Webber. Generally, it is assumed that problems are wicked not only because of their complexity but also because of multiple stakeholders' perceptions of them (Batie, 2008). Rittel and Webber wrote their article as a reaction to the failure of the initial twenty years of first-generation, functionalist systems thinking, which included complexity theory and which attempted to cope with wicked problems' biophysical complexity (Jackson, 2003: 24). They arrive at the conclusion that science is inadequate to the task of addressing wicked problems. This is because, they say, science cannot deal with open systems; neither can it deal with human values. As an alternative, they suggest a relativist, consensualist version of policy-making in which science, whether systems based or not, plays a relatively minor role, if any. By contrast, I argue that science must play a strong role in policy formulation, but in order to do so we need to adjust our view of what qualifies as good science. I believe that this will strengthen the democratic principles that allow us to be politically empowered in terms of decisions that relate to our well-being.

I begin by outlining the main methodological problems present in Rittel and Webber's concept of wicked problems. Nevertheless, many of their intuitive concerns are valid; it is their resolution of these concerns that I find problematic. Therefore, in the second part of the chapter I address certain of their concerns using critical realist principles. In so doing, I give an account of how to deal with wicked problems using the logic of retroduction. People use retroduction when they work out how the world must have been for something to be the way that it is. For example, a student might use retroduction to work out why their bank balance has gone into overdraft (most likely explained by too many nights out). A scientist might use retroduction to work out why our planet is experiencing climate change (most likely explained by an increase in carbon dioxide in the atmosphere due to human activity). In other words, retroduction is the move from an observation to a theory that accounts for the observation, preferably by choosing the simplest and most likely explanation. As retroduction is used by the lay person as well as the scientist, acknowledging its (currently unrecognised) validity and its place in science automatically reduces the power-differential between scientists and lay people, and is empowering for communities. This point, that retroduction-based science is not only philosophically more correct but also beneficial to democracy, will be a theme that recurs in both the first and second parts of this chapter.

Part 1: Methodological problems in Rittel and Webber's conception of wicked problems

Much of Rittel and Webber's analysis of wicked problems is familiar to critical realists. In an anticipation of the critical realist critique of mainstream science,[1] these theorists suggest that the pluralistic, open-system nature of wicked problems must necessarily result in the failure of scientific (mainstream evidence-based) social policy to solve them. However, unlike critical realists, Rittel and Webber respond to this critique of science-based social policy by suggesting that there is nothing wrong with the science. Rather, they claim that science has simply been over-valued as the basis for social policy and that we can solve the issue if scientists understand that when it comes to wicked problems, they must sit back and let communities take over. That is, Rittel and Webber want planners to adopt a different paradigm of social science, namely an irrealist–interpretative one; or, as climate change scientists Fullana *et al.* (2011) advocate, planners should accept that 'consensus beats reality' However, in practice, Rittel and Webber allow a variation on the theme of irrealism by also advocating an irrealist–pragmatist mixed methodology. Specifically, this mixed methodology is characterised as follows: the outcome determines the methodology to be used (hence its pragmatism); it is assumed that the paradigms are incommensurable; and thus truth becomes a relativist question arrived at in a variety of ways, such that we can choose a truth that best suits our agenda by choosing our research methodology.[2] Rittel and Webber candidly admit to this Machiavellian pragmatism. They say (p. 167) that in terms of wicked problems, the aim is not to find the truth but to improve some characteristic of the world. Relatedly, they also suggest that it is not the facts of the situation but what an analyst values, or their 'world view', that is the strongest determining factor in explaining a discrepancy and, therefore, in resolving a wicked problem. They state that 'everybody picks that explanation of a discrepancy which fits his intentions best and which conforms to the action-prospects that are available to him' (p. 145). While it is plausible that one's world view might largely decide their choice of action in response to an explanation of a discrepancy, I find it problematic to say that one's world view is the strongest factor in deciding on a truth, in this case in deciding on the explanation of an (ontologically real) discrepancy. Such a statement treads on dangerous relativist ground. It is an example of the kind of irrealism that I associate with extreme versions of postmodernism and interpretivism in which the measure of truth is simply an individual or community matter, perhaps a matter of consensus, or as (irrealist) pragmatist Rorty *et al.* (1980: 176) suggested, whatever your peers let you get away with. By contrast, I prefer to side with a rather different (ideal–realist) pragmatist, Pierce (in Haack, 2000: 31), who stated: '[When] it is no longer the reasoning which determines what the conclusion shall be, but … the conclusion which determines what the reasoning shall be … this is sham reasoning.' Such sham reasoning is, I argue, morally questionable and undermines the basic freedoms of a democratic society.

Allow me to illustrate this further with an example. If my world view is such that I am xenophobic, then according to the sham reasoning permitted by Rittel and Webber, it is to be expected that I will explain the long queues in the emergency hospitals as the result of too many immigrants, even though reliable evidence suggests that other factors such as spending cuts are a better explanation of the situation: this allows me to come to the (personally convenient) conclusion that we must reduce immigration. Thus my conclusion determines my reasoning. Given Rittel and Webber's assumption that sham reasoning is an unavoidable part of social policy, they have little scope to challenge such a conclusion, especially if it constitutes a consensus (remember that consensus supposedly beats reality). However, since reducing immigration is a solution based on an incorrect assumption, it will fail to address the ontologically existing issue of the inadequate emergency services. Thus the long queues will remain and a great deal of human suffering is likely to ensue.[3]

By contrast, critical realists respond to the critique of science-based socio-economic policy by redefining what it means to carry out quality science. They have therefore developed a scientific epistemology that provides a space for knowledge-making familiar to communities, and thus they reduce the gulf between scientific and lay knowledge: for them, the specialist methods of gaining empirical data (quantitative and qualitative) remain a technical necessity upon which to base the retroductive theorising that is a main objective of science and that is already carried out by scientists and lay people alike. Thus Bhaskar (2008b: 231–279) talks about the MELD (Table 7.1), which is a dialectic that can be thought of as an ontological–axiological chain (what *is* leads to action). When it relates to epistemology, it is called the DREI(C) and RRREI(C), or pure and applied science, respectively. When it relates to practical problem-solving to create a better society, it is called the DEA (see Diagram 1 for the meanings of the acronyms and further definitions). In its most basic form, this dialectic is the removal of absences, whether these be absences of what is known, leading to a more complete version of truth, or absences from society, leading to a more whole(some) version of society. Specifically, Table 7.1 compares the ontological–axiological dialectical chain (the MELD), pure science (the DREI(C)), applied science (the RRREI(C)) and the dialectic of progressive social change (the DEA), which exploits the DREI(C) and the RRREI(C). Usefully for policy-makers and those people deciding on action in the face of wicked problems, the possibility of methodological unity means that both

TABLE 7.1 Comparison of the MELD, pure science, applied science and practical problem solving

Dialectic in its general form of a dialectic or an ontological–axiological chain: the MELD	**Dialectic as pure science: the DREI(C) approach** Iteratively analogical–retroductive	**Dialectic as applied science: the RRREI(C) approach** Decompository–retrodictive	**Dialectic as practical problem resolution approach for progressive social transformation: the DEA approach**
First moment (1M) Ontology – being and knowledge are not conflated – acknowledges ontological stratification, i.e. non-empirical structures and mechanisms are real	**Transfactual theory unavailable** **Description** of the empirical law-like behaviour, i.e. data collection	**Transfactual theory available** **Resolve** the problem into its relevant components, as suggested by the theory/theories to be applied, i.e. data collection	**Transfactual theory available** **Diagnosis** a) Describe the problem in terms that are relevant to the independently validated normic theory or tendency statements, i.e. data collection
Second edge (2E) **Absence and negativity** – we deepen our thinking of being to encompass being as a process and change, using concepts of absence – the second edge is about interaction	**Description** b) Deepen the description of the situation in terms of contradictions, anomalies and other absences in current knowledge, i.e. begin data analysis	**Redescribe** these components in theoretically significant terms using the transfactual, retroductively derived theory of efficacious structures and mechanisms, i.e. consider the components in the light of the context in the situation at hand, specifically, the absences and contradictions, i.e. begin data analysis	**Diagnosis** b) Consider the processes that result in absences and contradictions in that context, i.e. begin data analysis

Third level **Totality** – this level includes relationships and normative statements, assuming totality rather than separation and leading to a naturalistic ethics; the *explanatory* critique is relevant here. In this level we think of being as being bound together	**Retroduction** leading to the absence of the absent knowledge, or the absence of the contradictions leading to an identification of a greater totality of *explanation* of the issue at hand **Elimination** – compare and eliminate competing theories – achieving, in so far as it is possible, subjective certainty	**Retrodiction** leading to an antecedent *explanation/s* of these absences and contradictions. Establish a full enough set of explanatory causes for a concrete applied explanation to have been provided, given one's explanatory objectives. If the available theory is inadequate to explain the situation, then retroduction may also be required **Elimination** – compare and eliminate competing theories – achieving, in so far as it is possible, subjective certainty	**Explanation** of the problem using **retrodiction**, perhaps using the seven laminations of scale (Bhaskar, 2010: 9–10), leading to a full enough set of explanations to achieve the objective of the intervention. If the available theory is inadequate to explain the situation, then retroduction may also be required **Elimination** – compare and eliminate competing theories – achieving, in so far as it is possible, subjective certainty
Fourth dimension **Transitive praxis** and **reflexivity** – equivalent to practice and leading to emancipation	**Identification** – use the theory, test it out – apply deductive experimental tests (if appropriate) until the claim is well established in the scientific community (achieves *inter-subjective* certainty) – it thus becomes a new phenomenon in turn to be explained. **Correction** – using the theory may suggest adjustments, i.e. praxis	**Identification** – check one's theories and establish them *inter-subjectively* in the scientific community – even small pieces of evidence should be explainable. As this is applied research, there will be implications that can be implemented and the success/failure of the interventions will contribute to the certainty that the theory is true **Correction** – using the theory may suggest adjustments – i.e. praxis	**Action** as suggested by the explanation and envisaged (by an *inter-subjective*, democratic process, perhaps requiring advocacy) as absenting the constraints to absenting absences. Success or failure of interventions based on the explanation will act to confirm/deny it. **Correction** – iterative feedback will allow agents to adjust their action in the event of unintended consequences, potentially leading to more adequate theory – i.e. praxis

scientists and lay enquirers must have the same responsibilities in terms of honest truth-seeking. An important aspect of the MELD is its transfactual theories, which are arrived at by the logic of retroduction. Transfactual theories are normic statements with factual instances (in the natural sciences) in the laboratory, and perhaps a few other effectively closed contexts, that constitute their empirical grounds; they need not, and in general will not, be reflected in an invariant pattern or regularly recurring sequence of events. That is, they are not necessarily reflected in correlations in the open system of the world (Bhaskar, 2008a). In social science, it is not usually possible to arrive at, or test, transfactual theories in a closed-system laboratory and therefore their truthfulness must be surmised from evidence such as from case studies or statistical surveys. Some natural science disciplines, such as ecology and cosmology, are similar to the social sciences in that their theories also cannot be arrived at, or tested, in laboratories.

In the xenophobic example above, we can dismiss the sham reasoning of the lay actor (even if it is a consensus) as easily as we could dismiss it if we came across it in the work of a scientist, and for the same reason: it is based on a wrong epistemology. Such fair play was one time not 'fair' at all, since positivistic science was able to be carried out only by trained scientists, and thus to insist that lay stakeholders play by the same epistemological rules effectively silenced them. If one was not a scientist, one's knowledge did not count for much. While critical realism allows the lay voice to be taken seriously, it nevertheless requires the same amount of integrity from the lay actor as the trained scientist in terms of honest truth-seeking. Currently, an inconsistency exists in which the lay consensus 'beats' reality (empirical data?)[4] – except when empirical data (reality?) beats the lay consensus – and those in power get to call what card is trumps according to what outcome benefits them.

Another reason Rittel and Webber are cynical about the potential for science to address wicked problems is that they suppose that facts cannot lead to values. They therefore assume that science can never, for example, contribute towards definitions of equity. To the contrary, critical realists assume that it is irrational to think that facts cannot lead to values (Bhaskar, 2008b: 300). Some examples which show that science can and does lead to values are: a) the scientific understanding of the role of bacteria in disease transmission has resulted in society coming to strongly value cleanliness in homes and public spaces; and b) in terms of equity, the scientific understanding of the transmission of the HIV virus has resulted in us being able to avoid discriminating against people living with HIV since we better understand that HIV is not transmitted through everyday contact.

However, commentators are right to be concerned that we should not use reified facts to advance ideological values. This is a different issue, and one which critical realism addresses by arguing against positivism, whose trademark is the reified fact, and by making the social aspects of science transparent through its conception of the transitive dimension of knowledge (Bhaskar, 2008a: 21–24). It is not in the scope of this chapter to fully explain how positivism results in reified facts, although it is well established in the literature.[5] The concern of science is not that we need to achieve reified objective facts, untouched by humans, in order to achieve truthfulness, but that we need to make the human, social contribution towards fact-making transparent so that we can make judgement calls as to the truth of the facts. Acknowledging the social aspect of epistemology suggests epistemological relativism, as we find in critical realism, such that two or more very different versions of a truth may nevertheless be equally as good at describing reality. However, we may prefer one version over the other simply because of an epistemologically pragmatic (rather than a Rorty-style, Machiavellian pragmatic) requirement for the way that the knowledge is to be used.

For example, the way that I describe a tree will be very different depending on whether I am a paper manufacturer, a carpenter, an evolutionary biologist or a poet, but essentially our accounts should remain faithful to the tree, unless, of course, one is purposefully being fictional. Furthermore, what counts as truth today, based on our best guess, may not be what counts tomorrow in the light of new developments such as new empirical evidence or someone arriving at a better understanding. For example, we were once confident that mammals do not lay eggs, but on the discovery of the duck-billed platypus, we had to revise that knowledge. Bhaskar (2008a: 249) describes epistemological relativism as follows:

> Epistemological relativism insists only upon the impossibility of knowing objects except under particular descriptions. And it entails the rejection of any correspondence theory of truth. A proposition is true if and only if the state of affairs that it expresses (describes) is real. But propositions cannot be compared with states of affairs; their relationship cannot be described as one of correspondence. Philosophers have wanted a theory of truth to provide a criterion or stamp of knowledge. But no such stamp is possible. For the judgement of the truth of a proposition is necessarily intrinsic to the science concerned. There is no way in which we can look at the world and then at a sentence and ask whether they fit. There is just the expression (of the world) in speech (or thought).

Notice how the lack of the possibility of a correspondence between the world and what we say about it means that scientists can never claim to have absolute truth in the sense that their reports are merely the 'truth-clay' upon which the stamp of reality is carried to policy-makers. Assuming the truth-clay version of epistemology leads to hypostatisation whereby empirical observations are incorrectly considered to be actual things. It also leads to reification, in which we assume that our theoretical, human-made facts, our interpretations of empirical measurements, such as causal correlations, are actual things. However, there is so much more to reality than the empirical, in the form of relationships, structures and mechanisms. Because we understand that the non-empirical real cannot be 'stamped in clay', it is not difficult to arrive at the incorrect conclusion that therefore the non-empirical does not exist; or that, at the very least, even if it did exist, we could not know about it. However, if one has an epistemology of non-correspondence or non-identity, then one can admit that even things that are non-empirical can be known and can be real. Unfortunately, the mainstream belief that what is real is only what is empirical, and that the only way to know causality is through constant conjunctions, has resulted in poor social policy.

Take the example of the UK government's social policy around its citizens' salt intake. It is well established that there is a correlation between reduced salt intake and a reduction in blood pressure (Dahl *et al.*, 1972; Meneely and Battarbee, 1976; Obarzanek *et al.*, 2003). To say that this proves that salt causes heart disease, perhaps going so far as to say that therefore this tells us that we must decrease our salt intake, is poor science. The first mistake (hypostatisation) is that it is assumed that high blood pressure simply *is* heart disease, yet high blood pressure is merely an empirical measurement often associated with heart disease. The second mistake (reification) is to assume that the correlation between high salt intake and heart disease (high blood pressure) is causal, yet in an open system, a correlation cannot be known to be causal and therefore we can have only a theory of causation, which must compete with other theories of causation (for example, an alternative theory is that the correlation is merely a chance artefact and is not causal). Furthermore, to assume that the only way to know causation is to use correlations is to remove the possibility of retroductively theorising deep structures and mechanisms that fully account for the observation or the problem. The third mistake (fetishisation) is to assume that therefore the correlation *tells* us to reduce salt, yet there can be many alternative actions suggested by a causal mechanism and it is people (including ourselves), who interpret the meaning of the mechanism and who *tell* us what to do. This hypostatisation–reification–fetishisation (HRF) triad can be avoided.[6]

In the salt example, hypostatisation (whereby the scientists/health policy-makers assume that high blood pressure is the same as heart disease, and that high salt intake measured in the laboratory is the same as high salt intake among real people in the non-laboratory-based world) removes the motive for collecting more data around this phenomenon. If one avoids the over-confidence of hypostatisation, one might feel obliged to ask more questions, such as: are there other ways to measure the ontological entity heart disease, other than high blood pressure, so that we can be (relatively) sure that this is what we are dealing with; or, are there other ways to measure the unsafe levels of salt intake in real human populations, so that we can be (relatively) sure that this is what we are dealing with?

In terms of reification, scientists/health policy-makers have assumed that a) the theory that there is a causal correlation between high blood pressure and high salt intake is the same as b) the causal link between high salt and heart disease. This removes their motive for collecting more data around this theorised link, and as it is based on the belief that only the empirical is real, it also technically disallows, and in practice it discourages,[7] retroductive theorising. If one avoids the over-confidence of reification, one might feel obliged to ask more questions, such as whether or not there are other theories that might better explain the correlation. If one has not hypostatised and thus not tended to over-simplify the empirical evidence-gathering phase, one will have a great deal of evidence that can be retroductively accounted for by whichever theory one eventually, albeit fallibly, deems is the most likely to be true.

In terms of fetishisation, scientists/health policy-makers have assumed that the correlation (constant conjunction) of increased salt intake and high blood pressure *tells us* that we must reduce our salt intake. However, if one has avoided hypostatisation and reification, then by the stage of deciding action one is likely to have a large amount of information to hand, to have explored the issue thoroughly, and to have arrived at transfactual retroductive theory about the causal structures and mechanisms involved. Given the complex system linking health to salt intake, one is likely to realise that there are trade-offs and side-effects to changing our salt-intake behaviour. For some people, reducing salt intake may be detrimental, such as for those people with Addison's disease, whose bodies excrete salt. For others, there may be a trade-off: low salt can worsen depression (Goldstein and Leshem, 2014) but improve blood pressure.

As it turns out, even as the British congratulate themselves for their successful policy intervention, which has significantly reduced the UK population's intake of salt (Shankar *et al.*, 2013), there is evidence that the advice is possibly incorrect as some research has found no correlation between relatively high salt intake and mortality (Alderman *et al.*, 1998). Other research suggests that reducing salt intake may be detrimental to health at the population level. For example, low salt intake has in some research been associated with higher mortality (Wenner, 2011; O'Donnell *et al.*, 2011; Stolarz-Skrzypek *et al.*, 2011), and people with diabetes and athletes have particularly high mortality rates if they have a low salt intake (Rosner and Kirven, 2007; Ekinci *et al.*, 2011).

A policy intervention as simple as how much salt we should eat has turned out to be a decidedly wicked problem, and the mainstream approach to the problem, based on HRF, as Rittel and Webber prophesied, is a doubtful success. However, the critical realist ontological–axiological chain (the MELD) improves on the positivist ontological–axiological chain (the HRF) in at least the following ways:

- It requires that a fact is placed into the open system of the world using information gathered from interdisciplinary science. An interdisciplinary explanation of the effects of salt in our lives would be something along the lines of the seven levels of scale, which is explained in more detail later in this chapter (see Table 7.2). It is advisable to avoid any kind of axiological claim based on a simplistic correlation only; in the salt case, a large-scale intervention was questionably rolled out on the basis of a correlation between salt and increased blood pressure.
- In attempting to understand the health implications of salt in an interdisciplinary way, we are likely to find that there are gaps in our understanding. Critical realism therefore requires that we understand the problem in terms of absences and anomalies. In the salt example, it would have required that policy-makers absent information such as how the lack of salt affected a variety of kinds of people, or whether or not the correlation between low salt and low blood pressure further translated into heart disease and low mortality.

- Critical realism requires that scientists not only retroductively theorise the facts at hand to fully understand the structures and mechanisms involved, but that they compare their theory to competing theories, and thus they are required to justify their choice of theory over other theories (critical realist judgemental rationality). In terms of the salt example, a competing theory to the one that suggests that people eat too much salt, and that salt intake must be reduced, is that healthy people have a tendency to self-regulate their salt intake towards optimum levels, especially if it is part of a healthy diet, and that salt requirements are significantly different for different kinds of people (McCarron *et al.*, 2009). The best theory will be the one that best explains all of the available evidence.
- Critical realism implies that lay actors can, and perhaps for reasons of democracy should, be involved in the retroductive reasoning process. Not only would this in theory help to avoid sham, ideological reasoning on the part of scientists from going undetected, but the process of retroduction itself might be enhanced through involving lay actors. Retroduction is a creative process in which new knowledge is generated by going outside of one's paradigm of what constitutes normal science (Kuhn, 2012). It requires that we mine cultural resources across a whole spectrum of society to generate a new concept. For example, words such as 'spin' and 'charge' are no longer used only in the old-fashioned way. Furthermore, career scientists may have too much invested in particular interpretations and beliefs to make it easy for them to risk their reputations on wild-card theories (Khun, 2012). However, lay actors are less likely to suffer from these restraints.
- Critical realism assumes that our knowledge is fallible – we may need to change our minds in the face of further evidence – and therefore it results in less powerful commitments to axiological claims. If we are not absolutely sure of our knowledge, and not sure of the outcome of an action, we are more likely to act in such a way as to be able to change direction if it turns out that we were wrong. Therefore, even if scientists decided that, on balance, policy-makers should advocate that people reduce their salt intake, they would nevertheless add certain caveats and would set up monitoring programmes to detect unintended consequences, allowing for a fast reaction if there seemed to be problems. They would also use language with lower modality, such as 'perhaps' or 'possibly' or 'to the best of our knowledge', making a turn-around in the advent of conflicting evidence less embarrassing.
- Critical realism assumes that there may be several feasible options to deal with the issue and that the affected people should have a democratic say in how the meaning of the fact is interpreted. By making the social aspect of the interpretation of the fact transparent (i.e. by refusing fetishisation which makes it possible for politicians to refuse responsibility for an intervention based on the claim that they were merely implementing policy suggested by evidence), communities can refuse to be manipulated and insist that all policy recommendations are framed in such a way as to make the steps of the ontological–axiological

chain transparent. Ideally, all research related to policy should be passed through a community discussion phase in which independent researchers explain the research findings to the community, and allow them to participate in the process of judgemental rationalism (choosing which retroductive theory best explains the evidence – possibly the community can at this point add their own retroductive theories to the mix). Advocacy by scientists or policy-makers for a particular theory or way forward may be necessary if awareness of the options is not high. Hopefully, by making all of the theoretical options clear, any ideologically based sham reasoning on the part of the scientists/policy-makers/development workers or the community will become apparent. Once a retroductive theory is decided upon as the most-likely-to-be-true rendition of the situation, the community[8] should consider the pros and cons of various options of action, perhaps leading to a vote on a particular way forward. This is where their world view, including, for example, cultural preferences, comes to the fore. This is not unlike a patient-centred medical context where a physician explains the several possibilities of diagnosis given the symptoms, considers what the patient has to say on the matter so that they together decide on the most likely diagnosis, and then explains the different treatment options, including possible side-effects and risks, so that the patient can be empowered to make their own decisions about their health from the position of well-informed choice and personal preference.

Part 2: Rittel and Webber's specific concerns revisited

Here I consider certain specific concerns discussed by Rittel and Webber (1973). For the most part, their concerns are valid, but they arrive at questionable conclusions. Critical realism offers a better way of addressing these concerns.

The planner has no right to be wrong

Rittel and Webber (p. 155) open their discussion of wicked problems by lamenting the public's loss of trust in the scientific community. They write: 'Few of the modern professionals seem to be immune from the popular attack whether they be social workers, educators, housers, public health officials, policemen, city planners, highway engineers or physicians.' Rittel and Webber assume they can avoid the attack by keeping science as it is but removing science from goal formulation, problem definition and issues of equity – which they suggest we leave to society (communities). Critical realists, however, prefer to include society in the process of epistemology, that is, in the science itself, and thus to change the science while at the same time using this socialised science (appropriate for studying natural and social phenomena) to help us to make educated choices for our goals, problems and equitable solutions. Incidentally, this achieves some of what Rittel and Webber seek, which is that scientists are not made fully responsible

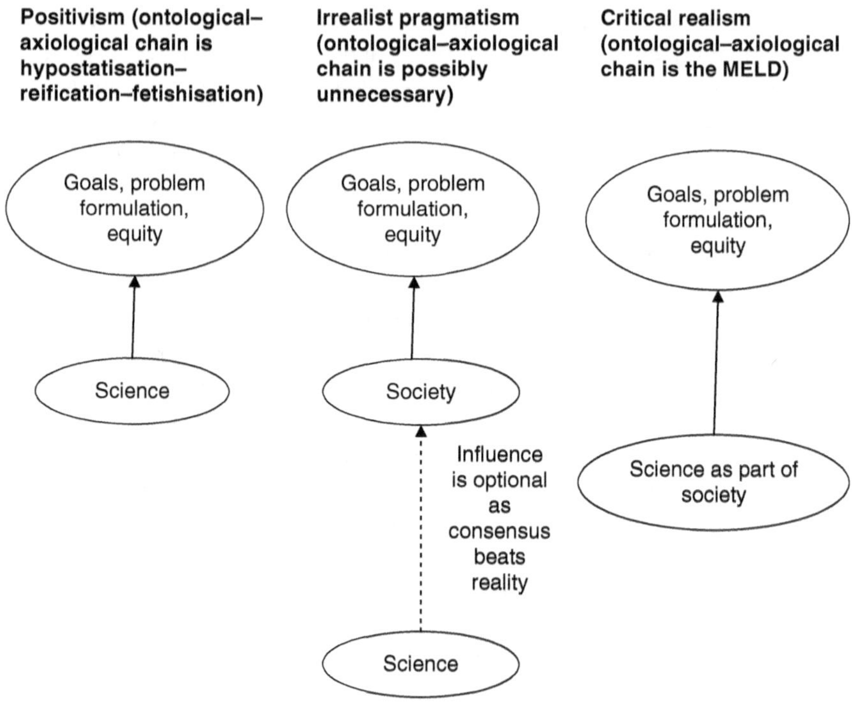

FIGURE 7.1 Dealing with wicked problems: positivism, irrealist pragmatism and critical realism

for wicked decisions; the community should also be responsible for these decisions. Figure 7.1 summarises the difference between positivism, Rittel and Webber's irrealist pragmatism and critical realism in terms of goals, problem formulation and equity.

Wicked problems are solved by a rich mode of reasoning

Rittel and Webber at times sound exactly like critical realists. For example, they write (p. 160):

> In dealing with wicked problems the modes of reasoning used in the argument are much richer than those permissible in the scientific discourse. Because of the essential uniqueness of the problem and lacking opportunity for rigorous experimentation, it is not possible to put hypotheses to a crucial test.

The rich *mode of reasoning* to which Rittel and Webber refer in the above quote is simply retroduction. The idea that we cannot use experimentation to deal with problems in an open system context is well described by critical realists (Danermark *et al.*, 2002[1997]: 100). This is precisely the critique of mainstream positivist science made by Roy Bhaskar (2008a). Whereas Rittel and Webber interpret this as proof that science cannot help much with wicked problems, Bhaskar (2008b: 109) resolves this problem by suggesting that we therefore need to enrich our modes of scientific reasoning by adding (or perhaps openly admitting to using) retroduction and retrodiction (similar to retroduction, but where we use already existing theory to explain something). Scientists have always used these modes of reasoning but have left them out of their formal theories of science. Wicked problems show how important it is that scientists stop making this mistake and join with communities in using retroduction to address complex bio/socio/economic problems. That is, scientists need to bring what they actually do in line with what they say that they do, which will bring them in line with lay agents, and in this way they will make science more democratic as it will allow both the scientists and the communities to be, methodologically speaking, 'on the same page'. Democracy is enabled because no particular group has epistemological superiority over the other. Thus no group has the right to choose what is true simply because they are dominant – as in mainstream science – or they are marginalised – as in stand point theory[9] whereby it is assumed that marginalised groups are the only ones able to see the truth of social situations. Such superiority equates to power over the other, as the work of Michel Foucault (1926–1984) has demonstrated. Instead, in some ways, truth is apolitical, even though different groups may differently interpret that truth and what it means for their socioeconomic–political purposes. So, for example, the truth that HIV is sexually transmitted can be interpreted equally validly as meaning that a) one should be monogamous, or b) that one should use condoms, depending on one's particular politics and world view. However, if someone refuses to take precautions because their world view is that HIV is not sexually transmitted, they may still contract HIV. Thus the truth is, in a sense, apolitical – reality will affect us no matter what we believe. It is therefore a good idea to try to keep one's beliefs as truthful as possible. Although it might be comforting to think that we can always rely on our community's consensus to give us the truth, this is not always the case.

Defining a wicked problem is the same as solving it

Rittel and Webber also sound like critical realists when they say (p. 161):

> To find the problem is thus the same thing as finding the solution... The process of formulating the problem and of conceiving a solution (or re-solution) are identical, since every specification of the problem is a specification of the direction in which a treatment is considered.

Again, instead of seeing this as simply a rather useful and indeed encouraging characteristic of science – that once we have explained the problem we are led immediately to the specification of an action, all other things being equal – Rittel and Webber claim this as proof that science is inadequate to the task. Bhaskar (2008b: 261–262) also makes the point that once we have explained a problem, we can then move directly to a relevant action.

> If … one can explain the falsity, then, subject to a ceteris paribus clause, in virtue of the openness of the social world and the multiplicity of determinations therein, one can move without further ado to a negative evaluation of the explanans and a positive evaluation of any action rationally designed to absent it.

It is when making this point in their chapter that Rittel and Webber most directly criticise first-generation systems theory by remarking on how systems theorists are told to first define their problem and then find a solution; yet for wicked problems, defining the problem is the solution. Here we see how Rittel and Webber (and first-generation systems theorists) are limited by a view of reality as being real only at the level of the empirical. Therefore they are limited to seeing causation in terms of shallow cause and effect based on constant conjunctions. However, Rittel and Webber intuitively know that we also can understand causation at a deeper level of reality. At this deep level of non-empirical reality the problem is explained in terms of structures and mechanisms. Thus the problem exists at two levels, but Rittel and Webber conflate them. Specifically, these levels are the level of the empirical, where a problem is described (D in the DREI(C)), and the level of the real, where a problem is explained using retroduction (R in the DREI(C)). Empirical description of the problem does not suggest solutions, but depth explanation of the problem does. Nevertheless, Bhaskar acknowledges that after a time, the original explanation of a phenomenon can become its definition. For example, the explanation of water as being made up of hydrogen and oxygen atoms is now the definition of water. Bhaskar (2008b: 110) writes: 'After a further elapse of time the firmly established structure may be held to be definitional of a natural kind.' This is consistent with the view of science as being iterative: today's structural explanation becomes tomorrow's description to be explained. For example, once we explained how water is made of hydrogen and oxygen, we then went on to detail how these atoms could be explained by the activity of sub-atomic particles.

Wicked problems overwhelm our intelligence?

Rittel and Webber consider wicked problems to be, by definition, overwhelming. This is because they are caught at the level of the empirical, and at this level all that they have to control the situation are millions of variables, which can affect each other in sometimes quite dramatic and surprising ways, illustrated by the butterfly effect of complexity theory. Critical realists, however, who acknowledge the real that emerges from the empirical, can work with structures and mechanisms based on a deep, interdisciplinary understanding of the problem at hand.

An analogy might be the way that the body manages complex problems, such as walking. If we try to consciously control every muscle in our body in the process of walking, the amount of information required and the amount of brain power required to analyse that information would be far too great. Instead, our body uses certain principles upon which to base its activity and it adjusts itself according to certain key empirical measurements, such as the information that it gets from our eyes or from the cochlea of the inner ear. This is why, when Rittel and Webber write that our 'theory is inadequate for decent forecasting; our intelligence is insufficient to our tasks' (p. 156), they are, metaphorically speaking, trying to walk by consciously controlling every single one of myriad variables. However, here we must understand that what they mean by *theory* is shallow compared with the critical realist understanding of theory. Mainstream theory is based on constant conjunctions or correlations theorised as being causal; in systems theory, multiple linear correlations are placed in a web of interacting variables which supposedly avoids linearity by providing feed-back loops and complex interactions. Senge (in Jackson, 2003: 71) hints towards using deeper theoretical principles to guide action in complex systems when he describes *archetypes*, which are 'regular patterns of behaviour' and which he claims is a way to make sense of, by simplifying, the massive amount of data required to manage complex systems. However, Senge sees these archetypes as groups of causal correlations that tend to be associated with each other. He does not take the step towards retroductively theorising deep causal structures and mechanisms.

In terms of the wicked problems of ecology and economics, there is a relevant transdisciplinary principle that growth cannot be unlimited and that it is necessary to live within one's means. Mainstream economists fail to follow this principle in terms of the exploitation of the Earth's natural resources and the destruction of the good-will, and sometimes the health and well-being, of their workers, whom the capitalists also exploit. At the level of the real, the as-yet-absent collapse of the ecological and/or economic system as we know it does not mean that the claim of the threat of failing to live within our means is not justified. As Rittel and Webber explain, we cannot rehearse these theories by first putting them to the empirical test, thus: 'Every solution to a wicked problem is a "one-shot operation"; because there is no opportunity to learn by trial-and-error, every attempt counts significantly' (p. 163). Being aware that we have one shot only and that we are breaking the principles of the trend or tendency for systems to fail when resources are over-used makes the economic policy-makers' disregard of the imminent ecological and social system failure all the more contemptible. However, given mainstream scientists' denial of the existence of structures and mechanisms at the level of the real, the politicians and economists can get away with their behaviour because the truthfulness of the structures and mechanisms supposedly 'can't be proved'. For example, the US Senate has repeatedly refused to acknowledge humanity's role in global climate change (Goldenberg, 2015). Climate change deniers have particularly well-developed arguments against climate change along the lines that it can't be proved or that there is no scientific evidence for it. However, if society generally understood science in a critical realist way, the logic of these commentators could be easily dismissed.

Wicked problems are by nature interdisciplinary

Rittel and Webber lament (p. 165):

> Every wicked problem can be considered to be a symptom of another problem...Removal of one cause poses another problem of which the original problem is a "symptom." In turn, it can be considered the symptom of still another, "higher level" problem. Thus "crime in the streets" can be considered as a symptom of general moral decay, or permissiveness, or deficient opportunity, or wealth, or poverty, or whatever causal explanation you happen to like best.

Critical realists might write exactly the same thing, but with a less exasperated tone. It is encouraging to see that Rittel and Webber acknowledge the layered nature of reality in this quote. Remarkably, they consider almost exactly the seven laminations of scale that Bhaskar (2010) identifies. However, Rittel and Webber describe these scales as contradictory, whereas for critical realists they are emergent and therefore they are all potentially correct, the higher-order problems being emergent from the lower-order ones. In Table 7.2, Rittel and Webber's analysis of the problem 'crime in the streets' is placed into the framework of Bhaskar's (2010: 9–10) seven laminations of scale.

TABLE 7.2 The wicked problem of crime on the streets

Bhaskar's seven laminations of scale	*Rittel and Webber's analysis of street crime*
(i) The sub-individual psychological level	Phrenologic aberrations (p. 166)
(ii) The individual or biographical level	Deficient opportunity, poverty (p. 166)
(iii) The micro-level studied, for example, by ethnomethodologists and others	Permissiveness, moral decay, cultural deprivation (p. 166)
(iv) The meso-level at which we are concerned with the relations between functional roles such as capitalist and worker or MP and citizen	Inadequately defined laws (p. 166) – which are one way that we define our relationships, roles and responsibilities to each other
(v) The macro-level orientated to the understanding of the functioning of whole societies or their regions, such as the Norwegian economy	A distressed economy resulting in too few computers (p. 165) or too few police officers (p. 166)
(vi) The mega-level of the analysis of whole traditions and civilisations	The tradition in the US of providing the police with arms, which is a different tradition from the UK where the police are unarmed (p. 164)
(vii) The planetary (or cosmological) level concerned with the planet (or cosmos) as a whole	Nothing suggested

Every wicked problem is essentially unique

Rittel and Webber state that, if they are right and every problem is unique, then 'the direct transference of the physical-science and engineering thoughtways into social policy might be dysfunctional, i.e. positively harmful' (p. 164). Once again, the theme of their article is revisited, namely that we must give up our scientific methodology when addressing wicked problems. However, critical realists are relatively optimistic and address this issue with their concept of the concrete universal and the concrete singular. While intuitively most of us understand the concrete singular, i.e. that every particular situation is unique, it is more difficult to understand the concept of the concrete universal. Bhaskar's version of the concrete universal depends on our acknowledgement of the layered nature of reality: specifically, the real, actual and empirical aspects of reality. According to Bhaskar (2008b: 128), *the concrete≠the actual≠the empirical*. Bhaskar (2008b: 132) describes a concrete universal as being a multiple quadruplicity made up of: 1) universal structures, 2) mediations, 3) singularities, and all of these influenced by 4) the passage of time (as processes or rhythmics) (Figure 7.2). If we take Marx's work, *Capital*, as a concrete universal description of the capitalist mode of production (universal structure), the intransitive object of its manifestation is capital in-concretion and it will be entirely unique (concretely singular) due to various open-system factors (mediations) yet nevertheless remain true to the essential nature of capitalism, assuming the truth of *Capital*. Mediations that may interact with intransitive capitalism include residues of previous economic modes, structures and mechanisms with which Marx did not attempt to engage and the timeline of that particular society's capitalist progression. Note that the concrete universal is not an abstraction; it is a real entity, emergent from all of the concrete singulars. In terms of the debate around the possibility of the existence of universals, the postmoderns were right to critique the idea of the abstract universal (Hartwig, in Bhaskar, 2008b: xviii). Thus Rittel and Webber were right to argue that it is dysfunctional to act on the basis of abstract universals, including statistical generalisations, which cannot account for each unique situation. However,

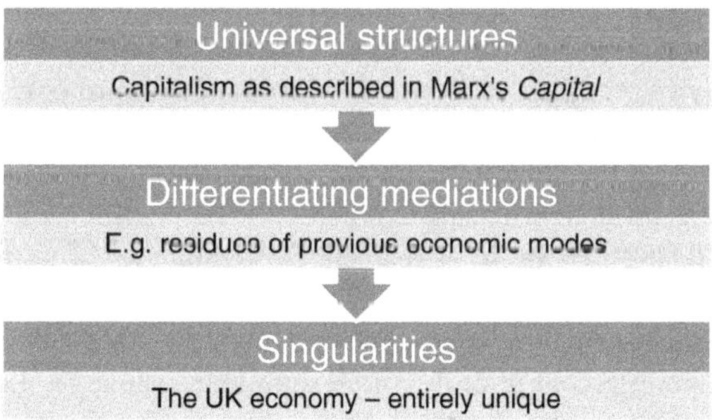

FIGURE 7.2 A concrete universal (influencing processes or rhythmics assumed)

by understanding the relationship between the concrete universal and the concrete singular, it is possible to have universal theories that usefully explain unique situations, and we can use these concrete universals to guide our actions. Climate change is a concrete universal, emergent out of all of the different contexts of climate change, but we can use the universal understanding of climate change to help us to respond to its unique contexts.

Conclusion

Rittel and Webber take a pessimistic view of science's ability to address wicked problems based on their correct acknowledgement that mainstream Humean-based positivist science cannot cope with the open-system nature of social problems. In the absence of faith in science to address so-called wicked social problems, they resort to relativistic notions that truth is historically and culturally defined and that when it comes to issues of social policy, truth is not an objective. Rather, the objective is that we manage to improve society. To the contrary, critical realists argue that without the help of a truthful epistemology, we are unlikely to improve society. If, like Rittel and Webber, we adhere to the assumption that the only way to know causality is through constant conjunctions, then the problems of social policy become wicked. However, critical realism tells us that this assumption is misguided. Correlations are neither the only nor a sufficient way to know causation. Although correlations can hint at causation, we need to move beyond correlations in order to understand why some entities might correlate with each other. The approach to know causation is therefore through transcendental realism, which allows us to arrive at deep explanations in terms of structures and mechanisms of the problems that exist at the level of the non-empirical real. Retroduction is used by both lay people and scientists. Democracy can be improved by creating spaces for community discussion which allow communities to be part of the retroductive theorising about depth causation of social problems, and allow communities to be part of the decision-making process in terms of actions designed to ameliorate problems that are based on a sound understanding of their causes. Current conceptions of mainstream science-based policy either a) make communities subordinate to science and simply consumers, rather than co-creators, of scientific advice, or b) make science subordinate to communities, which are not held accountable to the rules of epistemology and thus risk using incorrect knowledge to guide policy. In practice, policy-makers can switch between a) and b), depending on their particular agenda. Critical realism avoids this potentially dangerous situation by insisting that the epistemologies of both the scientists and the communities are commensurable. Scientists can thus be held accountable to the truth of their advice by communities, and vice versa. Critical realism thus offers a philosophically and ethically more sound alternative to the so-called 'consensus beats reality' version of policy-making.

Notes

1 It is customary to assume that the word 'science' refers to the empiricism essentially outlined by David Hume (1711–1776), but qualified by, for example, Karl Popper (1902–1994), Carl Hempel (1905–1997) or Willem Quine (1908–2000). Perhaps we might call this contemporary understanding of science 'science$_2$'. Perhaps we might call science that has been underlaboured by critical realism 'science$_1$'.
2 There is an acceptable way in which the outcome determines the research methodology to be used, but it is an epistemological outcome, not an outcome that is convenient to the researchers' personal agendas. So, for example, if I want to make policy decisions for a country around a health issue such as the incidence of heart disease, I ought to choose an epidemiological methodology, based on the nature of the problem. This is different from choosing a methodology based on my personal agenda, for example: say I am a whale conservationist and choose a participatory methodology (interpretivism) when I want to advocate *with* the community against coastal development, but a positivist methodology when I want to use facts to advocate *against* the community that wants larger whale hunting quotas.
3 While one can (perhaps) excuse a lay person from arriving at an ideologically based 'truth', since one might argue that they 'know not what they do', an objective scientist supposedly should know better. However, in contemporary versions of social science, a scientist can in practice achieve an ideological 'truth' while nevertheless keeping up appearances of objectivity. For example, if they too want to reduce the number of immigrants, they can choose an interpretative methodology (consensus beats reality) and thus allow the lay community to speak for them. If the evidence supports their position, even when the evidence is against the majority consensus, they can fetishise a statistical approach: 'you can't argue with the objective facts – it is not I who makes this argument but the facts.' That is, they can change their methodology depending on the outcome that they want and, in a clever sleight of hand, appear to be merely an innocent, disinterested messenger of an ideological 'truth'.
4 I place a question mark here because in mainstream science, empirical data and reality tend to be conflated, resulting in hypostatisation.
5 For a discussion of the positivism of mainstream science, see Bhaskar, R. (2009[1986]) 'The Positivist illusion: sketch of a philosophical ideology at work', in *Scientific Realism and Human Emancipation*, London: Routledge, pp. 224–308.
6 Bhaskar (2008b [1993]: 196) states: '"Reification" means the attribution of a purely thing-like characteristic to human beings, their products and/or relations, and in the fetishism of conjunctions, where "fetishism" means the attribution of animistic (ultimately, anthropomorphic) magical powers to things, attendant upon empirical realism.'
7 Empiricism merely discourages (rather than prevents) retroductive theorising because, despite themselves, scientists still tend to retroductively theorise; this is why we have a retroductive theory of anthropogenic climate change even though we cannot validate it using the empiricist notions of validity. Retroduction is thus occluded but cannot be entirely refused, since science depends on it; ideally, we should fully embrace it.
8 I realise that I have not defined what I mean by 'community'. Who should be included, and at what scales we should construct our definition, are important questions that I do not have the space to discuss here.
9 See Sandra Harding (1987) for an outline of stand-point theory.

References

Alderman, M. H., Cohen, H. and Madhavan, S. (1998). Dietary sodium intake and mortality: the National Health and Nutrition Examination Survey (NHANES I). *The Lancet*, 351(9105), 781–785.

Batie, S. (2008). Wicked problems and applied economics. *American Journal of Agricultural Economics*, 90(5), 1176–1191.

Bhaskar, R. (2000). *From East to West: Odyssey of a Soul*. London: Routledge.

Bhaskar, R. (2008a). *A Realist Theory of Science*. London: Routledge.

Bhaskar, R. (2008b). *Dialectic: The Pulse of Freedom*. London: Routledge.

Bhaskar, R. (2009). *Scientific Realism and Human Emancipation*. London: Routledge.

Bhaskar, R. (2010). Contexts of interdisciplinarity: interdisciplinarity and climate change. In Bhaskar, R., Frank, C., Høyer, K. G., Nœss, P. and Parker, J. (Eds.), *Interdisciplinarity and Climate Change: Transforming Knowledge and Practice for Our Global Future*. London: Routledge.

Dahl, L. K., Leitl, G. and Heine, M. (1972). Influence of dietary potassium and sodium/potassium molar ratios on the development of salt hypertension. *The Journal of Experimental Medicine*, 136(2), 318–330.

Danermark, B., Ekström, M., Jakobsen, L. and Karlsson, J. C. (2002) [1997]. *Explaining Society: An Introduction to Critical Realism in the Social Sciences*. London: Routledge.

Ekinci, E. I., Clarke, S., Thomas, M. C., Moran, J. L., Cheong, K., MacIsaac, R. J. and Jerums, G. (2011). Dietary salt intake and mortality in patients with Type 2 Diabetes. *Diabetes Care*, 34(3), 703–709.

Fullana, I., Palmer, P., Puig, R., Bala, A., Baquero, G., Riba, J. and Raugei, M. (2011). From life cycle assessment to life cycle management. *Journal of Industrial Ecology*, 15(3), 458–475.

Goldenberg, S. (2015). US Senate refuses to accept humanity's role in global climate change, again. *The Guardian*. January 22. Retrieved from www.theguardian.com/environment/2015/jan/22/us-senate-man-climate-change-global-warming-hoax.

Goldstein, P. and Leshem, M. (2014). Dietary sodium, added salt, and serum sodium associations with growth and depression in the U.S. general population. *Appetite*, 79, 83–90.

Haack, S. (2000). *Manifesto of a Passionate Moderate: Unfashionable Essays*. Chicago, IL: University of Chicago Press.

Harding, S. (1987). Introduction: Is there a feminist method? In Harding, S. (Ed.), *Feminism and Methodology*, pp. 1–14. Bloomington, IN: University of Indiana Press.

Jackson, M. C. (2003). *Systems Thinking: Creative Holism for Managers*. Chichester: John Wiley & Sons.

Kuhn, T. (2012). *The Structure of Scientific Revolutions: 50th Anniversary Edition*. London: University of Chicago Press.

Leshem, M. (2011). Low dietary sodium is anxiogenic in rats. *Physiology & Behavior*, 103(5), 453–458.

McCarron, D. A., Geerling, J. C., Kazaks, A. G. and Stern, J. S. (2009). Can dietary sodium intake be modified by public policy? *Clinical Journal of the American Society of Nephrology*, 4(11), 1878–1882.

Meneely, G. R. and Battarbee, H. D. (1976). High sodium-low potassium environment and hypertension. *The American Journal of Cardiology*, 38(6), 768–785.

Obarzanek, E., Proschan, M. A., Vollmer, W. M., Moore, T. J., Sacks, F. M., Appel, L. J., … Cutler, J. A. (2003). Individual blood pressure responses to changes in salt intake results from the DASH-sodium trial. *Hypertension*, 42(4), 459–467.

O'Donnell, M. J., Yusuf, S., Mente, A., *et al.* (2011). Urinary sodium and potassium excretion and risk of cardiovascular events. *JAMA*, 306(20), 2229–2238.

Rittel, H. W. J. and Webber, M. M. (1973). Dilemmas in a general theory of planning. *Policy Sciences*, 4(2), 155–169.

Rorty, R., Williams, M. and Bromwich, D. (1980). *Philosophy and the Mirror of Nature* (Vol. 401). Princeton, NJ: Princeton University Press.

Rosner, M. H. and Kirven, J. (2007). Exercise-associated hyponatremia. *Clinical Journal of the American Society of Nephrology*, 2(1), 151–161.

Shankar, B., Brambila-Macias, J., Traill, B., Mazzocchi, M. and Capacci, S. (2013). An evaluation of the UK Food Standards Agency's salt campaign. *Health Economics*, 22(2), 243–250.

Stolarz-Skrzypek, K., Kuznetsova, T., Thijs, L., *et al.* (2011). Fatal and nonfatal outcomes, incidence of hypertension, and blood pressure changes in relation to urinary sodium excretion. *Journal of the American Medical Association*, 305(17), 1777–1785.

Wenner, M. (2011). It's time to end the war on salt. *Scientific American*, 8 July. Retrieved from www.scientificamerican.com/article/its-time-to-end-the-war-on-salt/.

8

HOUSING STANDARDS, ENVIRONMENTAL SUSTAINABILITY, AND SOCIAL WELFARE

Petter Næss and Jin Xue

Introduction

In the Nordic countries, there is a saying that goes like this: "When it rains on the vicar, some drops will fall on the parish clerk." No similar English adage seems to exist, apart from, perhaps, the formulation "a rising tide lifts all boats." However, whereas the English formulation suggests that all boats are elevated equally much, the Nordic saying hints, more realistically, that the one receiving the most of what "falls down" (in the form of advantages) is the prominent person, while his subordinate gets a smaller advantage. Basically, the Nordic proverb refers to what economists have later termed a "trickle-down" effect.

Such plus-sum thinking has arguably been crucial for forging the class compromise on which the social-democratic Nordic welfare state model is based. By baking a bigger cake, tough conflicts on its distribution between members of society could be soothed. Economic growth, and the growth in consumption it facilitates and on which its continuation depends, has been a fundamental premise for "the Nordic model," which has internationally been considered to connote welfare politics and political progressiveness generally.

But what if the cake cannot, due to resource constraints, continue to be baked bigger? As argued elsewhere in this book, the idea of unlimited, environmentally friendly economic growth is illusory. This also applies to the housing sector. Literature has discussed the social distribution challenges of a non- or negative-growth society to a little extent. There was some discussion in the 1970s and onwards, especially by environmental activists, stating that consumption levels in rich countries should be reduced (or not grow) in order to make space for improved material standards in poor countries. But apart from a few examples (including Spangenberg, 2010; Martinez-Alier *et al.*, 2010), this logic has rarely been applied to the individual country.

Using the housing sector as an example, this chapter has as its purpose to illuminate social distributional aspects of non-growth or de-growth in the overall economy in affluent countries like the Nordic ones. What are the implications of securing an acceptable housing standard for all members of society in the case of a non-growing or shrinking economy?

The next section addresses environmental impacts of housing construction and the limited possibilities for decoupling housing stock growth from negative environmental consequences. Thereupon, the notion of acceptable housing standards is discussed, combining premises of environmental sustainability with notions of needs and welfare rights. The chapter moves on to discuss policies necessary to regulate the volume of housing consumption and its distribution between population groups if environmental sustainability and basic welfare for all members of society are to be obtained. The next section discusses some contradictions between such regulative frameworks and the inherent dynamics of capitalism, followed by brief concluding remarks.

Environmental impacts and decoupling within the housing sector

Environmental impacts of housing

Residential development and housing-related consumption cause several environmental impacts, comprising construction impacts and operational impacts. Construction impacts include environmental consequences resulting from the consumption of building materials, land for building sites, and the activities during the building process. Among the operational impacts, some occur in the building itself, such as energy and material consumption for space heating/cooling, maintenance, and so forth during the years of occupancy. Other operational impacts are locational. The latter category mainly refers to environmental consequences resulting from daily-life travel, as traveling distances and modes are influenced by the location of the dwelling relative to workplaces, schools, shops, leisure opportunities, and so on.

The environmental impacts from the housing sector are associated with housing types. Compared with detached single-family houses, apartments require less energy for space heating and cooling per square meter (Høyer and Holden, 2001; Brown and Wolfe, 2007), and even more so per dwelling due to their on average smaller size than single-family houses. In terms of land consumption, housing development based on apartment buildings often requires only 50–100 m^2 of land per dwelling, whereas the construction of single-family home areas typically consumes around 1,000 m^2 of land per dwelling.

Since land values usually vary with the distance from the city center (Alonso, 1964), and cultural conceptions of appropriate densities differ between inner-city and suburban contexts (Fishman, 1996), there is usually a clear center-periphery gradient in the density of population and jobs, with higher densities in inner than in outer parts of cities. If residential development takes place primarily as construction of detached single-family houses, new dwellings will likely be built mostly as suburban or exurban extensions of the built-up areas. Conversely, housing development in the form of apartments or other concentrated housing types is much more compatible with in-fill and transformation of vacant or poorly utilized areas within the existing urban fabric. This translates into different extents of pressure against undeveloped land from different kinds of residential development (single-family homes, row houses, apartment buildings).

Dwellings requiring a large site add up to low-density urban structures with long mutual distances between dwellings, workplaces, and service facilities. Low-density housing therefore contributes to increased needs for transportation. Density also affects travel modes, since it is economically unfeasible to provide a fine-meshed network of public transport lines with frequent departures in urban districts with a sparse population living along the lines. Walking distances from dwelling to public transport stops and waiting times for departures are therefore typically longer in single-family home areas than in higher-density housing districts. Low-density urban development also discourages extensive use of non-motorized modes of travel, since most trip destinations in a low-density city will typically be located beyond what the inhabitants consider acceptable walking or biking distances.

Car driving is facilitated in single-family house areas also because such housing normally provides parking space on each individual site in a garage or in the driveway. Although some apartments offer parking space in private basement garages, it is much more common that residents in apartment buildings (and row houses) have to walk to a common parking area some distance away from the entrance of the individual dwelling, or simply have to park along the street curb.

In line with the above mechanisms, overwhelming evidence exists showing that low-density cities and residential locations in outer suburbs or exurbs contribute to longer traveling distances, higher proportions of car usage, and higher energy use for transport, compared with denser cities and more central residential neighborhoods (Newman and Kenworthy, 1999; Ewing and Cervero, 2010; Næss, 2012).

Decoupling strategies

The various environmental impacts of housing development have made urban planners and researchers ask themselves how the detrimental effects of housing provision can be reduced. The *compact city* stands out as a relevant strategy to this end. According to this model, urban development will be more sustainable by adhering to the following recipe (Næss, 2001; Newman and Kenworthy, 1999): most new construction should take place as densification within existing urban demarcations. And most of the densification should be channeled to areas already substantially influenced by technical installations (for example, previous industrial or traffic areas), avoiding encroachments on parks and other intra-urban green recreational areas. Few or no detached single-family houses should be built; instead, apartment buildings and row houses should be prioritized. Strengthened transit provision and improved biking facilities should be combined with restrictions on urban motoring.

Building more densely implies more efficient land use. Channeling new buildings, for example, to derelict or abandoned industrial and dockland areas implies re-use of urbanized land. Increased resource efficiency and re-use are core elements in what has been termed ecological modernization theory (Mol and Spaargaren, 2000).

Norway's capital Oslo is in many ways a textbook example of ecological modernization within urban development (Næss, Næss *et al.*, 2011). Distinct from many other countries, urban sprawl in Norway has stagnated over the last decades. This tendency has been particularly pronounced in Oslo. Oslo's densification strategy has saved natural ecosystems, farmland, and energy. Yet, the city has only partially been able to decouple growth in building stock and infrastructure from negative environmental impacts (Næss, Strand *et al.*, 2011). A similar trend can also be found in the Greater Copenhagen region where, despite tightened land-use regulation emphasizing densification since the 1990s, metropolitan economic growth has been only relatively decoupled from growth in the built-up area. The same finding applies to residential energy consumption, which has grown at the aggregate level due to increased floor space (Xue, 2014).

Building stock growth entails increased consumption of building materials, land, and energy for space heating/cooling, lighting, and ventilation. This is true despite any reduction in resource consumption per built square meter resulting from technology that is more efficient. And although densification reduces conversion of undeveloped land into building sites, densification is not without negative impacts on intra-urban vegetation and ecosystems. Over the five-year period 1999–2004, open-access areas within the continuous urban area of Greater Oslo were reduced by 5 percent. And although the proportion of workforce participants traveling to their workplace by public transport, bike, or foot has increased, and the corresponding share of car drivers has decreased (from 59 percent to 46 percent between 2007 and 2012, according to the Highway Administration), the total road traffic volume has increased.

A large part of the densification on vacant urban space was possible only because manufacturing industries had closed down or moved out of Oslo, and because freight by ship had been replaced by truck transport. The partial decoupling of environmental impacts from building stock growth in Oslo and other Scandinavian cities is conditioned on environmentally harmful increase in truck traffic and relocations encroaching on nature elsewhere (for example, developing countries with lower labor costs and less restrictive environmental regulations). At the same time, out-location of factories has reduced inland consumption of energy and materials for manufacturing production, which misleadingly appears as decoupling between resource consumption and GDP in the national account.

The "low-hanging densification fruits" have been picked: it is relatively easy to obtain a reduction of environmental impacts per unit produced (for example, dwellings or office space) by re-using industrial areas as building sites. The (geographically limited) decoupling is, however, only temporary. Eventually, no more manufacturing industry will be left to relocate (and from a sustainability perspective, the extreme global division of labor on which post-industrial European and North

American cities depend is highly problematic). Exhausting of densification possibilities is, however, not confined to a Western urban context. In the city of Hangzhou, on the affluent Chinese east coast, residential development has to change from concentration in the inner city to suburban urban expansion areas due to the exhaustion of brownfield sites for in-fill development (Xue, 2014).

Construction of buildings and infrastructure is basically not an environmentally friendly endeavor. Unless the new buildings or infrastructure replace existing, more environmentally straining parts of the built environment, such development results in increased use of energy, land, materials, etc. The new developments will at best be ecologically favorable in a relative sense, i.e. compared with environmentally more straining solutions. This is particularly the case for impacts on biological diversity, natural areas, food-production soil, and landscape qualities from converting undeveloped land into building sites. Such conversion is practically impossible to reverse; at any rate this will often take hundreds of years. The same applies for agricultural areas.

Eco-efficient renovation of existing buildings with solar panels, heat pumps, better heat insulation, etc. can compensate to some extent for the environmental load caused by a growing building stock, but the growth in itself tends to increase the environmental load. In addition, eco-efficiency technologies render the use of resources less costly and thus tend to heighten consumption levels (Sorrel, 2007). This rebound effect undermines expected environmental gains from efficiency improvements.

The question is, then, to what extent renovating can compensate for the additional environmental load that construction of new buildings entails. For some "operational" environmental pressures, such as energy use for space heating and cooling, saving potentials are generally large, and an energy efficiency factor of 4, or maybe 10, or even higher appears possible in new buildings (Nordic Council of Ministers, 1999). Retrofitting existing buildings to such efficiency standards is, however, much more complicated and difficult. Such "extreme makeover" would also entail increased consumption of building materials, and it would obviously represent increased conflicts with building heritage protection. An average factor 4 of energy efficiency improvement for the existing building stock must be considered an optimistic estimate. This conclusion is supported when considering how energy use in Norwegian dwellings has developed over recent decades. Energy use per dwelling as well as per square meter of floor area decreased by less than 10 percent from 1993 to 2012 despite considerably higher heat insulation standards and a strong increase in dwellings with heat pumps during the last part of the period (Statistics Norway, 2014a).

For other operational pressures, such as daily-life, intra-metropolitan travel, the prospects for reduction seem even smaller unless people limit their choices among jobs, education, service facilities, leisure opportunities, and so forth much more to those available in the local neighborhood or city district. Such limitation is at odds with growth policies, however, since greater opportunities for choice is one of the key benefits that growth is assumed to provide, and because increased freedom of choice, and hence increased competition, is also an important assumed driver of growth. (Cf. current Norwegian as well as European policies for "region enlargement" through transport infrastructure construction.)

What is an acceptable housing standard in a Nordic context?

Environmental constraints imply a need for maximum standards

Environmental impacts are commonly understood as dependent on three main factors: population size (P), average affluence level measured in consumption or production per capita (A), and the environmental efficiency of the technologies in use, (T), where the environmental impact I = P*A*T (Commoner, 1972; Holdren and Ehrlich, 1974).[1] Applied to the housing sector, environmental impacts are determined by the size of population, residential floor area per capita, and eco-efficiency measures within the housing sector. Of these factors, the dominant discourse has been on "decoupling," focusing one-sidedly on the T factor. However, as argued earlier, although eco-efficiency improvements of existing dwellings can to some extent compensate for growth in the housing stock, the additional environmental load resulting from such growth will, if it continues for long, at some time exceed what is gained through improved environmental performance of existing buildings.

It is, of course, not possible to state exactly a level beyond which the total Norwegian housing consumption should not, from concerns of environmental sustainability and global equity, be further increased. Norway's share of the global population will be relevant in such a discussion, as will be the actual combination of local and globally reaching environmental impacts, and any context-dependent particular needs for housing space justified by, for example, cool climate. The environmental impacts from construction and use of dwellings occur in open systems where a multitude of factors influence the total environmental load as well as the proportion of it accounted for by the housing sector. Determining how large a part of the "acceptable" environmental load the housing sector should be allowed to account for, compared with other sectors, will probably also be a matter of disagreement, where prioritizations are likely to vary with geographical contexts and across time. And not the least, the question of whether or not the inhabitants of the Nordic countries should be entitled to a higher residential standard than the global average is a matter of political and ethical discussion. Rather than defining a ceiling for the volume of the total housing stock, the following discussion will focus on per capita residential floor area, leaving aside how a sustainable size of the Norwegian housing stock would be affected by the size of the global population and its distribution across national borders. The discussion will thus concentrate on the A factor of the IPAT equation.

The global population is forecasted to stabilize around 11 billion at the end of this century (United Nations Population Division, 2013). In a world of finite resources, securing a decent material standard of living for the billions of the global population that cannot today have their basic needs met may not be possible if the consumption level continues to increase among those parts of the global population who are already consuming a lot. Based on such considerations, as well as more general concerns of distributional justice, the concept of "environmental space" (European Environmental Agency, 2011) was developed in the 1990s, and was referred to as a guiding principle in environmental policy documents in certain countries, including Denmark (Environmental Protection Agency (DK), 1998).

Arguably, some kinds of environmental impacts of housing consumption in a Norwegian context are already above what would be environmentally sustainable and globally equitable. Norway is among the five countries globally with the highest residential floor area per capita; bringing the remaining countries up to that standard would require a vast amount of natural resources and entail severe environmental impacts. National forecasts for consumption growth indicate a threefold increase by 2060 (Ministry of Finance, 2013). Although the growth in floor area per capita has shown a stagnating tendency over the last two decades (Hille *et al.*, 2011), especially in the largest cities, the forecasted general growth in private consumption would most likely also involve growth in residential floor area. Moreover, Norwegian families increasingly have more than one dwelling they consider a "home." Such multiple-dwelling-home lifestyles include not only traditional cabins and apartments in mountain villages but also urban second homes and second homes abroad (for instance, along the Spanish sun coast).

Depending on how far eco-efficiency strategies can be implemented in practice, per capita housing consumption in the Nordic countries may already have passed the level at which housing consumption should not be increased further if global-scale environmental sustainability and a just international distribution of consumption are to be obtained. If this level has not yet been reached, the limit will sooner or later be passed, given the forecasted growth in purchasing power. It is therefore urgent to introduce maximum standards for housing consumption per capita.

If no overall escalation is to take place, increased floor area per capita among the population groups already having a high number of square meters of residential floor area per capita at their disposal will be possible only if the rest of the population reduce their floor area per capita. In a similar manner as the goal of raising the material standard of living in poor countries intensifies the need for affluent countries to reduce their CO_2 emissions, a national "ceiling" for the housing consumption per capita implies that increased floor space for those who already live in a spacious dwelling comes in direct competition with the wish to build for those who are lacking a dwelling, or who live in a substandard residence. If we intend to secure a certain minimum standard for everyone while not exceeding the "ceiling" on per capita consumption, it is necessary to practice a principle of selective standard improvement. Resources must then be allocated to raise the residential quality for the most poorly situated instead of increasing the standard further for the affluent groups. Maximum norms for housing consumption would be a highly relevant measure to this end, following the logics expressed by Gandhi already seventy years ago that the world has enough for everyone's need, but not enough for everyone's greed. In order to cater for possible rebound effects within the housing sector itself, the maximum standards should cumulatively include any second (and third, etc.) homes – cf. above.

Reducing the present level of inequality in housing consumption per capita seems inevitable if concerns of social welfare and environmental sustainability are to be combined. It is, of course, difficult to state a "reasonable" level of accepted inequality in housing consumption, since some people may value living in a rather high-standard dwelling while renouncing other kinds of consumption, whereas other people may be satisfied with a small dwelling, spending their money on different kinds of consumption instead. At the same time, the dwelling is a basic condition for shelter and family life, distinct from many other categories of consumption. It therefore makes sense to set a minimum standard for housing.

The difference in housing standard between the highest and lowest should also be reduced to diminish negative impacts of relative poverty, cf. Bartelmus (1999). A maximum acceptable size two or three times above the lower acceptable limit might perhaps be a guiding rule. Such a norm of course would not mean that people who have more floor area per capita should be evicted from their present spacious dwellings. However, policy instruments could be introduced to discourage people from occupying more residential floor space than the norm. Measures to enhance better utilization of the existing building stock in cities should also be employed, including policies to encourage subdivision of large residences into more units, and facilitation of co-housing schemes (Lietart, 2010).

Due to population growth, even if the per capita residential floor space becomes stable and does not increase, the aggregate volume of new dwellings will continue to increase. Considering the need to reduce inequality in residential space, the construction of spacious dwellings should be avoided. It therefore makes sense to set a quite narrow maximum size limit for new dwellings. If the maximum size of new dwellings had been set to, for example, 140 m^2, this would have led to a 26 percent reduction in floor area of the dwellings built from 2005 to 2009 in the Oslo region. Such a maximum size would in practice have ruled out the construction of detached single-family houses, since virtually all such dwellings constructed in the Oslo region in the period were larger than 140 m^2. With the given differences between dwelling types in energy use for space heating, a maximum size of 140 m^2 would have halved such energy use in the new dwellings. This, together with the fact that detached single-family houses are the housing type that exerts the heaviest environmental load in terms of land consumption, urban sprawl, and car dependency, speaks in favor of a ban on the construction of new single-family houses, at least in the major urban regions.

Needs, wants, and quality of life

The idea of setting minimum standards for housing is closely related to the notion of socially accepted needs. Different disciplinary traditions conceive of needs in different ways. Within biology, a need is said to exist when the organism is in a state that has to be changed (Østerberg, 1973), for example because it has a deficit or surplus of certain substances. In psychology, needs are commonly considered as circumstances that appear to be necessary for a person's prosperity and well-being, but cannot be explained physiologically (for instance, needs of stimulation and contact). Both in biological and psychological research, the innate, static, and objective nature of needs is often emphasized (Lian, 2000). Contrary to that, needs are conceived as purely subjective within economics, where market demand for commodities and services is considered an adequate indication of human needs (or preferences, which scholars within this tradition would prefer to say). Distinct from this, sociological research views needs as socio-culturally constructed (with the exception of biological needs related to mere survival). Sociologists also distinguish between needs and wants. We may need something that we do not wish, and we may wish something we do not need. For example, a child may be in need of nutrition from vegetables and not from soda water, but still wish to have soda water for all meals, and to be let off from eating vegetables. In practice, the distinction between needs and wants is often less clear-cut. For example, we may want a spacious luxury dwelling, while what we need is just plain shelter (where the latter encompasses a biological, psychological, as well as social component). If we buy a large single-family house, we may satisfy a need for shelter, but this need could also be met in a less resource-consuming way.

Needs evolve within certain historical and cultural contexts. There is a reciprocal influence between social development and needs. Apart from the physiological life necessities following from our biological constitution, prevailing opinions about necessary needs are social constructs. What are considered luxury needs in one historical period may at another point of time be considered necessary (Lian, 2000), and conversely, what is considered normal and necessary within a certain socio-spatial context (for example, the Norwegian middle class) might be considered luxurious in a future Norwegian context where the housing policy discourse has been strongly influenced by concerns of environmental sustainability and a fair distribution globally and locally.

The conception of needs applied in the above discussion of housing standards is normative, based on ethical considerations of welfare rights and distributive justice and a combination of sociological, psychological, and biologically defined needs with constraints set by ecological conditions and the environmental efficiency of relevant technologies. For such a definition of housing needs and maximum standards for housing consumption to become politically acceptable, a thorough and overall societal discussion on needs for and beyond material goods will be crucial. Reduction in the consumption level of residential floor area will not necessarily reduce people's life satisfaction and feeling of happiness. When satisfaction is met beyond basic needs, the gains from income growth and consumption of material goods tend to decrease gradually, a phenomenon known as the Easterlin Paradox (Easterlin, 1974). When quality of life is measured as the possession of material wealth, people are trapped in consumerism created by the growth society where people work more in order to consume more. Instead, a minimally sufficient material living standard will enhance quality of life through freeing up time and freedom for people to pursue non-materialistic sources of meaning and satisfaction, such as self-esteem, feeling of belonging, and possibilities to pursue their interests and values (Soper, 2008).

Welfare, rights, and ethics

Our argumentation for minimum and maximum housing standards is based on the position that values and norms can be subject to rational justification or critique (Bhaskar, 1998; Norrie, 2010). For example, taking the satisfaction of some basic human needs as a supposedly widely agreed-on normative premise, knowledge about the conditions causing deprivation of the physiological and psychological needs for shelter can be used to underpin norms of acceptable housing standards that can emancipate people from such deprivation (Bhaskar, 1998).

The notion of acceptable housing standard has traditionally nearly always been understood in terms of a minimum standard for what is an acceptable size of a dwelling, its usability, daylight conditions, technical equipment, and lately adaptability for wheelchair users as well. The notion of minimum acceptable standard is closely tied to the concept of welfare rights. Such rights are derived from conceptualizations of socially acknowledged basic needs. According to Assiter and Noonan (2007:185), "nutritious food, clean air and water, appropriate clothing and shelter are universal life necessities that must be safeguarded regardless of whatever else makes life meaningful for people." This line of thought is also represented in the Brundtland Commission's (1987) mentioning of food, water, clothes, shelter, work, energy, and hygiene as examples of basic needs. According to the Commission's definition of sustainable development, the notion of needs is one of the two key concepts contained within it, "in particular the essential needs of the world's poor, to which overriding priority should be given" (ibid.: 43).

Defining a minimum welfare standard, be it for housing or other goods, implies that the resources of society should be spent in such a way that no one is denied access to goods or services at this minimum standard. In a situation where the amounts of the goods in question are increasing, it is sufficient to allocate some of the growth in such a way that those not yet having obtained the minimum standard can have their standard raised up to that level. However, according to the Brundtland Commission (1987: 44), "living standards that go beyond the basic minimum are sustainable only if consumption standards everywhere have regard for long term sustainability." In a zero- or negative-growth situation, raising those living below the minimum standard up to this standard can be obtained only through redistribution. Such redistribution – or refusal to redistribute – explicitly or implicitly builds on certain ethical principles. Distributional ethics concern what is just and reasonable.

However, not all philosophers accept the notion of welfare rights or claims of the sort that usually go under the banner of "social justice" (Wolff, 1977). According to libertarian philosophers such as Robert Nozick (1974) and Tibor Machan (1984), every person is entitled to a "moral space" that must not be violated without compensation. The concept of moral space refers partly to the individual's body and a socio-psychological "personal space" around it, but partly also to property that an individual has acquired, regardless of how extensive it is, and regardless of how it has been acquired, unless by theft or fraud. If you have inherited two luxury dwellings and luxury vacation homes on the Norwegian coast, in the Norwegian mountains, and by the Mediterranean Sea, it would, following Nozick, be a violation of individual rights to prevent a person from continuing to own this much. Building on the liberal philosopher John Locke, Nozick considers no limits to exist as to how many more resources some may own over others, assuming that the distribution of holdings did not come about by fraud or theft. There is only one constraint – the so-called Lockean Proviso, or, more correctly, a weak interpretation of Locke's original condition. Whereas Locke held that one may own property just so long as "enough and as good" is left for others, Nozick considers that if the initial acquisition fails to make anyone worse off who was using the resource before, then it is justly acquired. A land owner who acquired a huge property of previously commonly owned land (perhaps as a gift from the king) centuries ago would then be in his full right to use this property according to his wishes (for example, for polluting mineral extraction, or ruthless exploitation of timber reducing its biodiversity and value for outdoor recreation), no matter if the present use makes other people worse off (Murray, 2015).

Nozick's argument does not take into consideration environmental and resource constraints to consumption growth. It is an example of the way of thinking termed "cowboy economy" (Boulding, 1966) or "frontier economics" (Colby, 1991) in the environmental debates some decades ago. More land was always assumed to be available, so if someone put up fences around a large parcel of land, this would not prevent other people from doing the same. Obviously, this condition does not apply in the contemporary situation of global ecological crisis and increasing scarcity of non-renewable resources. Yet, it is arguably still the implicit assumption of neoclassical economics and neoliberal policies.

Nozick, Machan, and other libertarian philosophers explicitly deny welfare rights; they only acknowledge (negative) liberty rights. This position is at odds with the United Nations Human Rights Declarations, which includes civil and political human rights as well as economic, cultural, and social human rights. Both categories of rights were incorporated in the UN Charter in 1945, in the Human Rights Declaration of 1948, and in two Human Rights Declarations of 1966.

The economic, cultural, and social human rights have relevance for what kind of welfare any human being is entitled to. In giving all people the same degree of entitlement to these requirements, they are also relevant with respect to a fair distribution of welfare. The distributional challenge will be particularly important in a situation where the total consumption level of a society cannot be raised. This is, as argued above, precisely the situation we are facing (or at least will have to face within a few decades) if crucial environmental objectives such as protection of biodiversity and sufficient soil for food production, and avoidance of more than two degrees' global warming, are to be achieved.

The renowned liberal moral philosopher John Rawls (1971) considered unequal distribution of benefits within a population to be morally defensible if this distribution is advantageous to all, including the least favored members of the population. Rawls' moral philosophy has been used to defend policies that result in an unequal distribution if they at the same time bring about a "trickle-down effect." This is, for example, the implicit assumption of the Brundtland Commission's (1987: 51) recommendation of high and continual economic growth in wealthy countries in order for them to act as "locomotives" in the world economy, pulling the poor countries out of poverty. According to the Rawlsian view, it would be acceptable to increase the gap in affluence between rich and poor countries if this resulted in the largest absolute increase in benefits also for the least favored individuals in the poor countries. However, as discussed above, such overall growth in affluence would not be environmentally sustainable, at least not in the long run. It would therefore make future generations worse off, especially the less privileged parts of those generations. Moving beyond anthropocentrism, what if the needs of non-human living beings are also to be taken into consideration and given some regard? The moral justification for high-consumptive lifestyles (including spacious dwellings) then becomes even more shaky.

Moreover, the "trickle-down" strategy implicit in the growth assumptions of the Brundtland Commission (and even more in contemporary strategies of the World Bank and the International Monetary Fund) disregards the non-material aspects of welfare. Within an overall societal context of competition and consumerism, the importance of relative wealth as a significant determinant of self-esteem and happiness should not be underestimated (Bartelmus, 1999). Particularly within individual nations, where contrasts between wealth and poverty are more easily visible than when comparing across continents, the psychological and social impacts of relative poverty must be taken into consideration when assessing whether or not a policy can be defended by referring to the Rawlsian criterion for morally defensible inequality.

In a world in which people's status and success are measured by their purchasing power, the poor will hardly be really better off from a policy increasing their purchasing power somewhat but also increasing the social and economic inequalities within the society. Their situation would arguably be improved more through a policy resulting in a lower increase in affluence also for the poor while reducing the economic and social inequalities considerably. In practice, the possibilities for individuals to maintain their (negative and positive) liberty rights are heavily influenced by their economic status. This adds to the difficulties in justifying claims that inequality-increasing policies are really advantageous for the least favored members of society.

Policies for securing environmental sustainability and social welfare in housing provision

Setting minimum and maximum standards for dwelling sizes as outlined above may seem utterly utopian today. It should still be remembered that the Scandinavian welfare states during the three or four decades subsequent to the Second World War had a number of policy instruments aiming in a similar direction. For example, the Norwegian State Housing Bank and Bustadbanken (another state bank financing farmhouses and other rural housing) together financed more than two thirds of all dwellings constructed in the last half of the 1950s. Such loans were given only to dwellings below a certain size limit (gradually increasing from around 90 m^2 in the 1950s to slightly above 100 m^2 around 1980). Moreover, an Act on the Distribution of Dwellings existed in Norway from 1955 to 1985, according to which municipalities could earmark large dwellings for households with many members.

What kinds of policies, then, would be relevant in a twenty-first-century Norwegian context to promote housing standards satisfying concerns of environmental sustainability as well as social welfare?

As mentioned above, banning the construction of new detached single-family homes in the major urban regions would be an important element of such policies. Partly, this could be done through land-use planning according to the Planning and Building Act. Municipalities could set aside areas for residential development only at locations suitable for apartments, row houses, and other more concentrated housing types. Local development plans should follow this up by excluding detached single-family houses from the kinds of housing types allowed in each development area. The government could issue national policy provisions to oblige the municipalities to implement these policies.[2]

The Norwegian State Housing Bank should align its lending policy for housing construction accordingly, and reduce the size limits for eligible dwellings (presently allowing up to 250 m^2 for two-story single-family houses) to those existing before the liberalization that has taken place during recent decades, for example to 100 m^2.

Whereas the Norwegian State Housing Bank and the previously state-owned Bustadbanken financed two thirds of the dwellings built in Norway in the late 1950s, the proportion of new dwellings financed by loans from the Norwegian State Housing Bank has been only 15–20 percent during recent years. Increasing the funds of the Norwegian State Housing Bank while putting restrictions on the conditions for private banks to give loans for housing construction would be necessary to prevent a large number of big dwellings still being built.

Policies for limiting the ecological footprint from the housing sector should, as mentioned above, also include measures to promote a more efficient utilization of the existing building stock by partitioning large dwellings into smaller units and by encouraging co-housing schemes. Heavy progressive taxation on the floor space exceeding the maximum norm could be one such measure. The tax could, for example, be zero for dwellings at the minimum acceptable standard, rising linearly to a medium level at the highest acceptable standard, and with exponentially increasing levels for standards above the maximum acceptable standard.

Apart from fees to discourage excessive housing consumption, economic measures and regulations should be in place to encourage eco-efficiency improvements (such as passive-house standards) in new buildings as well as in the existing building stock. Measures would also need to be in place to secure affordability of housing meeting the acceptable standard requirements. Rather than subsidizing such dwellings (which would tend to inflate prices), this should be done by setting a ceiling for the price per square meter of floor area. Another instrument for securing affordability could be a social housing scheme in which housing is built for rental permanently for low-income households. During recent decades, prices per square meter of floor area of dwellings in Norwegian cities, especially Oslo, have increased far more than construction costs. This has resulted in a situation where an increasing share of the population can only afford to live in dwellings smaller than the minimum standards set by the Norwegian State Housing Bank in the 1990s (unless they are willing to move to exurban locations where long car-based and environmentally unsustainable commuting would be required).

Environmental sustainability, social welfare, and capitalism

In contemporary crisis-ridden Europe, many debaters have called for a replacement of prevailing austerity policy with counter-cyclical economic policy. Such Keynes-inspired policy might perhaps reduce unemployment and hardship among victims of the economic crisis – although this seems less likely nowadays, due to strong neoliberal institutional arrangements (EU, IMF, WTO, and so forth). Keynesianism tries to circumvent the tough distribution issues through growth policies allowing the rich to become richer while also maintaining – or offering some increase in – the material standard of living among the non-affluent. But such "trickle-down" policies presuppose ever-increasing total volumes of consumption – which are not environmentally sustainable.

It can be imagined that the introduction of maximum size limits to new dwellings, and a ban on the construction of detached single-family houses, will meet resistance within the current neoliberal, capitalist society. Several counteracting mechanisms exist that make the policies restricting growth in consumption difficult to implement.

In the capitalist society characterized by an inherent growth imperative (Fotopoulos, 2010; Gordon and Rosenthal, 2003; see also other chapters of this book), non-growth in the housing sector will have to be substituted by more growth in other economic sectors, such as tourism, advertising, and consumption of non-residential products. This may be possible in the short term. However, given the significance of the housing sector in its contribution to economic growth, this scenario seems to be difficult to maintain in the long run. For example, the housing, transportation, and construction sectors together account for 20 percent of the Norwegian mainland GDP (Statistics Norway, 2014b). Among Norwegian households, the items "housing, lighting, and heating" and "transportation" account for half of their annual expenditures (Statistics Norway, 2014c). Disappearance of growth within these sectors would likely transmit to other sectors, and cause substantial deceleration of the overall economic growth.

Although a non-growing housing sector within a growing economy seems theoretically possible (Xue, 2014), empirical evidence speaks against this scenario.

Rapid economic growth has often been strongly associated with a building boom, as can be observed in Spain, Iceland, China, and some Middle East countries. In times of economic recession, where profitable investment objects are hard to find, long-term investments in built structures often appear as suitable outlets for surplus capital (Albrechts *et al.*, 1994).

The doctrine of neoliberalism says that the market mechanism is the best vehicle to provide goods and services to satisfy people's diverse demands. Neoliberalism takes individualism and freedom of choice as its essential values. Economic and social policies should not interfere with people's preferences but aim to satisfy them to the greatest extent. In the consumer society, this focus on free choice is further emphasized as the factor that should orient what is offered in the economic and social domains. Today, the market does not only satisfy demands but also creates new demands by massive consumerist propaganda through commercials and TV programs, and through the ways in which we generally speak and write (Fairclough, 2006). With the prevalence of the neoliberal agenda, any policy that aims at constraining the type and level of consumption will be considered as improper and thus be met with resistance.

Capitalism can perhaps stumble along without growth despite its growth imperative, but it would then be prone to frequent and severe crises and worsened living conditions for the majority of the population. Today, luxury dwellings (as well as other resource-consuming items of consumption) represent a "high-consumption reward" to the winners of the economic competition, and are a positional good showing the social status of the owner. Measures to curb luxury and excessive housing consumption would be a strong disincentive against the economic competition on which capitalist society is based. If the rich cannot obtain any material benefits from their wealth, what, then, is the point in being a capitalist?

Therefore, the introduction of a maximum housing standard is contradictory to the growth imperative of capitalism, as well as its incentive system. Implementation of maximum standards in a capitalist society will be difficult unless under some strong dictatorship (as in Singapore) imposing this regulation on its citizens. Under capitalism, it thus seems highly implausible to secure an acceptable housing standard for the working class and the unemployed while at the same time securing environmental sustainability.

Concluding remarks

A truly sustainable urban development in wealthy countries requires strategies that go beyond the current eco-modernization paradigm. Smarter designs of dwellings and cities can reduce the additional environmental load resulting from growth in the housing stock, but the possible "decoupling" between growth and environmental damage is only relative, not absolute (Xue, 2014). In order to prevent cities in affluent countries from becoming increasingly environmentally unsustainable, a shift toward non-growth or de-growth in the building stock seems necessary.

Such a decision in support of economic shrinkage – a planned and voluntary reduction of consumption levels, working hours, and the general busy-ness – is far beyond the agenda of the present society. Within the housing sector, non- or de-growth would aggravate conflicts about the distribution of available floor area between population groups. Growth in population and the number of small households further aggravates these conflicts. Although population growth is beyond the scope of this chapter, a growing population means a lower per capita affluence level if the biocapacity is limited. Therefore, policies counteracting population growth (at a global scale) as well as the trends toward smaller households are relevant.

While Keynesian demand-stimulating economic policy has been the traditional social-democratic strategy for improving the material standard of living among the least affluent groups of society, the continuing overall rise in total volumes of consumption that this implies is not environmentally sustainable. Instead, radical redistribution of living space per capita from population groups with high consumption of floor area per person to groups with low per capita floor area consumption is required.

A contraction of the economy must thus be accompanied by redistribution of wealth if it is to be socially sustainable (Martinez-Alier *et al.*, 2010). Obviously, strong social institutions and policies must be in place to manage the double challenge of reversing the growth trajectory of the economy while securing the quality of life for all members of society. Such institutions and policies would find themselves in inevitable and intense conflict with the individual capitalists, as well as the interest organizations of the capitalist class. Combining environmental and social sustainability in housing provision therefore seems implausible within the confines of capitalism, be it in its neoliberal or in a more Keynesian form.

Acknowledgment

Thanks to Magnus Boysen for valuable comments on an earlier version of the chapter.

Notes

1 The IPAT model has been criticized for omitting important factors such as the prevalent values and political conditions, which may influence the P, the A, as well as the T factor. In response, attempts have been made to nuance and develop the model further (Dietz and Rosa, 1994).

2 Such policies might seem to be at odds with prevailing housing preferences in some countries (notably the USA, the UK, and Australia). However, housing preferences are neither universal nor static. For example, in Norway, centrally located apartments have become more popular over the last decades, and Norwegian cities (especially Oslo) have experienced a strong increase in population density (Næss, Strand *et al.*, 2011; Næss, 2016).

References

Albrechts, L., Baeten, G., and Spithoven, A. (1994). Politics, economic crisis and the planning of transport infrastructures. In *Planning Theory and Social Theory in Front of the Sustainable Development Problematique – Are Local Strategies Possible?* Tampere, Finland: International Conference, 22–25 September.

Alonso, W. (1964). *Location and Land Use*. Cambridge, MA: Harvard University Press.

Assiter, A., and Noonan, J. (2007). Human needs: a realist perspective. *Journal of Critical Realism*, 6(2), 173–198.

Bartelmus, P. (1999). *Economic Growth and Patterns of Sustainability*. Wuppertal Papers no. 98. Wuppertal: Wuppertal Institute.

Bhaskar, R. (1998). *The Possibility of Naturalism. A Philosophical Critique of the Contemporary Human Sciences*, 3rd ed. London/New York: Routledge.

Boulding, K. E. (1966). The economics of the coming spaceship earth. In H. Jarrett (ed.) *Environmental Quality in a Growing Economy*, pp. 3–14. Baltimore, MD: Resources for the Future/Johns Hopkins University Press.

Brown, M. and Wolfe, M. (2007). *Energy Efficiency in Multi-Family Housing: A Profile and Analysis*. Washington, DC: Energy Program Consortium.

Brundtland Commission (World Commission on Environment and Development) (1987). *Our Common Future*. Oxford: Oxford University Press.

Colby, M. E. (1991). Environmental management in development: the evolution of paradigms. *Ecological Economics*, 3(3), 193–213.

Commoner, B. (1972). The environmental cost of economic growth. In *Population. Resources and the Environment*, pp. 339–363. Washington, DC: Government Printing Office.

Daly, H. E. and Cobb, J. B. Jr. (1989). *For the Common Good*. Boston, MA: Beacon Press.

Dietz, T. and Rosa, E. A. (1994). Rethinking the environmental impacts of population, affluence and technology. *Human Ecology Review*, Summer/Autumn, 1.

Easterlin, R. A. (1974). Does economic growth improve the human lot? Some empirical evidence. In Abramovitz, M., David, P. A., and Reder, M. W. (eds.) *Nations and Households in Economic Growth: Essays in Honour of Moses Abramovitz*. New York: Academic Press, Inc.

Environmental Protection Agency (DK) (1998). *Økologisk Råderum – en sammenfatning*. Copenhagen: Ministry of the Environment and Energy, Environmental Protection Agency.

European Environmental Agency (2011). *The Environmental Space Concept*. Copenhagen: European Environmental Agency. Downloaded May 8, 2015 from www.eea.europa.eu/publications/92-9167-078-2/page003.html.

Ewing, R. and Cervero, R. (2010). Travel and the built environment. *Journal of the American Planning Association*, 76, 1–30.

Fairclough, N. (2006). *Language and Globalization*. London/New York: Routledge.

Fishman, R. (1996). Bourgeois utopias: visions of suburbia. In Fainstein, S. and Campbell, S. (eds.) *Readings in Urban Theory*, pp. 23–60. Malden, MA: Blackwell.

Fotopoulos, T. (2010). The de-growth utopia: the incompatibility of de-growth within an internationalized market economy. In Huan, Q. (ed.) *Eco-socialism as Politics: Rebuilding the Basis of Our Modern Civilisation*. New York: Springer.

Gordon, M. J. and Rosenthal, J. S. (2003). Capitalism's growth imperative. *Cambridge Journal of Economics*, 27(1), 25–48.

Harvey, D. (2010). *The Enigma of Capital and the Crises of Capitalism*. London: Profile Books.

Hille, J., Simonsen, M., and Aall, C. (2011). *Trender og drivere for energibruk i norske husholdninger. Rapport til NVE*. Sogndal: Vestlandsforsking.

Holdren, J. P. and Ehrlich, P. R. (1974). Human population and the global environment. *American Scientist*, 62, 28292.

Høyer, K. G. and Holden, E. (2001). Housing as basis for sustainable consumption. *International Journal of Sustainable Development*, 4(3), 48–59.

Lian, O. S. (2000). En sosiologisk forståelse av behov. *Tidsskrift for den norske lægeforening*, 120, 111–114.

Lietart, M. (2010) Cohousing's relevance to degrowth theories. *Journal of Cleaner Production*, 18, 576–580.

Machan, T. S. (1984). Pollution and political theory. In Regan, T. (ed.) *Earthbound: New Introductory Essays in Environmental Ethics*. Philadelphia, PA: Temple University Press.
Martinez-Alier, J., Pasqual, U., Vivien, F.-D., and Zaccai, E. (2010). Sustainable de-growth: mapping the context, criticisms and future prospects of an emergent paradigm. *Ecological Economics*, 69, 1741–1747.
Ministry of Finance (Norway) (2013). *Meld. St. 12 (2012–2013) Perspektivmeldingen 2013*. Oslo: Ministry of Finance. Accessed February 2015 at www.regjeringen.no/nb/dokumenter/meld-st-12-20122013/id714050/.
Mol, A. P. J., and Spaargaren, G. (2000). Ecological modernization theory in debate: a review. *Environmental Politics*, 9(1), 17–49.
Murray, D. (2015). Robert Nozick: political philosophy. In *Internet Encyclopedia of Philosophy*. Retrieved March 21, 2015 from www.iep.utm.edu/noz-poli/print.
Næss, P. (2001). Urban planning and sustainable development. *European Planning Studies*, 9(4), 503–524.
Næss, P. (2012). Urban form and travel behavior: experience from a Nordic context. *Journal of Transport and Land Use*, 5(2), 21–45.
Næss, P. (2016). Housing culture, residential preferences and sustainability. Forthcoming in Nielsen, L. M., Reitan, J. B., and Skjerven, A. (eds.) *Design for a Sustainable Culture. Perspectives, Practices and Education*. Abingdon: Routledge.
Næss, P., Næss, T., and Strand, A. (2011). Oslo's farewell to urban sprawl. *European Planning Studies*, 19(1), 113–139.
Næss, P., Strand, A., Næss, T., and Nicolaisen, M. S. (2011). On their road to sustainability? The challenge of sustainable mobility in urban planning and development in two Scandinavian capital regions. *Town Planning Review*, 82(3), 287–317.
Newman, P. W. G. and Kenworthy, J. R. (1999). *Sustainability and Cities: Overcoming Automobile Dependence*. Washington, DC and Covelo, CA: Island Press.
Nordic Council of Ministers (1999). *Factors 4 and 10 in the Nordic Countries – the Transport Sector – the Forest Sector – the Building and Real Estates Sector – the Food Supply Chain*. Copenhagen: Nordic Council of Ministers.
Norrie, A. (2010). *Dialectic and Difference: Dialectical Critical Realism and the Grounds of Justice*. London: Routledge.
Nozick, R. (1974). *Anarchy, State, and Utopia*. New York: Basic Books.
Østerberg, D. (1973). *Behov*. [Needs.] Article in the *Pax dictionary*. http://lotus.uib.no/norgeslexi/paxlex/alfabetet/b/b06.html.
Rawls, J. (1971). *A Theory of Justice*. Cambridge, MA: Belknap Press of Harvard University Press.
Soper, K. (2008). Alternative hedonism, cultural theory and the role of aesthetic revisioning. *Cultural Studies*, 22(5), 567–587.
Sorrel, S. (2007). *The Rebound Effect: An Assessment of the Evidence for Economy-wide Energy Savings from Improved Energy Efficiency*. London: UK Energy Research Center.
Spangenberg, J. H. (2010). The growth discourse, growth policy and sustainable development: two thought experiments. *Journal of Cleaner Production*, 18, 561–566.
Statistics Norway (2014a). *Energibruk i husholdningene, 2012*. Oslo: Statistics Norway. Retrieved March 20, 2015 from www.ssb.no/energi-og-industri/statistikker/husenergi/hvert-3-aar/2014-07-14.
Statistics Norway (2014b). *Table: 09170: Produksjon og inntekt, etter næring*. [Production and income, according to trade.] Retrieved July 7, 2014 from www.ssb.no/statistikkbanken
Statistics Norway (2014c). *Table: 10237: Utgift per husholdning per år, etter vare- og tjenestegruppe og landsdel*. [Annual expenditures per household, according to commodity and service group and part of the country.] Retrieved July 7, 2014 from www.ssb.no/statistikkbanken.

United Nations Population Division (2013). *World Population Prospects. The 2012 Revision. Highlights*. New York: United Nations, Department of Economic and Social Affairs.

Wolff, R. P. (1977). Robert Nozick's derivation of the minimal state. *Arizona Law Review*, 19, 7–30.

Xue, J. (2014). *Economic Growth and Sustainable Housing: An Uneasy Relationship*. London/New York: Routledge.

9

SYSTEMIC ISSUES WITHIN THE CRISIS OF GLOBAL CAPITALISM

The case of land and food

Robert Biel

Introduction

This chapter explores ways in which general systems theory can help us understand the meaning of crisis under capitalism. We focus specifically on food/land issues, both as an illustrative case and as a fundamental factor underpinning more general issues of social structure.

The question of how to arrive at a critical perspective on systems theory is an important one in social science, and more specifically in the critical realist approach (for example, Mingers 2011) that guides this book. Therefore, the chapter will seek to interrogate systems theory itself, more specifically around issues such as 'pattern', determinism and teleology. Any system requires radical phase transitions if it is to continue regenerating its structure. The fact that capitalism experiences crisis is therefore not in itself a sign it is 'finished', it may even be a sign of continued vitality; which is not to say that such vitality is a good thing: capitalism's structure disproportionally benefits only the few, while the costs of building it are borne by the majority.

We first ask how systems in general employ order and disorder. Emphasising those aspects of self organisation and co-operation that make complex systems work, we explore parallels between general systems theory and dialectics, and briefly present a model of the capitalist international political economy (IPE) as it moves through successive waves or regimes. Second, we consider why the current crisis may be different from previous ones, notably because of chaotic factors, and the human system's interplay with a natural system itself prone to sharp extremes. Of course, humanity has many times in the past confronted extremes (ice ages, pandemics). The specific handicaps we face today are due to (a) the damaging legacy of the *illusion* of control or dominance over nature (Merchant 1980), which we inherited from the capitalist revolution; and (b) the vulnerability and lack of resilience that occur when highly simplified systems confront complex problems, an issue well demonstrated in the case of food systems which have become dependent on a narrow range of crops and strains, and where knowledge and innovative capacity are centralised, rather than being distributed as would be required for the recovery of a system disrupted by extreme events.

On an optimistic note, there has historically existed a faculty to re-invent food systems from below whenever they collapse at the centre/top under pressure of climate or pandemics (Thirsk 1997). The issue is to re-activate this response today, and to do so quickly. We therefore thirdly emphasise the role of agency, which imparts its specific imprint to human systems: there is still an equivalent to the bifurcations of physical systems, but mediated through choice and, most importantly, struggle, an issue which we concretise by specific reference to the era of imperialism.

Fourth, we introduce our case study of land/food issues, emphasising factors evident at this enhanced level of detail which might be missed at the level of the IPE as a whole. Finally, we apply our earlier hypothesis about the chaotic nature of the recent phase transition, notably with respect to food price, concluding by considering the relevance of this argument for a new generation of struggles.

How systems work with order and disorder

Complexity is good for a system: if the bits that make it up are diverse and not too constrained, they will, when necessary, be able to self-assemble into new kinds of order, thereby allowing the system to access the free energy of self-organisation. Thus, 'complex systems may produce emergent order … *without a prescription for the pattern existing beforehand*' and 'a higher order complexity can result from the cooperativity of simpler components' (Thelen 1989: 80; our italics[1]).

The above argument does not deny the existence of pattern, quite the contrary; the point is simply that the features of that pattern cannot be predicted deterministically from the parts: 'We do not understand what will happen in any situation – only that something interesting will' (Lucas 2005). The implication of this argument would go against a reading of dialectics which is either deterministic or teleological: the liberatory aspect of systems thinking is precisely to access an *open* future (Prigogine 2003). 'Openness' is here employed in two distinct but interrelated ways. First, a system is open where it possesses a 'surroundings' into which it can *dissipate* (shed its disorder), in which case it can escape the seemingly fatalistic descent into entropy prescribed by the Second Law of thermodynamics. Second, by this very process, it is able to access the creative forces for non-deterministic development, thus its future becomes open-ended.

Pursuing the theme of a system's development, complexity is associated with its being in flux. It is therefore not a desirable goal simply to 'settle into' some stable or balanced condition and remain there. In fact, 'We now know that simplicity and stability are exceptions', beyond which we encounter '*an unexpected intrinsic structure of reality*' (Prigogine and Stengers 1984: 216; italics in the original). So in this sense, structure in a system is actually in contradiction to equilibrium: 'A universe in equilibrium cannot be complex, because the random processes that bring it to equilibrium destroy organization' (Smolin 2013: 202). Randomness here means the 'loss of pattern' (or of the faculty to generate pattern); such a loss would draw the system into entropy, understood as a kind of dead equilibrium where 'nothing interesting' happens.

The creative, low-entropy situation can degenerate in two seemingly opposite directions, which nevertheless converge since they are both manifestations of entropy. We can illustrate this in a 'Scrabble' model (Figure 9.1).

It follows that disturbance has a useful role to play in preventing stagnancy. In Holling's study of the evolution of physical ecosystems, cyclical 'rift' is intrinsically needed to break up stagnant equilibria (Holling 2001). Even (or perhaps especially?) those forces in appearance most inimical to order may play unexpected roles in creating it: even entropy does so, for example in the role of supermassive black holes (Scharf 2012) as a regulating force in the organisation of galaxies.

This in turn brings us to the notion of chaos. In one sense, chaos is seen as the disruptive force that counters too much balance (structure, order). If 'complexity involves an interplay between chaos and non-chaos' (Baranger ND), then the issue would be to allow the right dose of chaos without letting it tear the system apart. 'Crisis' might then constitute an interlude of chaos functioning to break up a stagnant order.

But there is another perspective on chaos, in which we see it as being *itself* an organising principle: 'Recent research has shown that chaos may actually be useful under certain circumstances, and there is growing interest in utilising the richness

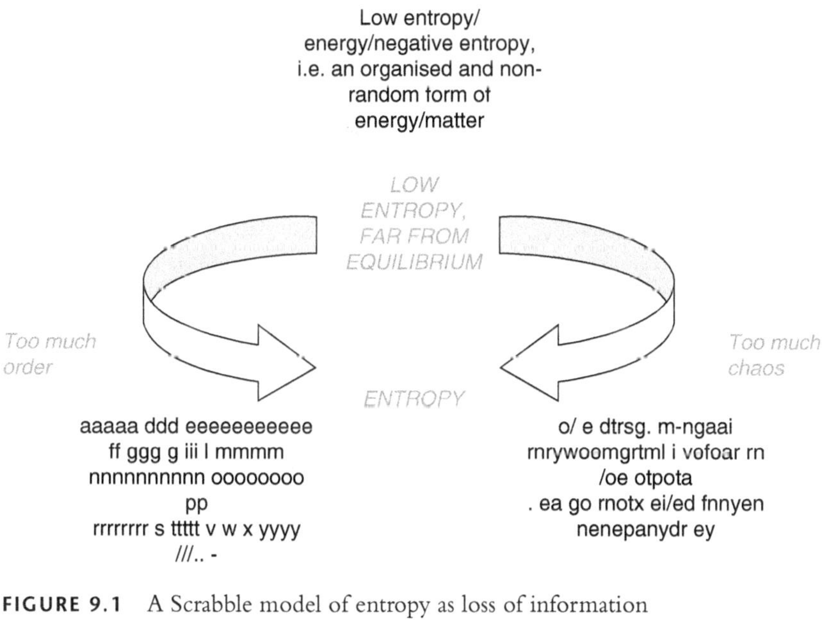

FIGURE 9.1 A Scrabble model of entropy as loss of information

of chaos' (Ivancevic and Ivancevic 2007: 10). For example, in brain dynamics, the brain's 'controlled chaos' is not just an accidental by-product of complexity but an intrinsic feature of its regulation (ibid.). The organisational role of chaos is often represented by the term 'attractor', a concept to which we will return in the final section of this chapter.

Chaos holds within it a promise of organisation, under the right conditions.

The whole of the above argument ought to sit well with Marxism, because dialectics is premised on embracing contradiction as a dynamic force, and a universe in constant flux. And, in fact, the systems perspective comes from the same root as dialectics: from its origins, general systems theory drew upon the pre-Socratic philosophers (Drack 2008), and thus the ancient Asiatic knowledge systems filtered through them. Hegel drew from this same source in framing the dialectics later developed by Marx. For example, Hegel's remark in his lecture on Heraclitus – 'It is a great advance in thought to pass from Being to Becoming' (Hegel 1995) – closely parallels Prigogine and Stengers' statement about non-equilibrium systems revealing 'a glimpse of the road that leads from being to becoming' (Prigogine and Stengers 1984).

So let us now consider how this model may be useful to a critical perspective on capitalism. Like any system, capitalism moves through phases: temporary periods of relative stability punctuated by crises. While such disruptions threaten to rip apart the mode of production, they are nevertheless functional. This duality is captured by Schumpeter's term 'creative destruction' (Schumpeter 1976) – even if I personally find the term itself more interesting than Schumpeter's own exploration of it. It has been observed that the 'creative destruction' idea is very much in the spirit of Marx (Schubert 2013); it should therefore come as no surprise that the period immediately following the Russian Revolution saw an interesting debate (cf. Day 1981), exploring the extent to which capitalism remained capable of generating new structure. Particularly important in this respect was the work of Nikolai Kondratiev (influential under Lenin, suppressed and eventually killed by Stalin). Given our focus on the rapprochement between Marxist dialectics and general systems theory, it is significant that the idea of 'Kondratiev waves' has received a certain confirmation from complexity theory (Korotayev and Tsirel 2010).

Let us now represent a succession of phases, or in Kondratiev's vocabulary, 'waves' (Figure 9.2). It should be noted that the approach we employ is one of political economy, i.e. it addresses the mode of production in its largest sense (including all military and political aspects), itself embedded within the environment, in distinction from the apolitical and economistic way in which 'waves' are sometimes addressed.

Since capitalism is for the time being the ruling mode of production, the figure is 'about' it. Thus, the plateaus represent phases when, having established a certain structure, it can explore and eventually exhaust the potentials of that structure; the troughs are intervening episodes, punctuated by crisis, where structure is weak.

It should be noted that neither the ordered phases nor the disordered ones are necessarily preferable from the standpoint of the livelihoods of the mass of the people.

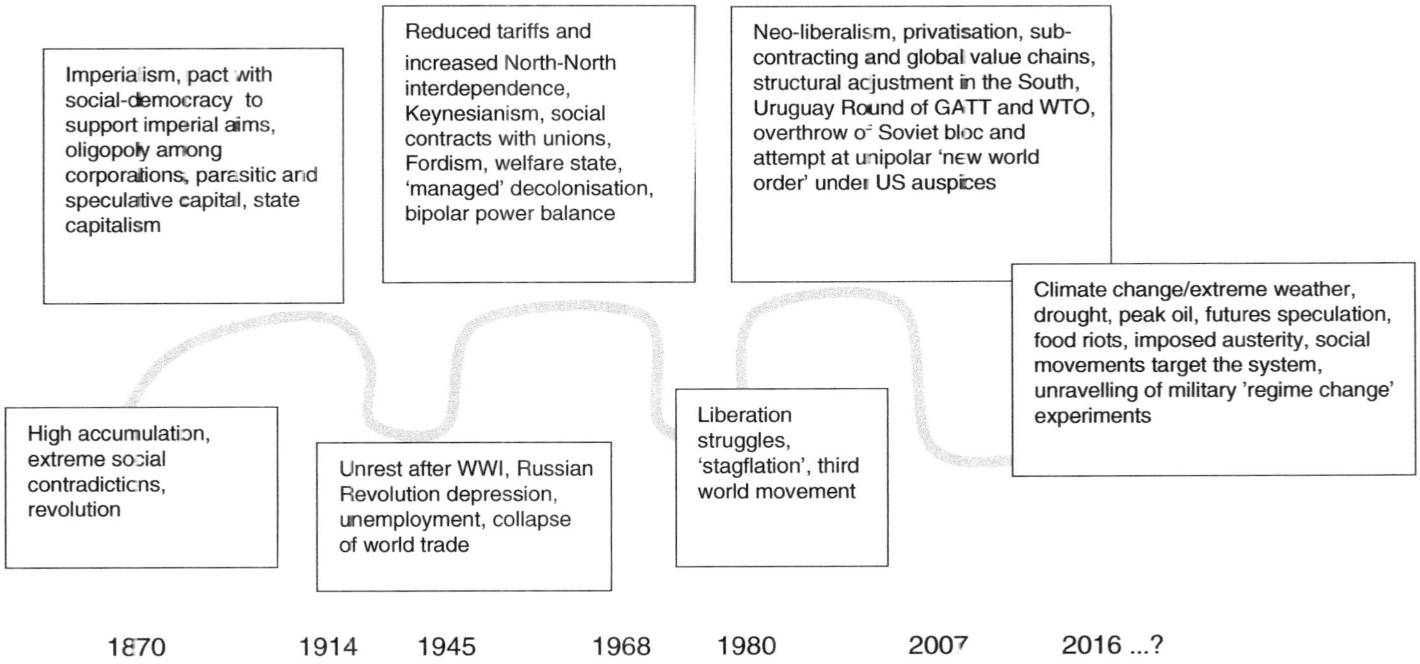

FIGURE 9.2 A succession of structural regimes in the international political economy, punctuated by phases of low order
Source: adapted and developed from Biel 2006

The former, because if the order itself is inherently exploitative, when it is working well it is simply more efficient at exploiting; the latter because the ruling system tends to export downwards, both onto the working class and (following Foucault's argument) onto the most marginalised, the destructive aspect of creative destruction, while reserving the creative side for itself. The people therefore tend to experience the worst aspects of both chaos and repressive order. It is true, nevertheless, that phases of low order, while they often bring intensified deprivation and suffering, are also phases of opportunity for counter-systemic struggle. During such phases, capitalism is unstable not just through the operation of its internal contradictions in some abstract way but primarily through the agency of social struggle and revolution. In turn, from capitalism's perspective, the goal is to find a form in which it can successfully either repress struggle – through political or military means – or co-opt it. Hence an ongoing dialectic of struggle, which is in fact the main point we are making in Figure 9.2.

Although we have said that structure is not predictable from the parts, there is indeed a kind of predictability in capitalism, which we can understand in the sense that as long as it remains the dominant mode of production, it restricts the scope of innovation by ruling out anything that is not compatible with continued capital accumulation. While there are huge structural revolutions within capitalism, they still embody the same basic rules, with the predictable result of an increasing concentration of wealth/power, so in that sense nothing changes (except that it gets worse).

Let us now consider more closely the meaning of crisis. The term would make sense as a time of acute disruption reflecting the overthrow of one particular structural form and the prelude to a new one. This should imply some sense of things 'coming to a head'. In medicine, for instance, 'if the crisis state cannot be distinguished from noncrisis states, the whole concept is meaningless' (Slaikeu 1990: 13). It would therefore seem an elementary error to apply the term to any condition that continues indefinitely.

But that is precisely the error that came to dominate Soviet theory from the 1930s onwards, with the notion of a 'general crisis' of capitalism, which was not only absurd (Lotta and Shannon 1984) but politically damaging to the left (Biel 2015a) – it could not explain why capitalism has its ups as well as its downs and can recover dynamism periodically. By the 1980s, the notion of a continuous crisis spanning half a century had become simply ridiculous. Alongside such a stagnant vision of capitalism, its complementary opposite might logically be a stagnant socialism, which is effectively what seems to have happened in the Soviet bloc where boringness and predictability became almost a virtue, reflecting the definition of entropy as a kind of death by excessive order (Figure 9.1, above). Whatever the shortcomings of Mao Zedong's Cultural Revolution, it was consciously designed to provoke a crisis within the dead equilibrium of the Soviet model – and may even have succeeded.

Why today's crisis may be different

From the standpoint of where we are today, the obvious question posed by Figure 9.2 is: what could be the recipe for a new 'up' phase?

Yet there may be a deeper question: might the crisis beginning around 2007, even though at first glance it appears similar to previous ones, in reality be qualitatively different? And might the difference have something to do with the function of chaos? Following the twofold perspective on chaos outlined above, we could broadly say that in the conventional interpretation of 'creative destruction', chaos is not considered itself as an organising principle but merely as a necessarily destructive punctuation between two phases of order. This arguably makes sense in interpreting earlier crises, but does not necessarily hold true today. In the phase that began in the late 2000s, there still exists structure, but not in the old sense of a fairly established set of rules which governed the system predictably, as in the Keynesian or neo-liberal regimes. Instead, the system may be ruled in a way that partially, at least, embraces its chaotic features (Biel 2012). 'Certain unstable systems have a tendency to settle into patterns which still fluctuate, but fluctuate within parameters that are comprehensible enough to produce an illusion of concreteness' (Teed Rockwell 2005). This, in turn, would have significant implications for how we exercise agency. In a moment we will explore these implications practically, but first let us consider the proposition in a conceptual way.

Systems that keep encountering their resource constraints will tend to enter into an oscillating behaviour (being periodically 'bounced back' from those constraints whenever they bash into them); even if they are chaotic, there is nevertheless a kind of 'rhythm' to the chaos (Gharajedaghi 2006: 117–18). This in itself is an interesting notion with respect to the current crisis, but we would have to take it one step further because the actual situation is not one where the resource environment simply confronts the human system as a static (Malthusian) 'wall' or 'ceiling'. Rather, I will argue, the resource environment has itself entered a somewhat chaotic, or at least discontinuously extreme, form. There are therefore three elements to consider: a different behaviour of nature, a different behaviour of capitalism, and how the two interact. This is represented schematically in Figure 9.3.

Precisely because – as highlighted by general systems theory – all systems have some fundamental common features in the way they evolve, capitalism and nature both move through phase transitions, and similar terminologies can be applied to both. For example, the term 'regime', meaning a mode of organisation, is used both in political economy (for example, Lipietz 1987: 14 ff.) and in studies of the physical environment (for instance, Holland and Webster 2007). Of course, the existence of these similarities does not mean the two systems are compatible; quite the opposite. The cycles of capital – expanded reproduction – are antagonistic to the cycles of reproduction of nature. But again, the fact that the two systems are mutually antagonistic does not deny that there can be interaction between them – mostly of a bad kind.

Against this background, let us consider the thesis that something changed qualitatively with the current crisis, making it different to previous ones. This has two basic aspects. First, with respect to nature, a regime shift occurred some time around the very end of the twentieth century and the first few years of the twenty-first. This can most easily be depicted as transition to an era where extreme events become the norm – for example, a regime shift to extreme weather (Lyall 2013), or in a more general

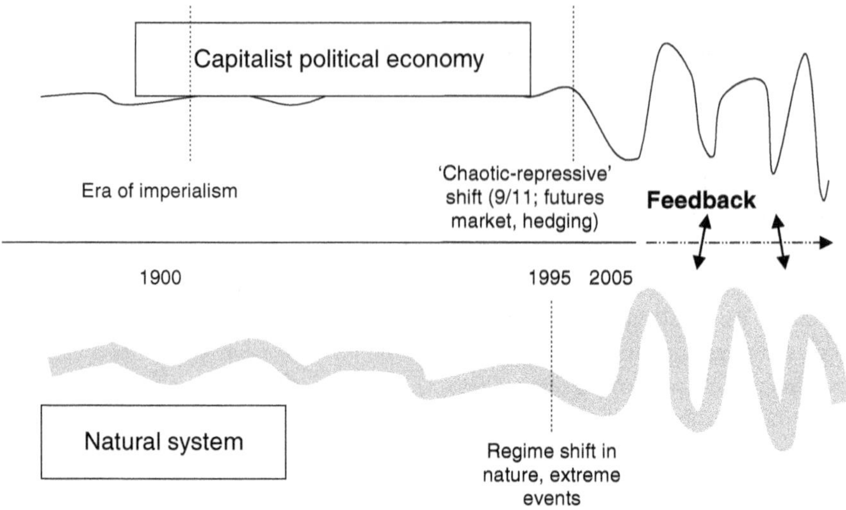

FIGURE 9.3 A representation of the interaction of two systems – socio-economic and natural – which at roughly the same time enter into a more chaotic or extreme behaviour.
Note: Vertical dotted lines indicate some important regime shifts

sense, 'disasters'. In many of the indicators with respect to weather and disasters we can spot a watershed at some point at the end of the 1990s and very beginning of the 2000s. In some cases, cycles or waves can be identified before that point as well as after, the difference being that now (a) the fluctuations are more extreme, and (b) each peak tends to be higher than the last.[2] In terms of real impact, there is a qualitatively greater threat to livelihoods because extreme events are hard to recover from. This regime of extremes seems set to continue, irrespective of what happens in the political economy; it would thus form the backdrop to any future phase of capitalist structure, or lack of it.

Second, within capitalism itself, certain latent features developed in a new way, the effect of which was to create positive feedbacks whereby signals in one system amplify extremes in the other. The clearest expression is the tendency for speculative finance capital to seize and parasitise upon risk, turning risk itself into a source of profit, of accumulation. The regime shift in nature occurred roughly at the same time that cracks began appearing in the accumulation regime, which had resolved the crisis of the 1970s. Even if this were pure coincidence, the effect has been to lock the systems together to some extent. But, in fact, it is not merely coincidence, because the structural changes in capitalism, with the rise of the futures market and hedging, were a response to opportunities presented by a new dispensation of risk and disaster.

The above argument suggests that capitalism has, partly under the impact of opportunities gifted by the climate regime, evolved important new structural features. But at the same time, since we are talking about parasitism and the dominance of finance capital, these are features latent within capitalism but which the recent context has allowed/encouraged to assume exaggerated and distorted forms, so in this sense the new forms are exploring a potential that was already there. In order to deepen our understanding of this issue, let us revisit the area of Marxist theory that first identified these tendencies more than a century ago: the debate on imperialism.

Imperialism and the role of agency

Marxism is social science, but in the revolutionary tradition – the point is not to understand the world but to change it. The point of the imperialism debate of the early twentieth century was to understand an epoch of revolution, the transition from capitalism to a new social order. In revisiting this debate from the standpoint of its relation to systems/complexity thinking, our purpose is principally to identify the openings for radical struggle existing in today's situation. As we will argue, a key conceptual tool in a systems understanding of imperialism has been dialectics. Let us therefore briefly consider how far we can conceive of dialectics in a non-teleological way.

An example of the worst kind of teleology presents history as a set of stages with a kind of logic which happens to coincide with Western 'civilisation' as the highest point: this was the racist, social-Darwinist doctrine which developed through the nineteenth- and early twentieth-century colonial/imperialist quest for world domination, and then through Cold War modernisation. The good use of dialectics, on the contrary, would see that there is a kind of logic in the movement to overthrow oppressive social systems; since the latter negated the open-endedness of human creativity, their own subsequent negation will restore this (i.e. the Negation of the Negation).

If we concretise this in relation to our own topic, that of land/food systems, we find two key features: (1) the socio-institutional organisation of farming (who 'owns' the land, whether it is enclosed or communal, and so forth), and (2) the technical organisation of the way in which land and cropping systems are managed. It should be noted that whereas the progressive movement is immediately an overthrow *of* capitalism, it profoundly questions class society as a whole, since both (1) exploitative agrarian social structures and (2) problematical practices of farming technique (monocropping, deep ploughing) began long before capitalism, and were subsumed by it.

With respect to the use of dialectics by Marx and Engels, I would argue that, while they mostly resisted the dominant Eurocentric teleology, they made a significant fault of omission in failing to expose and criticise it (Biel 2015a). However, Engels is correct in the defence he mounts, in *Anti-Dühring* (Engels 1969 [1894]), of the use of dialectics, and notably of the Negation of the Negation, in their own theories: Marx's and Engels' arguments are derived from reality, not from theory, and dialectics serves as a way to represent that reality – an approach we could consider very much in the tradition of critical realism of a 'conceptually mediated' (Fleetwood 2004) appraisal of reality. Significantly, Engels' argument aiming to show how dialectics is embedded in the material world draws on issues such as plant evolution and soil structure (Engels 1969 [1894]: 162–4).

This argument connects us in an interesting way back to the issue of randomness. Evolutionary theory is often presented as a random process, but this misses an important point: in Brian Goodwin's argument (Goodwin 1994), drawing on the phenomenon of convergent evolution, although mutations may be random, the selection of these mutations for viability is not. There are certain patterns which re-assert themselves. This perspective could have an applicability to social science and, in terms of the topic of this chapter, it could include both areas (1) and (2) referred to above. With respect to (1), while Marx was concerned not to lay down abstract blueprints because the point was to let society self-organise (both in the obvious sense of power from below and in the more theoretical sense of emergent order – his interest lay in studying the forms actually developed by the proletariat, as in *The Civil War in France*), at the same time the existence of a certain logic should not be downplayed: the pattern or structure of today's land/food-related struggles, such as Mexico's Zapatistas, does somehow rediscover co-operative explorations of the past. With respect to (2) some re-connection with sustainable techniques of biomimicry are already widely explored in agroecology, permaculture, natural systems agriculture, low-impact and no-till methods, and so forth, which draw inspiration from indigenous tradition. The excitement and open-endedness of the future open system will be seen in the unfolding potential of these approaches, which has so far merely been hinted at.

Our specific focus in this chapter is the application of dialectics to systemic crisis. In this context, it is interesting to note that the early twentieth century was an extraordinarily rich and creative period in human thought, witnessing a major re-ordering of the way we apprehend nature. Thus, relativity and quantum theory broke through the restrictions of reductionism and linearity, at least at a broad conceptual level (it is another matter with corporate-dominated applied science, for example in agriculture/food systems where highly simplistic approaches still hold sway to a significant extent). There was something about the Zeitgeist that lent itself to questioning reductionist dichotomies and developing insights on the chaos–order question. These revolutions are not normally discussed in the same breath as imperialism theory, but perhaps they should be. The time of imperialism's beginnings was one where it became possible to glimpse the possibility of something new, a transitional, and in some respects deeply troubled process, unfolding over an era. The outlines of this were still hazy, necessarily so in that both the broader picture and the details would be on the one hand emergent (not predictable from first principles), on the other arising only through struggle. The huge transition phase marked by imperialism is where it would begin. Although this coming era in one sense would still be imprisoned within the 'predictability' of successive structures of capital accumulation, it was also the era in which the anti-systemic forces would begin generating alternative structures. This duality is reflected in the process represented in Figure 9.2, which is driven by the struggle of opposites. As anyone with experience of such struggles will know, the big issue is to avoid becoming the thing you are fighting, but at least if one is conscious of this danger one can resist it as far as possible.

To create a social science of imperialism was not easy, and what's often missed is how Lenin anticipated the general theory of systems by drawing insights from nature in doing so. Thus, he undertook deep studies of dialectics (Lenin 1972 [1914–16]) in the period when *Imperialism, the Highest Stage of Capitalism* was under preparation, and it is precisely dialectics which embodies the consciousness of principles of complexity and the transformation of opposites of traditional thinking. As Capra points out (Capra 1992), the early twentieth-century scientific revolution re-connects us with the traditional insights – derived from nature – that had been suppressed by the reductionism and linearity of early capitalist thought.

To theorise this era correctly would be crucial, precisely because the theory would serve as a guide to radical practice. This does not at all preclude an important role for structure. While structuralism has a bad press – deservedly so if we think of a linear, teleological and reductionist reading – a complexity-based structuralism would simply reflect the existence of certain objective processes of self-organisation, and even co-operation, an understanding of which is essential precisely because it forms the condition for our exercising agency; this was really the point of developing socialism 'from utopia to science' (Engels 1966).

The era of imperialism would certainly not be stagnant. Nevertheless, its developmental features would take the form of a sharpening of antagonisms, a playing out of tendencies to decay. Two outstanding contributors to the imperialism debate, Hobson and Luxemburg, highlighted both the continued scope for change and development remaining within imperialism and its limitations. Each step is in this sense a depletion of future developmental potential, in Luxemburg's argument, the depletion of a 'milieu' (Luxemburg 1913). The question is what would happen once this process reached a point where capitalism/imperialism has exhausted its capacity to develop in a 'normal' way, i.e. in a way where chaos plays only an intermittent role in mediating periods of order. Then, might it not embark on a phase where chaos *is* the only order? In this case, a more 'embedded' form of chaos would take over, perhaps less 'crisis-like' and more endemic.

The early phase of imperialism one hundred years ago (the First World War and the Russian Revolution) signalled the possibility of a qualitative loosening of order, an issue brilliantly highlighted by Yeats in his phrase 'the falcon cannot hear the falconer (Yeats 1963 [1919]: 211). At that time, the loosening was not yet definitive, but perhaps this latent tendency has now, partially at least, been actualised. In today's circumstances, the creative potential of chaos can no longer really be mastered by the system, beyond simply exporting it downwards onto the oppressed segments of society. The creative potential is nevertheless not abolished; it still exists, but now it can be enlisted only for a project coming from outside the dominant order. 'Outside' means the excluded, which we might assume in the Marxian argument to mean primarily class. Nevertheless, we should not forget that Engels saw the gender issue as the basis for all forms of social oppression, and we can add to this all categories of the excluded: those oppressed on 'racial' lines, indigenous peoples, etc. In relation to our case study, there are many issues around feminist and indigenous perspectives on nature which make this of great qualitative importance to humanity's future.

Specificities of food regimes

A brief case study is now offered, partly to concretise the general model of political economy/ecology, but also, more importantly, to reveal a finer level of detail which may question higher-level generalisations and suggest different insights, notably on the structure-agency issue.

Within the overall compass of political economy/ecology, sub-structures regulate specific areas and embody in a concrete way the general issues of high or low order at various historical stages. We could therefore develop our earlier model with specific reference to land/food issues (Figure 9.4).

Once again, the politico–military dimension must be stressed. While the Cold War was formally a mode of organisation for the sphere of international political and military relations, it cast its shadow on all areas of life through the Keynesian long cycle (from 1945) to the beginning of the pure neo-liberal cycle (early 1980s) and notably food regimes, where it explains how 'food as a weapon' was deployed to control the global South (cf. Biel 2000, 2015b).

The role of agency/struggle assumes its own particular form within each of these areas. Thus, as with regime shifts more generally, the development of food regimes is not produced either purely out of structure itself or out of agency (c.f. Potter and Tilzey 2005), but through some interaction between the two.

The specific form of this interaction can be understood if we think how food relates to the overall driving force of capitalism, i.e. accumulation. The structural ingredient, in Marx's theory, is supplied by a kind of logic which tends to reduce wages to the cost of subsistence. But Marx was extremely clear that this structural factor acts only as a context for agency, i.e. struggle (Marx 1969 [1865]): the actual degree of exploitation has no fixed level but is determined by the point at which one force (struggle) halts the other, the tendency to drive wages downwards (it should be noted that this refers to 'day-to-day' struggle within the limits of the current system, not the more strategic struggle for system-change, which we will address in a moment).

Within the cost of subsistence, food price obviously plays a key role. Powerful structural pressures therefore exist within capitalism to cut food costs. The economistic side of this is first to maintain the rate of profit by reducing the value of labour power, and second (in the mass consumption phase) to reduce the proportion of earnings spent on food, thus leaving more purchasing power for consumer goods; the political side is to avoid the mass unrest that occurs when people go hungry. All these factors united to push capitalism into the productivist paradigm also within the food supply sector: wholesale introduction of chemical fertilisers and pesticides and – for the global South – all the political dimensions of the Green Revolution.

But there are also counter-forces pushing the opposite way, to drive food prices up. There are two aspects to this: factors internal to capitalism and ecological constraints.

(1) In relation to capitalism itself, let us begin by considering a theoretical, purely industrial mode of accumulation, where the rate of profit depends on food costs

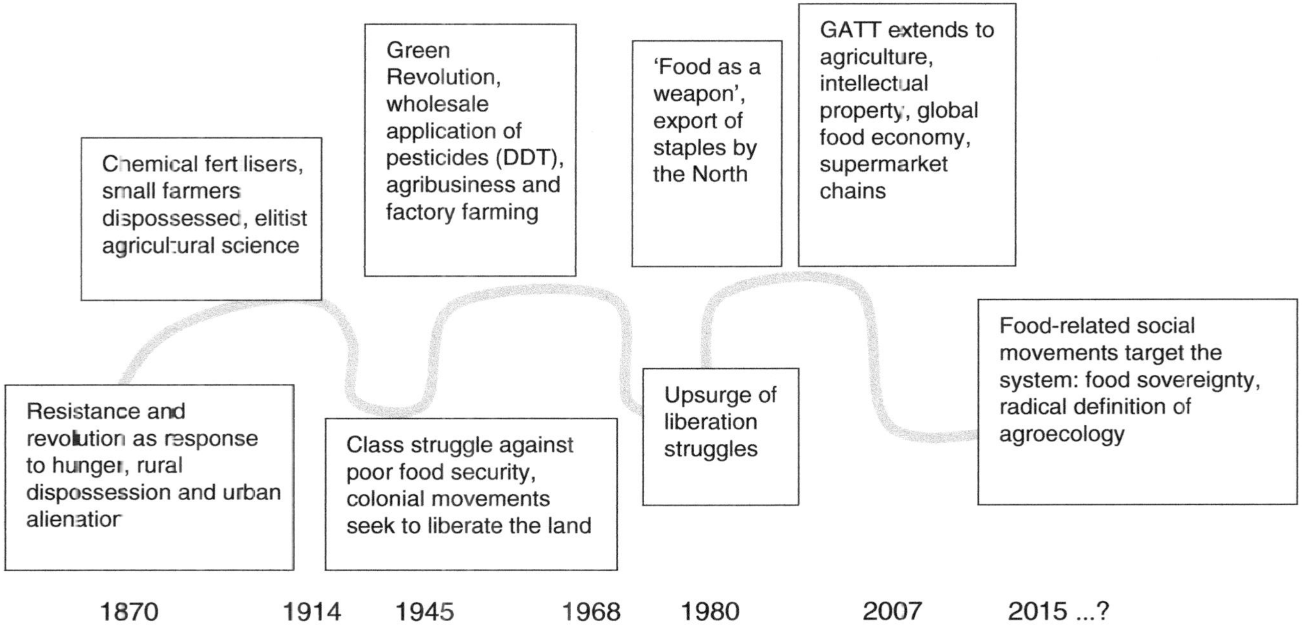

FIGURE 9.4 A succession of 'waves' in the capitalist political economy of food, punctuated by phases of crisis

being minimised. Although never wholly realistic, this did make a certain sense at least up to the structural crisis of the 1970s. But then there occurred a shift: instead of simply being a condition for accumulation in industry, agriculture now became a major player in accumulation in its own right, a process further accentuated with its full incorporation into the world trade system through the Uruguay Round of GATT (1986–1994), the formation of the WTO (1995) and the current (at the time of writing) trade agendas (TTIP, and so on) whereby corporate interests seek unprecedented power over many food-related issues, for example food standards.

Viewed in this context, certain more recent food regime trends, signalled for example by McMichael (2009: 284) – dispossession of small farmers by agribusiness, increased dependence of consumers on the corporate food sector, strong elements of monopoly in food marketing – can be recognised as further developments of a trend going back more than four decades to push up prices, in this case through the monopoly element of buyer-driven chains, a factor that would be absent if small farmers were the main suppliers. It should be emphasised that neither the forces pushing prices down nor those pushing them up have been favourable either to the global South or to small producers. Under the regime of low food prices, the lack of income for small farmers led to a failure of accumulation 'from below' in the rural sphere, upon which alone meaningful development could have been based, a factor which limits to the South's capacity to develop (even industrially) in a truly independent way (Gakou 1987: 63), while today, corporate control is sufficient to prevent Southern producers, or farmers more generally, recouping any benefit from higher prices to the consumer.

But the above trends, though interesting in themselves, are only manifestations of a deeper logic which does not just go back four decades but has always been latent in capitalism. This is precisely why we have to think in terms not just of food but of land. Right from the onset of capitalism, when it seemed on the surface very much an industrial mode of production, Marx discerned land ownership as the foundation of the whole structure: 'The history of landed property… would indeed be the history of the formation of modern capital' and 'The inner construction of modern society, or, capital in the totality of its relations, is therefore posited in the economic relations of modern landed property' (Marx 1973: 252, 275). In this sense, seemingly new phenomena, such as the agricultural basis of accumulation and the role of monopoly in food price, are merely expressions of a deeper reality. Today's 'land grabs' are its most obvious expressions, but in a more general way the issue is both political – the power conferred by monopoly of the means of production – and economic: the 'rents', i.e. income, derived from that power. These features in turn have a wider and more general significance extending beyond ownership of the land itself, most notably into the realm of science and knowledge; thus 'intellectual property' – a key feature of the post-Cold War food regime from the second half of the 1980s onwards – similarly serves both as a means of monopoly control and a source of rents.

(2) The ecological factors have in turn two aspects: (a) the limits of the productivist model itself: diminishing returns from chemical-based farming, exhaustion of the

soil, exhaustion of the natural immunities and resilience when plants are fed excessive nutrients, exhaustion of the wider ecosystem upon which agriculture depends (natural predators, pollinators); even the FAO – historically quite subservient to mainstream/corporate agendas – now finds itself obliged to call for a 'paradigm shift' (Graziano da Silva 2015); (b) the regime of natural extremes which exposes the deficit of resilience in highly simplified systems depending on a narrow range of crops and strains. These environmental factors have reinforced the issues internal to capitalism, more especially in the most recent period, i.e. since about 2007.

The exhaustion of productivism is a good example of how we can perceive important things from a specific case study – food systems – which would not be visible at a higher/broader viewpoint on accumulation regimes in general. Thus, whereas the old linear and reductionist paradigms were in a general and conceptual sense undermined by the twentieth-century scientific revolution, they still hold sway in many applied fields, and none more so than the application of science to agriculture – the mainstream paradigm still tends to reduce everything to chemical inputs, underestimate the properties of complex soil systems, shrink the diversity of crops and strains, and cheerfully destroy complex ecologies. In this, it is of course anchored by the vested interests of imperialism, viewed as an intermeshing of, on the one hand, military power and on the other, corporate profit motives. Nevertheless, even from a socialist perspective, it is important to understand the particular as well as the general. Even Lenin, who in an overall sense left a brilliant legacy on dialectics, was less assured in his approach to agricultural applied science. While he correctly picked up on Marx's insights on the absurdity of capitalism's failure to channel urban sewage back to the land (Lenin 1938: 98–9), this was not on the basis of an understanding that a sustainable agriculture must intrinsically be organic, Instead, he attacked the notion of diminishing returns as Malthusian, and seemed to recognise no limits to the application of science to agriculture (Lenin 1938: 59). The key point which this argument misses is that the real issue in mainstream farming has always been the intensified application of reductionist science to agriculture. As a result, diminishing returns are a reality which can easily be demonstrated (for example, between the beginning of the 1960s and the mid-2000s, global fertiliser inputs per ha. increased 5.5 times for a 2.5 times increase in per ha. cereal yield – HM Govt. 2011: 79) for the very good reason that they deplete the soil's own complex mineral/biological system. The fundamental fact is therefore that, as Marx observed, under capitalism 'all progress in increasing the fertility of the soil for a given time is a progress towards ruining the more long-lasting sources of that fertility' (Marx 1954 [1887]: 506). In many respects, what we witness today is the playing out of this tendency, latent from the early period of capitalism but only fully brought to realisation now. Hence, an exhaustion of the soil, and with it of the mode of production as a whole, underpins much of its current crisis.

On the basis of the above argument, let us consider the specificities of where we are today, within the historical succession of accumulation regimes and periodic crises. During previous phases of 'good order' in the international political economy/ecology, the ruling paradigm of the moment tended to be somewhat stable and coherent. Today, this is no longer true, the system being instead ruled by a number of forces pushing in contradictory directions: those imperatives which tend to decrease food prices are still in play, juxtaposed with those acting the opposite way; the old productivist paradigm, even though severely challenged, is similarly still partially intact. One could imagine that such contradictory forces might cancel each other out and settle into some smooth and stable mean, but this is exactly what does not happen; instead, they propel the system into wild and unpredictable swings. I will argue that this could be a symptom of the peculiarly chaotic form into which the system has settled.

If this is the case, there would be an important deduction: the contemporary structural crisis would differ from previous ones due to the presence of a quality of disorder too intense to be harnessed in the service of the 'normal' creative destruction whereby capitalism has in the past used crisis itself to fuel a new accumulation regime, a type of disorder which may in fact be impossible to process within the bounds of capitalism at all. Hence the challenge facing the social movements: if humanity cannot impose control upon, or eliminate, chaos, the only choice is to use it to fuel a fundamental system change. In the final section, we will briefly examine some implications of this idea.

Chaos as background to a new generation of struggles

In the general political economy/ecology model proposed earlier, we advanced the following points: (1) that both natural and human systems shifted, around the early 2000s, to a more chaotic state; (2) that a kind of interaction between the two systems acts to amplify extremes. To concretise this argument in relation to our case study, let us consider the indicator of food price.

In Figure 9.5, we may discern two phase transitions which embody some features of the transitions represented in a schematic way in Figure 9.4. The first, at the beginning of the structural crisis of the 1970s, is reflected in a doubling of food price (the destructive side of 'creative destruction' being exported onto the masses in the shape of food insecurity), followed by a long period of relative stability (fluctuation around a consistent line) until about 2007, at which point we find a second phase transition: a precipitate rise (a further doubling), followed by wild fluctuations and the apparent absence of a stable equilibrium point. This may reflect a conflicted phase in capitalism, which no longer has clear paradigms.

Though it is impossible to say for sure that such fluctuations will continue, there are reasons to expect they will do so. From the angle of the ecological system, climate/disaster extremes – upon which food prices partially depend – they are practically certain to continue – as we argued earlier, the ecology does not merely confront the human system as a static Malthusian 'limit' but has its own extreme behaviour. From the angle of the socio-economic system, there are features that have evolved, partly as a culmination of long-term trends within capitalism, but also partly as a response to this new phase in the ecology. Let us consider this interaction.

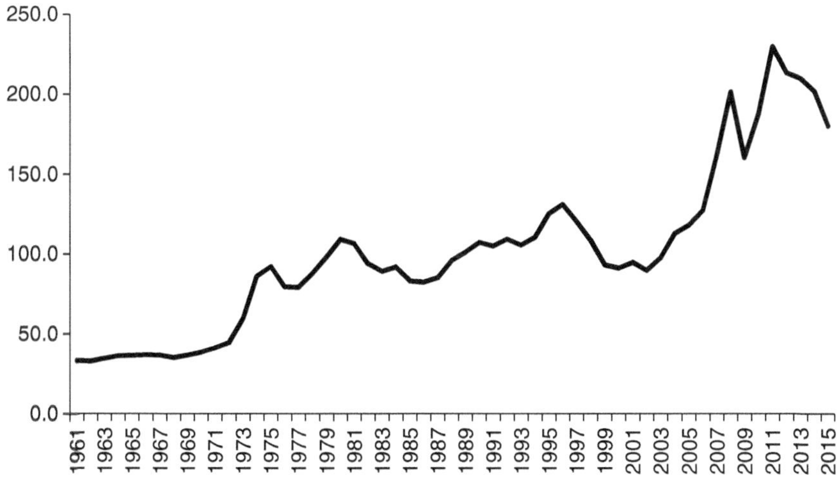

FIGURE 9.5 Food Price Index (2002–2004 = 100)
Source: the author, data taken from UN FAO at www.fao.org/worldfoodsituation/foodpricesindex/en/

While the rise of parasitic finance capital is one of the long-term tendencies of imperialism, as we discussed earlier, it hits a qualitatively new stage once the ecology presents it with plenty of risk to parasitise upon. The response is a new vocabulary of speculation, notably the futures market and hedging.

A reductionist view (for example, Kaufman 2011) that food crisis is essentially caused by speculation cannot be correct because ecological instability is a reality in its own right – we could, for example, point to direct effects of El Niño events on agriculture (Cai *et al.* 2014), which would exist even in the absence of the finance system. But speculative capital undoubtedly responds to and embraces such risk. The point is that capital cannot stand still – it has to maintain expanded reproduction somehow, and in practice what happens is, in a general sense, for parasitic capital to embrace the 'risk society' as a source of profit (Biel 2012). Thus, the director of agriculture trading at leading commodities broker Glencore typifies this: 'The environment is a good one. High prices, lots of volatility, a lot of dislocation, tightness, a lot of arbitrage opportunities' (quoted in Cusick 2012). Barclays (under the leadership of Bob Diamond, forced to resign in 2012 over the Libor manipulation scandal) grabbed a quick £0.5 billion profit in two years from food commodity funds (Bawden 2012). While this might appear (in terms of our argument at the beginning of the chapter) as one more instance of 'crisis-as-opportunity', it is certainly different from 'creative destruction' in the Schumpeter mould: nothing is created!

In analysing such an unstable and fluctuating system, there is important scope for the application of complexity theory. An example would be research by the New England Complex Systems Institute (NECSI) in this context. Thus, in relation to causes, there is recognition that 'according to researchers [from NECSI], commodity speculation – investors betting on food prices – will amplify the drought's market signals' (Keim 2012). The hypothesis of resonances between the two systems (nature's regimes on the one hand and the current structure of capitalism/imperialism on the other), which we sketched in Figure 9.3, can therefore be seen in action here. Moreover, with respect to effects, NECSI again highlights an interesting point: a strong correlation between high food prices and social unrest (Lagi *et al.* 2011). In Figure 9.6 we see how the two post-2007 peaks observed in Figure 9.5 coincide with heightened incidences of societal conflict.

The level of fine detail revealed in Figures 9.5 and 9.6 is important in sharpening up our broad-brush approach to accumulation regimes. In Figure 9.4, where we simply represented the post-2007 phase as a uniform 'low order', we might be missing the main point: it is precisely the horizontal squeezing of peaks and troughs within a short time lapse that imparts its specific chaotic flavour to the current regime.

This realisation may lead us to some insights. One of the most interesting things about complexity theory is that one can deduce certain projected behaviours. Thus, even in purely physical systems, volatility may be indicative of impending paradigm shift: 'It is remarkable that near-bifurcations [sic] systems present large fluctuations. Such systems seem to "hesitate" among various possible directions of evolution' (Prigogine and Stengers 1984: 14). We could make an analogy with oil prices, which

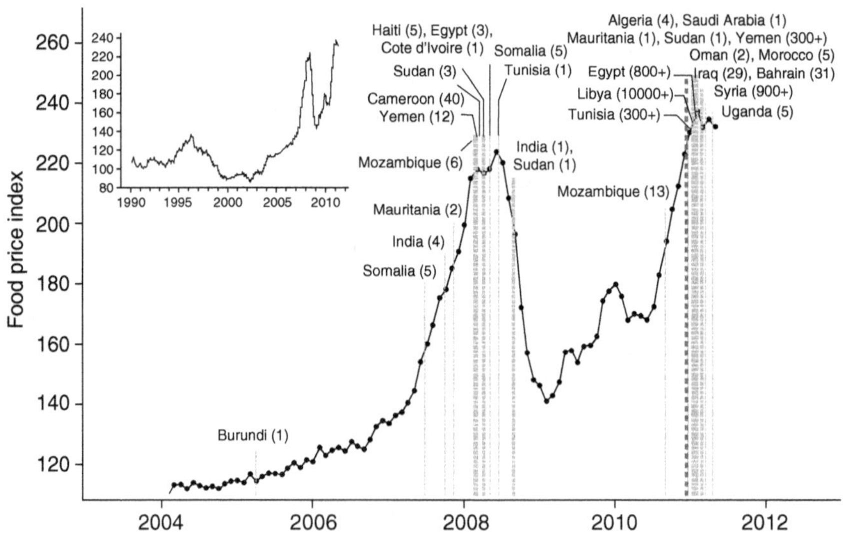

FIGURE 9.6 Time dependence of FAO Food Price Index from January 2004 to May 2011.

Note: Dashed vertical lines correspond to beginning dates of 'food riots' and protests associated with major unrest in North Africa and the Middle East. Overall death toll is reported in parentheses

Source: Lagi *et al.* 2011: 3; diagram reproduced from: http://necsi.edu/research/social/img/fig1_crises.pdf; reproduced with permission

also appear caught between two conflicting tendencies, namely tendencies to both high and low prices, each of which could be bad for the fossil economy (high prices encourage a shift to renewables, low ones damage the viability of fracking, tarsands, etc.), and on this point, Fred Pierce makes an interesting observation: 'Maybe we are seeing the death throes of our addiction to fossil fuels' (Pierce 2015: 23). So, in a similar vein, we could ask, do the chaotic features of food indicators herald the death throes of chemical/fossil fuel-based farming, as the system feels its way into a paradigm shift?

Up to a point, the above line of argument could be viewed as 'structuralist'. However, even at that level, it is not structuralism as we know it, at least if we assume this to mean something simplifying or deterministic: complexity theory and dialectics would, in complementary ways, view structures as intrinsically dynamic, capable of passing through chaotic insecurity into regime change.

But of course, in human systems the actual vector of change is agency. On this point, mainstream complexity analysis such as that of NECSI tends to be quite conservative (Drury King and Currier 2012), viewing social struggle as a dependent variable merely reactive to factors such as food shortage. In contrast, a Marxist complexity approach would go the crucial step further in its commitment to the exercise of agency to change the world.

Agency probably has a special role in 'near-bifurcation' systems, because the very notion of bifurcation somehow implies a responsibility of choice. This is the point of the notion of 'transition' in social movements (c.f. Hopkins 2008), specifically around low-carbon futures, within which the alternative food movement is very much situated: if a system is 'hesitating', we should push it the way we want it to go. Food sovereignty can itself be seen as part of the low-carbon transition, either because it permits improved energy return on energy invested (EROEI) (Martinez-Alier 2007) or because it helps escape fossil fuel dependency (Wright 2009). But in a deeper sense, food sovereignty/agroecology is also part of a larger agenda to re-integrate human society with nature. The new farming paradigm thinks about agriculture differently, and while this appears revolutionary in comparison with the dominant approach, it is at the same time a return to a straightforwardly rational realisation that one cannot conceive of farming outside the natural system in which it is embedded. This refers on the one hand to the long-term issues that have always been there – for example that we cannot focus only on the farmed portion of the earth without sustaining the wider ecosystem within which it is inserted (Odum 1969) – and on the other to systemic challenges specific to today's regime of nature – for example, that our farming system must be judged not just on the criterion of yield but on that of robustness (Darnhofer *et al.* 2010: 548).

If farming is being thought of differently, so should the organisation of society. It is precisely this shift of paradigms from two directions – on the one hand, the organisational forms of struggle, on the other, the concrete application of new ways of working to physical reality, in this case farming – that embodies the coming (back) together of human and natural systems.

The capitalist mode of production is currently ruled in two contradictory ways: through repressive order and through chaos, and in neither respect can the dominant order relax and feel 'secure'. On the one hand, with respect to central/top-down repressive rule of the old type, a mighty edifice of dominance has been built, through land monopoly, rents, intellectual property, control over staple food exports to the global South and the elimination of their traditional staples, such as the capture of genetic resources, the new biotech, land grabs and TTIP-style trade pacts. However, like any citadel or Bastille, such symbols of control become targets of struggle. This explains part of what is happening with food sovereignty and various grassroots land/food movements today, and in this particular sense the struggle can be viewed as a coming to fruition of secular militant traditions. Thus, the five interrelated tasks formulated in the land and freedom movement of the 1970s (c.f. Hobbs, 1976: 136) – protection of the land, production of food, distribution of land, creating new human settlements, and providing for exchange learning of skills and knowledge – constitute a bridge linking centuries-old peasant and anti-colonial movements with today's food sovereignty/agroecology. From this angle, it is the continuity of struggle that is emphasised.

On the other hand, the second aspect of capitalist rule – the chaotic side – might lead us to formulate tasks and organisational approaches in a new way, appropriate to complexity and emergence. Thus, 'environmental direct action, resistance taken from outside the dominant culture, as in protests, blockades and sabotage by indigenous peoples, workers, anarchists and other activist groups, increases dissipation within the coupled system over fast to intermediate scales and pushes for changes in the dominant culture that favor transition to a stable, sustainable attractor' (Werner 2012). 'Attractor' here refers to the way in which chaotic systems acquire a certain ordered configuration. This does not mean an imposed or centralised or artificially unified order, but an emergent self-organisation, which could in turn imply a redefinition of forms of struggle. For example, parallels are noted between the Mexican Zapatistas and the Kurdish PKK in exploring a new paradigm of revolutionary movement closer to principles of social ecology (Stanchev 2015), a development which for some time has been predicted with dread by US thinktanks because such struggles would be emergent and hard to pin down (Biel 2012). It must be stressed that we are not arguing that the 'old left' should be scrapped, simply that an era of a new type – wherein some new system arises from the death throes of the old – implies an exploratory process which in some sense recognises that the chaos unleashed by capitalism, and uncontrollable by it, will be available in strange and unexpected ways as creative raw material for a new age.

Radical popular movements around land/food could be seen as a concrete expression of this historical logic. All modes of production have to be based on nature, the peculiarity of capitalism being simply its failure to recognise this. In this respect, the FAO's belated call for a new agricultural approach from a position of weakness: if radical movements from below are allowed free rein to explore the agroecological paradigm, that paradigm might emerge in threatening ways unacceptable to ruling interests. It is not surprising, then, that the establishment should step in with its own, 'safe' definition; nor is it surprising that popular struggles should in turn continually regenerate (both conceptually and in practice) agroecology and food sovereignty from below, and flesh out their transformative implications.

With the land, it has always been the direct producers who are responsible, both for keeping alive the universal principles of sustainable cultivation (such as biomimicry, intercropping, compost, mulches, succession) and for understanding the micro-characteristics of the particular plot where these are implemented. Land reform, a prolongation of peasant movements and then anti-colonialism, is never only a change of ownership but more profoundly an assertion of stewardship, which in turn is linked to a more decentralised and open-source approach to resources in general, and more specifically of knowledge. In the words of Brian Goodwin: 'The whole metaphor of evolution, instead of being one of competition, conflict and survival, becomes one of creativity and transformation. … Nature as we read it now is a much more complex, coherent and creative type of process than the one we have in our social and economic system' (King 1996). The point of the new attractor is to seek a similarly complex, coherent and creative form for society, and thus bring human and natural systems back together along similar operational lines. The food system forms an excellent point of departure for achieving this.

Notes

1 It is interesting to note here that 'co-operation' is seen as an objective property of physical systems, which hints at how deeply embedded the co-operative principle might be for human futures.

2 As examples the reader could refer to statistics on damage from natural disasters at www.emdat.be/disaster-trends (graph displayed at http://imgur.com/a/KdyTV#4) or the annual frequency of North Atlantic tropical storms at http://climate.org/topics/extreme-weather/index.html.

References

Baranger, M., ND *Chaos, Complexity, and Entropy*, discussion paper, Center for Theoretical Physics, Laboratory for Nuclear Science and Department of Physics, Massachusetts Institute of Technology, at www.necsi.org/projects/baranger/cce.pdf.

Bawden, T., 2012 'Outrage as bank revealed to be major speculator while millions face starvation', *The Independent*, 1 September.

Biel, R., 2000 *The New Imperialism – Crisis and Contradictions in North–South Relations*. London: Zed Books.

Biel, R., 2006 'The interplay between social and environmental degradation in the development of the international political economy', *Journal of World-Systems Research*, 12, 1, http://jwsr.ucr.edu/archive/vol12/number1/pdf/jwsr-v12n1-biel.pdf.

Biel, R., 2012 *The Entropy of Capitalism*, Leiden: E.J. Brill.

Biel, R., 2015a *Eurocentrism and the Communist Movement*. Montreal: Kersplebedeb Publishing.

Biel, R., 2015b 'Food and imperialism' in Ness, I. and Cope, Z. (eds.) *Palgrave Encyclopedia of Imperialism and Anti-Imperialism*.

Cai Wenju, C., Borlace, S., Lengaigne, M., van Rensch, P., Collins, M., Vecchi, G., Timmermann, A., Santoso, A., McPhaden, M.J., Wu, L., England, M.H., Wang, G., Guilyardi, E. and Jin, F.-F., 2014 'Increasing frequency of extreme El Niño events due to greenhouse warming', *Nature Climate Change*, 4: 111–116. www.nature.com/nclimate/journal/v4/n2/full/nclimate2100.html.

Capra, F., 1992 *The Tao of Physics*, 3rd edition. London: Flamingo.

Cusick, J., 2012 'We'll make a killing out of food crisis, Glencore trading boss Chris Mahoney boasts', *The Independent*, 23 August, at www.independent.co.uk/news/world/politics/well-make-a-killing-out-of-food-crisis-glencore-trading-boss-chris-mahoney-boasts-8073806.html.

Darnhofer, I. *et al.*, 2010 'Adaptiveness to enhance the sustainability of farming systems – A review', *Agronomy for Sustainable Development*, 30: 545–555.

Day R.B., 1981 *The 'Crisis'and the 'Crash' – Soviet Studies of the West (1917–1939)*. London: New Left Books.

Drack M., 2008 Ludwig *von Bertalanffy's Early System Approach*, von Bertalanffy Lecture, ISSS Conference, Madison WI, at http://journals.isss.org/index.php/proceedings52nd/article/viewFile/1032/322.

Drury King, R. and Currier, B., 2012 'Food shortages, social unrest and the low-input alternative', *Union for Radical Political Economics Newsletter*, Fall, pp. 10–14.

Elliott, J.E., 1980 'Marx and Schumpeter on capitalism's creative destruction: a comparative restatement', *Quarterly Journal of Economics*, 95(1): 45–68.

Engels, F., 1966 *Die Entwicklung des Sozialismus von der Utopie zur Wissenschaft*. Berlin: Dietz.

Fleetwood, S., 2004 'The ontology of organisation and management studies' in Ackroyd, S. and Fleetwood, S., eds., *Realist Applications in Organisation and Management Studies*. London: Routledge.

Gakou, M.L., 1987 *The Crisis in African Agriculture*, London: United Nations University/Zed Books.

Gharajedaghi, J., 2006 *Systems Thinking: Managing chaos and complexity*. Burlington, MA: Butterworth-Heinemann.

Goodwin, B.C., 1994 *How the Leopard Changed Its Spots: The evolution of complexity*. New York: Charles Scribner's Sons.

Graziano da Silva, J., 2015 *Agriculture must change – FAO Director-General speaks at International Forum on Agriculture and Climate Change*, Paris, 20 February, at www.fao.org/news/story/en/item/278192/icode/.

H.M. Govt. 2011 *Foresight. The Future of Food and Farming: Challenges and choices for global sustainability Final Project Report*. London: The Government Office for Science.

Hegel, G.W.F., 1995 *Lectures on the History of Philosophy*, Volume 1; trans E.S. Haldane. Lincoln, NE: University of Nebraska Press, p. 278ff., at www.marxists.org/reference/archive/hegel/works/hp/hpheraclitus.htm.

Holland, G.J. and Webster, P.J., 2007 'Heightened tropical cyclone activity in the North Atlantic: natural variability or climate trend?', *Philosophical Transactions of the Royal Society A*.

Hopkins, R., 2008 *The Transition Handbook – from oil dependency to local resilience*. Totnes: Green Books.

Ivancevic, V.G. and Ivancevic, T.T., 2007 *High-Dimensional Chaotic and Attractor Systems: A comprehensive introduction*. The Netherlands: Springer.

Kaufman, F., 2011 'How Goldman Sachs created the food crisis', *Foreign Policy*, 27 April.

Keim, B., 2012 'U.S. drought could cause global unrest', at www.wired.com/wiredscience/2012/07/drought-food-prices-unrest.

King, D., 1996 'An interview with Professor Brian Goodwin', *GenEthics News*, Issue 11, March/April, 6–8, at http://ngin.tripod.com/article8.htm.

Korotayev, A.V. and Tsirel, S.V., 2010 'A spectral analysis of world GDP dynamics: Kondratieff Waves, Kuznets Swings, Juglar and Kitchin Cycles in global economic development, and the 2008–2009 economic crisis', *Structure and Dynamics*, 4(1), at http://escholarship.org/uc/item/9jv108xp#page-7.

Lagi, M., Bertrand, K.Z. and Bar-Yam, Y., 2011 'The food crises and political instability in North Africa and the Middle East', *arXiv:1108.2455*, 10 August; see in particular the visual correlation of the data on http://necsi.edu/research/social/img/fig1_crises.pdf.

Lenin, V.I., 1938 [1901–7] 'The agrarian question and the "critics of Marx"', *Selected Works*, Volume XII (Theory of the Agrarian Question), London: Lawrence and Wishart.

Lenin, V.I., 1939 *Imperialism, the Highest Stage of Capitalism*. New York: International Publishers.

Lenin, V.I., 1972 [1914–16] 'Conspectus of Hegel's book The Science of Logic', Lenin *Collected Works*, Vol 38 (Philosophical Notebooks), Moscow: Progress Publishers.

Lipietz, A., 1987 *Mirages and Miracles – The crises of global Fordism*. London: Verso.

Lotta, R. and Shannon, F., 1984 *America in Decline*, Vol 1. Chicago: Banner Press.

Lucas, C., 2005 'Perturbation and transients – the edge of chaos', at www.calresco.org/perturb.htm.

Luxemburg, R., 1913 *Die Akkumulation des Kapitals – eine Beitrag zur Ökonomischen Erklarung des Imperialismus*. Berlin: Paul Singer.

Lyall, S., 2013 'Heat, flood or icy cold, extreme weather rages worldwide', *New York Times*, 10 January, www.nytimes.com/2013/01/11/science/earth/extreme-weather-grows-in-frequency-and-intensity-around-world.html?pagewanted=all&_r=0.

Marx, K., 1954 [1887] *Capital*, Vol. 1. Moscow: Progress Publishers.

Marx, K., 1969 [1865] 'Wages, price and profit', *Marx and Engels Selected Works*, Vol 2. Moscow: Progress Publishers.

McMichael, P., 2009 'A food regime analysis of the "world food crisis"', *Agriculture and Human Values*, 26: 281–295.

Merchant, C., 1980 *The Death of Nature – Women, Ecology and the Scientific Revolution.*, San Francisco, CA: Harper.

Mingers, J., 2011 'The contribution of systemic thought to critical realism' *Journal of Critical Realism*, 10(3): 303–330.

Odum, E.P., 1969 'The strategy of ecosystem development – an understanding of ecological succession provides a basis for resolving man's conflict with nature', *Science*, 164(3877): 262–270, at http://habitat.aq.upm.es/boletin/n26/aeodu.en.html.

Pierce, F., 2015 'Over a barrel', *New Scientist*, 3004, 17 January.

Potter, C. and Tilzey, M., 2005 'Agricultural policy discourses in the European post-Fordist transition: neoliberalism, neomercantilism and multifunctionality', *Progress in Human Geography*, 29(5): 581–600.

Prigogine, I., 2003 *Is Future Given?*. Singapore: World Scientific.

Prigogine, I. and Stengers, I., 1984 *Order out of Chaos*. London: Heinemann.

Scharf, C., 2012 *Gravity's Engines – the Other Side of Black Holes*. London: Allen Lane.

Schubert, C., 2013 'How to evaluate creative destruction: reconstructing Schumpeter's approach', *Cambridge Journal of Economics*, published online 22 January.

Schumpeter, J., 1976 [1943] *Capitalism, Socialism and Democracy, 5th Edition*. London: George Allen & Unwin.

Slaikeu, K.A., 1990 *Crisis Intervention: A Handbook for Practice and Research*. Boston, MA: Allyn & Bacon.

Smolin, L., 2013 *Time Reborn*. London: Allen Lane.

Stanchev, P., 2015 'From Chiapas to Rojava: seas divide us, autonomy binds us', *ROAR* Magazine, 17 February, at http://roarmag.org/2015/02/chiapas-rojava-zapatista-kurds/.

Teed Rockwell, W., 2005 *Neither Brain Nor Ghost: A Nondualist Alternative to the Mind-brain Identity*. Cambridge, MA: MIT Press.

Thelen, E., 1989 'Self-organisation in developmental processes – can systems approaches work?', in Gunnar, M.R. and Thelen, E. (eds.), *Systems and Development: The Minnesota Symposia on Child Psychology*, Volume 22. New York: Psychology Press.

Thirsk, J., 1997 *Alternative Agriculture, A History: From the Black Death to the present day*. Oxford: Oxford University Press.

Werner, B., 2012 *Is Earth F**ked? Dynamical Futility of Global Environmental Management and Possibilities for Sustainability via Direct Action Activism*, Discussion paper, Fall Meeting, American Geophysical Union, San Francisco, 3–7 December.

Yeats, W.B., 1963 'The Second Coming', from Michael Robartes *and the Dancer, Collected Poems of W.B. Yeats* London: Macmillan.

10

THE ILLUSION OF GREEN CAPITALISM

Petter Næss

Introduction

In 1987, the UN World Commission on Environment and Development (often referred to as the Brundtland Commission) launched its report *Our Common Future*. With this report, the concept of sustainable development was put on the international political agenda. Distinct from many previous environmental reports, such as the 1972 *Limits to Growth* report by the Club of Rome, the Brundtland Commission (1987) claimed that economic growth and environmental sustainability could be combined. Indeed, "reviving economic growth" was pointed out as one of the "critical objectives" of sustainable development. The Commission underlined that the content of growth must be changed so that it could take place within the limits of what is ecologically sustainable. In line with the parallel discourse on ecological modernization, the Brundtland Commission pointed at eco-efficiency and substitution as the ways to decouple economic growth from negative environmental impacts.

Twenty-five years later, the final declaration of the United Nations Earth Summit on sustainable development in Rio de Janeiro in 2012 (Rio + 20) emphasized "green growth" as a global concept for the future. This was considered an important result, as several countries had until then rejected the idea that a greening of the economy would be conducive to growth. The idea that the pathway toward a sustainable future is continual growth, also in the "developed" countries, was thus strengthened at the Earth Summit.

Before moving on to my main line of argument, let me first make it clear the statements presented in the following about the environmental unsustainability of continual economic growth do not imply that I consider that growth in affluence should never take place for any country, population group, or sector within society. Increased material standard of living is a legitimate aspiration for the world's poor – but not for the rich, given the ecological constraints we are facing. Similarly, growth within certain sectors of society (for example, organic food production for domestic consumption, local/regional public transport services, and renewable energy supply) could be promoted, at least up to a certain level, but in order to be compatible with environmental sustainability this would have to be balanced by a radical shrinking of other sectors (such as meat production, construction of motorways and luxury dwellings, and the oil industry).

This chapter contends that the ideas of green growth and green capitalism are illusory. The idea of green growth is based on flawed conceptions of the diversity of environmental impacts, the possibilities for efficiency-increasing technologies and recycling schemes, and the scope for compensating for growth in the volume of consumption through changes in its composition. At the same time, capitalism depends on growth in order to avoid running into severe crises. In the next section, the main theoretical arguments in favor of the possibility of decoupling economic growth from environmental degradation will be reiterated, and some strategies for decoupling will be described. I will then put forth arguments that the scope for decoupling growth in production and consumption from environmental degradation is limited, and that the decoupling strategy is unable to keep up with unlimited growth. First, I will give some examples of how reduction of the material resource input and environmental load per unit produced can be pursued and what has actually been obtained within different fields of society. Thereupon, theoretical potentials for eco-efficiency will be discussed, including an assessment of recycling as a resource-saving scheme in a growth economy and the prospects of substituting material consumption with consumption where the input of material resources is low compared with the economic value. Arguments will then be put forth about the insufficiency of the frequently mentioned Factor 4 and Factor 10 objectives, seen in a growth perspective beyond our current century. The growth compulsion of capitalism will then be discussed as a plausible main reason for the widespread but illusory belief in unlimited, green growth. A few brief concluding remarks round off the chapter.

Ecological modernization and the idea of decoupling

Historically, economic growth has been closely tied to increasing consumption levels as well as increasing loads on the environment. Unless this trend is broken, growth will lead to steadily aggravated environmental degradation and resource depletion. Moreover, a number of studies indicate that the present level of consumption of natural resources and environmental pollution is already higher than what can physically be sustained in a long term (WWF, 2014). The growth in the consumption of raw materials, energy, and land leads to impoverishment of the natural base, loss of biodiversity, and scarcity of a number of non-renewable natural resources within the foreseeable future. The increasing combustion of fossil fuels contributes to dramatic climate change, unwholesome pollution in urban areas, and damage to vegetation and wildlife. Growth in material resource consumption is not environmentally sustainable at a global scale, and in particular not in wealthy nations if the inequality between rich and poor countries is to be reduced, as recommended by the World Commission on Environment and Development.

Combining environmental sustainability with economic growth would require that the hitherto close connection between economic growth and growth in the consumption of natural resources be broken. Such a disconnection, or "decoupling," which is the most common term used, is a key assumption in the ideology of green growth (OECD, 2002). Decoupling means cutting the link between economic growth and environmental degradation through increased eco-efficiency and substitution. The former refers to the production of commodities of unchanged or better quality while reducing the resource consumption and negative environmental impacts associated with the production and products. Improved technological solutions are the crucial means in order to obtain higher eco-efficiency. Substitution is used as a term for a change in the pattern of consumption from environmentally harmful to less environmentally harmful forms of consumption. Dematerialization is a joint concept including both eco-efficiency and substitution, and refers to a (more or less strong) contribution to decoupling of economic growth from resource consumption and negative environmental impacts.

The belief in the possibility of decoupling economic growth from negative environmental consequences is in particular pronounced within the theory known as ecological modernization (Mol, 1995; Young, 2000). According to this theory, solutions to environmental problems can be found within the context of industrial capitalism. However, the capitalist economy in its present form is limited by the capacity of the natural environment to absorb the effects of economic growth and to supply necessary resource inputs. Resource depletion and recipient overload will in the long term not only undermine natural ecosystems, human health, and quality of life, but also destroy the possibilities for continual economic growth. Capitalism must therefore undergo a process of transformation if it is to be sustainable in the long term. Along with strong efforts in environmentally sound technology development, changes in legislation and tax systems are advocated in order to promote environmental policy integration across sectors and tiers, and to create incentives for market mechanisms to contribute to eco-efficiency. According to ecological modernization theory, society in its present form need not be changed, as pressures from customers, environmental groups, legislators, etc. will force organizations to take environmental responsibility and come up with technological solutions (Strannegård, 1999).

The so called Factor 4 and Factor 10 objectives are often used to concretize the idea of eco-efficiency. The Factor 10 objectives were originally formulated by environmental researchers in order to illustrate the magnitude of the required reductions of resource consumption and environmental load in rich countries, compared with contemporary levels, in order to achieve environmental sustainability (Schmidt-Bleek, 1993). The "factor" thinking was modified by "green capitalism" proponents who instead referred to a reduction of the environmental load and resource consumption per unit produced. Factor 4 came to be used as an objective of "doubling wealth while halving resource use": if the resource consumption and environmental load per unit produced of a commodity or a service can be reduced to one fourth, that is, by a factor 4, then the negative environmental impacts can be halved even if the production is doubled (Von Weizsäcker *et al.*, 1998).

Besides increasing the efficiency of production, the Brundtland Commission (1987) recommended a change in the content of growth by giving priority to the parts of the economy requiring the least amounts of energy and raw materials (i.e. substitution from environmentally harmful to less harmful types of production and consumption). Here, the Commission pointed at the service sector in general, and knowledge production and culture in particular. If you go to ballet performances instead of using your money to buy a second car, or buy books for reading at home in your living room instead of, for example, going on autumn vacation to the Canary Isles, then the environmental load per euro spent will be reduced.

There is an apparent connection between the theory of ecological modernization and the hypothesis of an Environmental Kuznets Curve (EKC) (Stern, 2004). According to this hypothesis, growth in already affluent societies will contribute to improve rather than reduce environmental quality, because increased wealth implies that more money may be spent on the development of environmentally friendly technologies. In this way, technological development in the wealthy part of the world is believed to compensate for the increased environmental load resulting from the industrialization of less affluent countries. Moreover, as people become more affluent, they are also expected to develop more post-materialistic values (Inglehart, 1995), which are in turn assumed to contribute to a substitution of material-intensive consumption with consumption categories involving less material throughput, such as culture, entertainment, and services.

Decoupling so far: at best only partial

Despite the fact that decoupling has been on the sustainability agenda for nearly thirty years, the attempts to compensate, through increased eco-efficiency and substitution, for the increased pressure against the environment resulting from economic growth have only been able to slow down the environmental degradation. Within most sectors, and for most impact categories, the annual environmental load is higher today than thirty years ago, both in total and when measured per capita. The accumulated environmental degradation and resource depletion, for example in terms of concentration of CO_2 in the atmosphere, extinction of species, loss of farmland, and exhaustion of finite energy sources and minerals, are far more extensive today than in 1987 when the Brundtland Commission published its sustainability report.

Admittedly, rising GDP levels accompanied by reduced emissions have been found for certain pollutants at a local scale. However, for a number of other types of environmental impacts there is far less evidence of such decoupling. Minimizing the consequences on one impact category may also sometimes result in increased environmental load on another impact category. According to Spangenberg (2001), no indication of an environmental Kuznets curve can be found when using measures accounting for the total use of energy, materials, and land.

During the period 1974–2013, global CO_2 emissions increased steadily along with economic growth, while there was non-growth or reduction in the emissions in three periods of economic downturn (in the early 1980s, 1992, and 2009). For the first time during the whole forty-year period in which the International Energy Agency has been collecting data on carbon dioxide emission, 2014 showed no increase in CO_2 emissions despite economic growth (IEA, 2015). It remains to be seen whether the 2014 result, which IEA attributes to greater generation of electricity from renewable sources in China, and increased energy efficiency and more renewable energy in OECD countries, will continue. Anyway, zero-growth in CO_2 emissions is far from sufficient in a situation where a reduction of 90 percent or more within the next fifty years is called for in order to avoid "dangerous climate change." Moreover, without the 3 percent global growth in 2014, the emissions would probably have decreased instead of remaining constant, as they did in 2009 when the global economy also had a downturn due to the financial crisis.

In a somewhat older study, Azomahou and Van Phu (2001) investigated economic growth and CO_2 emissions in one hundred countries during the period 1960–1996. Using non-parametric regressions, they found a correlation between economic growth and increased CO_2 emissions among poor countries, middle-income countries, and wealthy countries. Within all three groups of countries, the CO_2 emissions tend to increase with higher gross domestic products.

To the extent that correlations between affluence levels and emissions of some pollutants (notably NO_2, carbon monoxide, and sulfur dioxide) consistent with the EKC hypothesis have been found, this may in part be due to the limitation of many such studies to a confined geographical scale (e.g. cities). According to Stern (2004), the total pollution emissions tend to rise with increasing income rather than follow an inverted U-shaped curve. Pollution concentrations may still follow the curve predicted by the EKC hypothesis due to urban and industrial decentralization, taller smoke stacks, and so forth. Moreover, reduced emission levels in wealthy countries may be a result of outsourcing polluting industries to third world countries. Another case in point is the fact that the emission reductions obtained for impact categories where some evidence for the EKC hypothesis can be found are invariantly resulting from strong governmental regulations. While the EKC hypothesis is often used in the environmental debate to create an image of a "self-regulatory" market economy, the empirical examples referred to in supporting this hypothesis were dependent on precisely the type of regulations that are usually fiercely opposed by its proponents.

The fact that dematerialization to a degree sufficient to counterweigh the impacts of economic growth has not taken place until now does not in itself rule out the possibility for a stronger and more successful dematerialization in the future. The prospects for this still do not seem very promising in the light of the nearly forty-five years that have passed since the publication of the *Limits to*

Growth report, and the nearly thirty years since the publication of the Brundtland report. Decoupling growth from environmental degradation has been on the agenda during the very same period when only partial or local evidence of the EKC hypothesis has been found. Moreover, many of the lowest-hanging fruits have probably been picked in this period. Improving eco-efficiency further will often require technologically more challenging and socially more controversial measures. This may be the reason why some more recent studies indicate that in the longer term, the Environmental Kuznets Curve tends to be N-shaped instead of following the originally hypothesized inverted U shape. This suggests that pollution increases as a poor country becomes industrialized, decreases once a threshold affluence level is reached, and then begins increasing again as national income continues to increase.

In much of the debate about economic growth and decoupling, there has been a tendency to focus solely on emissions of various pollutants (and in recent years a rather one-sided concentration on CO_2 emissions only), whereas negative environmental impacts resulting from land take and land fragmentation have tended to be overlooked. The prospects for decoupling growth from the latter kinds of impacts may be even less bright. This is particularly the case for the direct impacts on biodiversity, natural areas, food-production soil, and landscape qualities from converting undeveloped land into building sites or technical infrastructure such as roads and power plants. The few studies carried out on loss of biodiversity suggest that further economic growth in an already wealthy country or region is accompanied by higher biodiversity losses (Mills and Waite, 2009; Tevie *et al.*, 2011).

Theoretically, it is possible to imagine a "Factor 4" or "Factor 10" reduction of the land use per produced unit by building more densely and higher, as well as placing most of the buildings in areas that are already technically affected, such as traffic areas and derelict industrial estates/brownfields. However, unless the new buildings or infrastructure replace existing, less environmentally favorable parts of the built environment, construction of new, eco-efficient buildings or infrastructure will at best be ecologically friendly in a relative sense, i.e. compared with environmentally more straining solutions (Xue, 2014; see also Chapter 8). In the USA, farmland is reduced ten times faster than the influx of new cultivated land, and in China the reduction of farmland is 30–40 times faster than the supply of new soil for food production (Steigan, 2011). Phosphorus is another natural resource of key importance to food production. According to Cordell *et al.* (2009), the peak of phosphorus production may be reached already within 30–40 years, and the known sources of phosphorus may be exhausted within 50–100 years.

Some of the raw materials used in renewable energy production, such as lithium, are also becoming increasingly scarce (Defra and BIS, 2012). Along with a number of other so-called rare minerals (including beryllium, cobalt, and tantalum) used in computers, mobile phones, aircrafts, communication satellites, and rechargeable batteries, lithium is on the "critical list" identified by a panel of sixty-nine executives of key global companies in seven different industries (PricewaterhouseCoopers, 2011).

Limits to decoupling

What would be required to obtain a decoupling between economic growth and negative environmental impacts strong enough to avoid continual environmental degradation? First, the decoupling would need to be absolute, not only relative (i.e. compared with current practice). The correlation between economic growth and environmental impacts would have to be zero or negative – it would not be sufficient that the correlation remained positive but weaker than before. Second, the absolute decoupling would need to apply to all types of environmental impacts, not only a few selected ones. Decoupling thus would have to encompass not only greenhouse gases and pollutants such as sulfur dioxide, nitrogen oxides, and soot, but also impacts such as loss of species, encroachments on ecosystems, deforestation, loss of soil for food production, and shrinking drinking water resources. Third, and importantly, for several categories of impacts, non-growth of impacts would not be sufficient. This applies, among others, to greenhouse gas emissions, where present annual emissions are way above what would be an environmentally sustainable level. Fourth, institutional frameworks and mechanisms would have to be in place to secure that technical possibilities for decoupling were actually implemented – not only in isolated pilot projects or by particularly motivated actors, but everywhere.

Different categories of environmental impacts may be of different importance for human life and health. Some environmental qualities (such as water) are crucial, whereas others may be important to people's quality of life but not imperative for human survival. Some economists have differentiated between "critical natural capital" and "substitutable natural capital," where the latter category refers to amenities that may be important to many people's quality of life but still not necessities for survival, and hence negotiable against "human-made capital." According to this view, loss of a forest for outdoor recreation could be outweighed by economic gains enabling nearby residents to purchase, for example, new and more advanced smartphones and iPads. Whether or not such a forest should actually be protected would then be a question of willingness-to-pay. All of nature's diversity and richness is thus considered reducible to one category, namely money. However, apart from the severe validity problems of willingness-to-pay investigations (see Chapter 4), the differentiation between "critical" and "substitutable" nature capital is based on an entirely anthropocentric view according to which nature has no value beyond what is useful, enjoyable, or interesting for humans. If we consider (as I do) that nature has value apart from this, and that we have moral responsibilities for other parts of nature than just our own species (Vetlesen, 2011), the idea that ecosystems, biodiversity, and species are substitutable with an increased supply of commodities and services becomes highly problematic.

Limits to eco-efficiency increase

As mentioned above, technical possibilities for more eco-efficient production and consumption would not be sufficient – institutional frameworks securing their implementation would also need to exist. However, such institutional frameworks (for example, legislation, regulations, taxation, and subsidies) for changing the quality of growth are largely absent today. In addition, private enterprises, as well as many politicians, have been strong opponents of the introduction of such institutional arrangements.

More fundamentally, even if institutional frameworks were eventually established, serious doubt may be raised against the possibility of making continuing economic growth environmentally sustainable. In its physical dimension, the economy is an open subsystem of the earth system, which is finite, non-growing, and materially closed (with the exception of the influx of solar energy and occasional solid particles, such as meteorites). As the economic subsystem grows, it incorporates an ever greater proportion of the total ecosystem into itself and must reach a limit toward 100 percent, if not before (Daly, 1993). Institutional arrangements that may change the quality of growth are thus only able to postpone the encounter of ecological limits to economic growth; they cannot enable humanity to trespass such limits.

The so-called cradle-to-cradle strategy has received considerable attention during recent years as a technological pathway to allow environmentally benign economic growth (McDonough and Braungart, 2002). Based on a consistent recycling of waste and large-scale transition toward renewable energy supply, a future society is envisaged where the same resources are used again and again, the energy is supplied from environmentally friendly and renewable sources, and the buildings, instead of being dependent on energy supply from elsewhere, are producing their own renewable energy, and are even able to export a surplus of energy via "smart grid" electricity networks. Some even envisage roads where solar cells produce energy not only for maintenance but also for the propulsion of the vehicles driving on the roads, rendering traffic growth unproblematic from a climate perspective (FEHRL, 2015).

However, even if it were possible to meet the energy demand in buildings and for transportation without negative impacts (which would probably not be the case since, for example, the production of photovoltaic cells and cables depends on scarce minerals, and entails considerable pollution during the production process), the increasing consumption of materials associated with continual growth would hardly be environmentally neutral. With steadily rising numbers of products, buildings, and infrastructure, the circulation rate must also increase continually to secure sufficient input of recycled resources for the growing economy. In practice, this implies that the products, buildings, and infrastructures tying up resources must be taken out of use with a shorter interval each time. In a recycling-based growth economy, innovation will therefore have to address the question of how the lifetime of products and built environments can be reduced (Høyer, 1997). However, recycling is not environmentally neutral; it ties up and consumes energy and material resources, and even more so if the circulation rate is increased. Moreover, many materials begin to fail after a couple of recycling cycles and have to be put to different, less quality-demanding use, or become waste.

In a growth-oriented economy, the lower flows of energy and other resources made possible by higher efficiency tend to be *rebound* because of the quest of the economy for higher flows. Such rebound effects also include increased environmental loads from other activities made possible as a result of reducing an environmentally harmful activity (Nørgaard, 2008). As long as purchasing power remains the same or increases, resource efficiency improvement resulting in money saving is like squeezing the balloon. Avoiding such effects seem impossible unless the purchasing power decreases. Needless to say, this poses a huge challenge to the dematerialization strategy: unless you manage to dematerialize all products, services, and activities of society simultaneously, reduced consumption within one field is likely to be compensated by increased consumption in another field. In a situation with economic growth, the metaphoric balloon is on top of that, pumped up with more and more gas.

Can changing consumption patterns make limitations on consumption volumes unnecessary?

Substituting material consumption with consumption where the input of material resources is low compared with the economic value has been mentioned as a way of sustaining economic growth while avoiding its adverse environmental effects. Replacing energy- and material-intensive types of consumption with consumption of arts and services is often used as an example. If you spend your money on expensive art instead of going for a spring trip to Australia, the environmental load per money spent will be reduced. But how will the owner of the gallery where you buy expensive paintings use the income from these sales? Maybe he will spend the money on a four-wheel-drive SUV, or a trip on a cruise liner. Thus, in order for substitution to bring about a degree of decoupling sufficient to make economic growth environmentally sustainable, it must take place among most members of society, not among only a few environmental enthusiasts. The question then immediately arises: can art and care make up the sought-for bases for eternal economic growth? The fact that the day and night consist of only twenty-four hours may pose a limit: how many novels can one person read during a given time, how many movies or art exhibitions can she watch, and how often would she like to have her hair styled?

Moreover, the resource consumption within the service sector – often described as a less environmentally loading trade – is perhaps not so low after all. Basically, almost all kinds of services represent the results of human labor in connection with some capital asset. Any increase in service activities in order to obtain economic gains would need to be performed without any increase in these service-oriented capital assets if the ecological requirements were to be met (Commoner, 1971). Many of these service businesses are quite transport intensive. The food and beverages served in a restaurant, for example, are often imported from far corners of the world. Even though buying expensive wine at a restaurant ties up money that might have been used to buy gasoline, for example, and the alcoholic content of the wine means that you cannot drive home by car, it is not obvious that the overall environmental load will be lower than if you take the car to the cinema in the evening.

There are significant environment and resource problems linked to the "new" industries as well. In the first place, they are linked to consumption of products. Computers, printers, and so forth, as well as microchips, are increasingly short-lived as new and upgraded models make older models incompatible with network facilities and difficult to have repaired in the event of breakdown. Some of the core material tools of allegedly environmentally benign knowledge industries thus have a very heavy ecological rucksack. Scientific work is also increasingly based on heavily polluting international air travel (Lassen, 2010). Moreover, new scientific knowledge often facilitates extended material consumption, for example through technological development.

Virtual growth?

In addition to arguments emphasizing dematerialization strategies, some economists have posed another and quite peculiar argument in support of the view that a decoupling between economic growth and environmental degradation is possible. According to economic theory, economic growth is a measure of changes in the economic activity, defined as volume times price for all commodities and services. Growth in the economy from one year to another might therefore theoretically be a result of the average price of all commodities and services having increased, without any increase in the volume of goods and services. On this basis some economists have argued that increased economic growth does not necessarily mean increased consumption (Johnson, 1998). This is a purely theoretical argument, however. The fast rise in the stock values of a number of so-called dot.com companies in the late 1990s without any corresponding growth in these companies' substantive assets, and the rapidly increasing market values of dwellings in the years preceding the financial crisis in 2008/2009, may have inspired the idea of an entirely virtual economic growth. Historically, however, economic growth has clearly been linked to increased consumption. The fact that the connection is not necessarily one-to-one does not mean that a complete disconnection between economic growth and consumption will be possible.

Even if it were somehow possible to raise the average price of all goods and services without increasing the total volume of goods and services, two questions arise immediately. First, how will the consumers be able to afford to buy the new, more expensive goods to the same extent as before if there is no substantial basis in the form of increased production? Second, how will those who reap the fruits of the growth in the form of greater affluence use their surplus if it cannot be spent on consumption of goods and services? As far as I can see, the only way in which economic growth could be totally de-coupled from growth in production and consumption of commodities and services is if the increase in monetary values is solely a result of inflation. But what would be the purpose of such a "consumption-less" economic growth? And would this type of "growth" satisfy the requirements of the capitalist economic system?

"Doubling wealth while halving resource use" – but what will happen afterward?

As can be seen above, it may prove highly demanding to achieve a Factor 4 improvement in the average eco-efficiency for all sectors of society. Given an annual growth rate of 2.1 percent (similar to the growth experienced in Western European countries in recent years until the financial crisis), the production will be doubled within thirty-three years. A reduction of resource consumption and the environmental load per produced unit down to one fourth must therefore be obtained within this time horizon in order to reach the goal of halving the total, annual environmental load. But what will happen afterward? For how long will it be possible to compensate for a continual growth in the volume of production by increasing the eco-efficiency?

Those who believe that economic growth can be de-coupled from environmental loads and resource consumption will probably answer that we must become even more proficient in the art of dematerialization. But as growth continues over a long time span, quite dramatic reduction factors will be needed in order to prevent the resource consumption and environmental load from increasing. With a global economic growth rate of 2.1 percent, the world's total production would be eight times higher after one hundred years, sixty-four times higher after two hundred years. And after five hundred years? The absurdity of these examples illustrates how obviously untenable it is to believe that exponential growth in consumption and production can continue infinitely without running into ecological limits. The dogma of the possibility of decoupling growth in production and consumption from exploitation of natural resources and environmental degradation is therefore not valid, at least not in a long-term perspective.

One could, of course, imagine a lower growth rate of, for example, only 1 percent annually, or linear instead of exponential growth (i.e. a stable annual increase in the volume of the economy, which would imply gradually reduced percentages of growth). Such reduced growth would still only postpone the times at which various kinds of ecological and social limits become serious obstacles to continued expansion of the economy (although linear growth would imply considerably lower long-term environmental load, compared with exponential growth). Moreover, as we will discuss below, such reduced growth rates would cause serious difficulties in a capitalist economy.

Fragmented analyses

Typical for neoclassical environmental economics are fragmented analyses, where both the environmental impacts and their causes are looked at in separation from their environmental and social context. For example, economic analyses of the environmental problems related to car traffic and the possibilities of reducing these problems often focus on only one part of the problem (for instance, the emissions from the combustion of fossil fuels) while disregarding other aspects (such as the encroachments on nature and urban environments from road construction in order to facilitate traffic growth, barrier effects, reduced mobility for people who for some reason are not able to drive a car, and so on). Such fragmented analyses are the result of a reductionist approach where the multi-causal situation in open systems is ignored. They tend to result in a relocation of environmental problems (temporally, spatially, and topically) instead of a solution to the problems. Distinct from this fragmented approach, critical realism considers that physical, biological, psychological, psycho-social, socio-economic, cultural, and normative kinds of mechanisms, types of context, and characteristic effects are all essential to the understanding of the phenomena in fields such as the study of environmental problems. It would also be necessary to take into consideration a hierarchy of more macroscopic or overlying and more microscopic or underlying kinds of structures or mechanisms which may be involved in social explanation (Bhaskar and Danermark, 2006).

The belief of neoclassical economics in the possibility of limitless economic growth is a consequence of the separation of mainstream economics from any material context, illustrating the "autistic" character of the dominant parts of the discipline, where the axiomatic assumptions are, so to speak, immune to any corrective inputs from other sciences (Fullbrook, 2004). Neoclassical economics fail to realize the fact that reality is hierarchically stratified, where each higher-level stratum includes the powers and mechanisms of the lower strata, in addition to the new powers and mechanisms emerging at the higher stratum. Such lack of acknowledgment of the dependency of society and the economy on the natural environment is an example of the anthropic fallacy, i.e. the exegesis of being in terms of human being (Bhaskar, 2008: 205). This position feeds the fantasy that there are no ecological or environmental limits to human activities. Such anthropism serves to legitimize the "nature-blindness" of neoclassical economics, in particular its failure to acknowledge any ecological limits to economic growth. Whereas social life cannot be reduced to the powers and mechanisms of lower strata, it still necessarily involves the powers and mechanisms of, among others, physics, chemistry, and biology (Bhaskar, 1998). The assumption of infinite economic growth (and infinite dematerialization) represents a particular kind of "downward conflation" (Archer, 2000), where the powers and mechanisms of the natural world are considered totally controllable by humans as if they were mere epiphenomena of the human world.

Why growth?

Through the preceding examples I have tried to show that the belief that long-term economic growth can be "decoupled" from negative environmental impacts is untenable. Why is this belief still so widespread? Fairclough (2006: 58) characterizes economic growth as "an assumed good" and questioning economic growth as a value as "a scandalous thing to do in most contexts in most countries." According to Bhaskar (1998: 173–174), a set of ideas can be characterized as "ideological" if the set of ideas is false and at the same time more or less necessary for those whose interests would have been threatened if the practices among the population had not been strongly influenced by this belief. So let us see what might have rendered necessary the belief in the possibility of decoupling economic growth from environmental impacts.

Several reasons have been mentioned for the desirability of economic growth (see Chapter 5), including growth as a contribution to quality of life, growth as a measure to reduce poverty, social inequality and social unrest, and growth as a necessity to maintain the health of the economic system.

Although economic growth entailed improved conditions of living for earlier generations, the contribution of continued growth to human need satisfaction, personal development, and happiness in wealthy countries has diminished as the general level of affluence has increased. There is considerable evidence indicating that people will not become happier from consuming ever more commodities and services, once a threshold value has been reached (Easterlin, 2005; Jackson, 2009). Economic growth in rich countries is therefore hardly conducive to the quality of life of their inhabitants, and it is clearly incompatible with meeting the needs of the world's poor and future generations of humans.

According to Max-Neef (1995), quality of life may even begin to deteriorate if growth continues beyond such a threshold level. Growth does not only necessitate increased productivity through technological innovations, we all also have to run faster. At all planes, the growth demands an increasing acceleration of society (Rosa, 2010). In wealthy countries, more and more people find it difficult to keep up with the pace of the steadily faster-rotating carousel. There is a tendency that work becomes limitless and demands our full involvement with life and soul, putting heavy pressure on our physical, psychological, and social resources. Large population groups find themselves worn down, stressed, and suffering from work-related depressions. At the same time, the labor market has become more characterized by increased competition and insecurity due to the proliferation of temporary employment, project terms, and freelance work (Nielsen, 2011).

According to many debaters, economic growth (in wealthy as well as in developing countries) is needed to reduce poverty (Krueger, 2004). Many also hold that inequalities in the affluence levels of different population groups will be reduced as the economy grows. The latter hypothesis was first put forth by the economist Kuznets (and was later extended by environmental economists to the field of environmental protection, cf. above). However, global economic growth has proved to be extremely inefficient in reducing poverty, and has become even less effective during recent years. Between 1990 and 2001, for every $100 increase in the world's average per capita income, only $0.60 contributed to the UN Millennium Development Goal of reducing poverty among those who earn less than $1 a day (Woodward and Simms, 2006).

Since neither contribution to quality of life nor reducing poverty and inequality appears to be a convincing argument for continual economic growth in already wealthy countries, let us move to the third explanation for the strong prioritization of growth policies: the growth imperative of the capitalist economy. According to Marx, expansion is the very essence of capitalism. The capitalist, *qua* historical type, finds his raison d'être in an insatiable toil for more monetary wealth, attainable through a constant growth of the economic system. Marx used the simple formula M-C-M' to illustrate how the locomotive of the capitalist economy is limitless accumulation. In a capitalist economy, all things – raw materials, human labor power, and the products resulting from this work – can be regarded as interchangeable commodities (referred to as C in the formula). To ordinary people, commodities have "use values" enabling us to fulfill various needs and wants. In the capitalist economy, however, commodities have a different principal function: to render possible the conversion of some amount of "exchange value" – or money, M – into a greater amount M'. And, argued Marx, it does not stop here:

> If capital increases from 100 to 1000, then 1000 is now the new point of departure, from which the increase has to begin; the tenfold multiplication; profit and interest themselves become capital in turn. What appeared as surplus value now appears as simple presupposition.
>
> *(Marx, 1993: p. 335)*

A company may have increased its capital one hundred times, yet continued growth remains its main ambition. Companies such as Microsoft and Toyota have expanded their capital tremendously over the last couple of decades, but they are no less growth-hungry today than they were twenty years ago. It is rather the opposite: the profit motive becomes more pronounced compared with other concerns that a company might have, the larger and more faceless the company grows (Nielsen, 2011). The more money-capital rules, the more corporations are removed from contact with nature as an object of care, and the more nature is reduced to mere abstraction (Kovel, 2002).

At an aggregate level, economic growth emerges as a result of the capitalist mode of production, based on the need for each capitalist to make profit and the competition between the capitalists (Gordon and Rosenthal, 2003). Companies are harassed to grow at a rate at least as high as their competitors in order not to lose momentum in the continual race for survival (Nadal, 2010). A firm (or a nation) that wishes to stand still may find that it falls back as its competitors increase their productivity and lower their prices. In addition, inflation implies that money will become steadily worth less unless it is growing. The neoliberal globalization over the past three or four decades has intensified the pressure for competition and created an endless competitive struggle between the world's nations as well as at an individual level. Consumption has increasingly become an individual competition where you have to constantly improve your skills and adapt yourself to changing conditions in order not to fall back. New and continually more demanding norms for socially acceptable levels of consumption are rapidly established (Nielsen, 2011; Sennett, 1999).

Admittedly, capitalism has survived periods when there was little or no economic growth, for example the worldwide recession in the wake of the breakdown of the Wall Street stock market in 1928, and more recently the economic downturn following the 2008 financial crisis. Such periods tend to entail high social instability, including numerous bankruptcies, unemployment, destruction of means of production, poverty, social unrest – and often also war. Non-growth also implies that some regions or countries must become poorer to the same extent as other regions or countries become richer. Needless to say, such a situation will sharpen conflicts over the distribution of wealth, also between nations, and cause increased geopolitical instability.

As can be seen from the above, there is a strong inherent dynamic in the capitalist economy making up a structural imperative of growth. The growth rate in a particular country in a particular year is contingent on the combination of a number of causal powers, such as world trade conditions, the competitiveness of domestic companies compared with foreign companies, national economic policies, etc. But capitalists *tend* to accumulate capital, even though some of them fail to do so and go bankrupt. Productivity increases and technological innovations stimulated by the fierce competition between the capitalists are important elements of the growth dynamics of capitalism, making it possible to avoid the zero-sum game situation (or, in other words, a state of non-growth) where the gains of one capitalist necessarily imply the losses of another capitalist. These technological changes, in their turn, tend to result in a faster exploitation of natural resources and more environmental pollution (although cleaner technologies and more efficient resource utilization may also occur).

Although disagreeing with Marx on a number of other issues, mainstream economic theory agrees on the necessity of economic growth if a capitalist economic system is to maintain its stability. Some economists still deny that a capitalist economy must necessarily expand. The English philosopher and economist John Stuart Mill claimed that capitalism can evolve into a balanced, steady state. This position is shared by some influential growth-critics within the "ecological economy" tradition (for example, Daly and Cobb, 1989). However, zero-growth capitalism would require strong institutional frameworks to prevent capitalists from expanding the scale of the economy. Without such regulations, any capitalists who voluntarily abstained from growth would be ousted by their less gentle counterparts. Moreover, in a non-growing economy, any increase in the wealth of the richest implies a reduced affluence level among the rest of the population. If we want to avoid increasing poverty and social marginalization, strong regulations would need to be in place to counter the spontaneous tendency of the market to concentrate wealth in the hands of the rich as well as to prevent the non-growth situation from creating mass unemployment. Such frameworks would be in inevitable and intense conflict with the individual capitalists as well as the interest organizations of the capitalist class – if the rich cannot get richer, much of the point in being a capitalist would disappear.

There are important psychological mechanisms at work here as well, both among the capitalists and among the general population of a capitalist society. According to Kovel (2002), capitalism selects for mentalities that are recklessly eco-destructive, particularly the desire to win at all costs. Capitalism's relentless competition assures that only the sufficiently self-seeking and ruthless are selected to control the higher ranges of capital. Moreover, in a society characterized by high inequality, relative wealth is a significant determinant of happiness, and the consumption levels of the affluent make up an important trigger for wishes for increased consumption among the less privileged parts of the population (Hirsch, 1976; Bartelmus, 1999).

Concluding remarks

There is a fundamental contradiction between a growth-oriented economic system and long-term environmental sustainability. Since economic growth without growth in the production and consumption of commodities and services is meaningless, while increased production and consumption necessarily involve some natural resource consumption and impacts on the environment, continual economic growth without negative consequences to nature and the environment is an illusion. A decoupling of economic growth from resource depletion and environmental degradation is at best possible only within certain sectors or product types and within relatively short time perspectives.

Yet the health of the capitalist economic system is dependent on the very same growth that inevitably leads to increasing environmental degradation. There is thus a fundamental contradiction between capitalism and environmental sustainability. The dream of a green capitalism is an illusion.

The widespread belief in this illusion is important in order to secure continuous acceptance and support of the capitalist system. Neoclassical economy plays an important role in establishing and maintaining the hegemony of this belief. The assumptions of neoclassical economists about infinite economic growth (and infinite dematerialization) represent a fallacious ontology according to which the powers and mechanisms of the natural world are considered totally controllable by humans as if they were mere epiphenomena of the human world. Fragmented environmental analyses based on a reductionist approach ignoring the multi-causal situations characteristic of open systems also contribute to underestimate the limitations of the dematerialization strategy.

The impacts of growth within a particular sector, geographic area, or period are contingent on the combination of a number of causal powers, for example the local natural conditions, the technologies involved, the lifestyles of the consumers, environmental regulations, and so forth. Within a particular spatial and temporal context, changes in the latter causal powers may produce environmental gains outweighing the increased pressure on the environment resulting from growth. Nevertheless, there is a causal mechanism by which increased production and consumption creates an increased pressure on nature and the environment. Without it, the ecological situation would have been radically different. In the long run, this is likely to be the dominant mechanism, since the natural resources (except solar radiation) are finite, and it is impossible to reduce the average resource consumption and environmental load per unit produced of all products down to zero.

In addition to capitalism's growth imperative, it is difficult to establish the institutional conditions in a capitalist society necessary in order to change the quality of growth in a more environmentally friendly direction. Individual capitalists tend to oppose the constraints on their economic freedom that would be necessary in order to achieve a high degree of eco-efficiency (for example, bans or high taxation on particular materials and products), and collectively the capitalist class has normally been a strong opponent of such policies. Capitalism thus contributes to increase the pressure against nature and the environment both through its growth dynamics and through the tendency of individual capitalists to resist the introduction of institutional frameworks necessary to obtain collective benefits, including the realization of potentials for dematerialization. In a society where the production is determined through democratic political decisions instead of profits, the introduction of such institutional frameworks will theoretically be more attainable. However, not even in such a society will a de-coupling of economic growth – defined as growth in the total monetary value of all commodities and services – from growth in negative environmental impacts be possible. Provided that the society in question is democratic and not totalitarian, there may be improved opportunities for growth in knowledge, skills, human care, and solidarity, and growth in such qualities does not need to consume natural resources or reduce environmental qualities. However, such growth is something quite different from GDP growth.

References

Archer, M.S. (2000). *Being Human. The Problem of Agency*. Cambridge: Cambridge University Press.

Azar, C., Holmberg, J., and Karlsson, S. (2002). *Decoupling – Past Trends and Prospects for the Future*. Gothenburg: Chalmers.

Azomahou, T. and Phu, N. (2001). *Economic Growth and CO2 Emissions: A Nonparametric Approach*. Leuven: Université catholique Louvain.

Bartelmus, P. (1999). *Economic Growth and Patterns of Sustainability*. Paper No. 98, Wuppertal Institute, Wuppertal, Germany.

Bhaskar, R. (1998). *The Possibility of Naturalism: A Philosophical Critique of the Contemporary Human Sciences*. Third Edition. London and New York: Routledge.

Bhaskar, R. (2008). *Dialectic: The Pulse of Freedom*. London and New York: Routledge.

Bhaskar, R. and Danermark, B. (2006). Metatheory, interdisciplinarity and disability research – a critical realist perspective. *Scandinavian Journal of Disability Research*, 8: 278–297.

Brundtland Commission (1987). *Our Common Future*. Oxford and New York: Oxford University Press.

Commoner, B. (1971). *The Closing Circle: Nature, Man and Technology*. New York: Alfred Knopf.

Cordell, D., Drangert, J., and White, S. (2009). The story of phosphorus. Global food security and food for thought. *Global Environmental Change*, 19: 292–305.

Daly, H.E. (1993) Sustainable growth: an impossibility theorem. In Daly, H.E. and Townsend, K.N. (eds.), *Valuing the Earth: Economics, Ecology, Ethics*. Cambridge, MA: Massachusetts Institute of Technology.

Daly, H.E. and Cobb, J.B. (1989). *For the Common Good*. Boston, MA: Beacon Press.

Defra and BIS (2012). *Resource Security Action Plan: Making the most of valuable materials*. London: Department for Environment Food & Rural Affairs.

Easterlin, R.A. (2005). Feeding the illusion of growth and happiness: A reply to Hagerty and Veenhoven. *Social Indicators Research*, 75(3): 429–443.

Fairclough, N. (2006). *Language and Globalization*. London and New York: Routledge.

FEHRL (2015). *Forever Open Road. Redefining road transport for the 21st century*. Woluwe-Saint-Lambert: Forum of European National Highway Research Laboratories. Accessed June 25 at www.youtube.com/watch?v=AKuoO3nG5iM&feature=player_embedded.

Fullbrook, E. (2004). Broadband versus narrowband economics. Introductory chapter in Fullbrook, E. (ed.), *A Guide to What's Wrong With Economics*. London: Anthem Press.

Gordon, M.J. and Rosenthal, J.S. (2003). Capitalism's growth imperative. *Cambridge Journal of Economics*, 27(1): 25–48.

Hirsh, F. (1976). *Social Limits to Growth*. New York: Harvard University Press.

Høyer, K.G. (1997). Recycling: issues and possibilities. In Brune, D., Chapman, D., Gwynne, M.O., and Pacyna, J.M. (eds.), *The Global Environment: Science, Technology and Management*, Vol 2. Weinheim, Germany: VCH Publ.

Inglehart, R. (1995). Public support for environmental protection: objective problems and subjective values in 43 societies. *Political Science and Politics*, 28: 57–71.

IEA (2015). *Global energy-related emissions of carbon dioxide stalled in 2014*. Paris: International Energy Agency. Accessed June 18, 2015 at www.iea.org/newsroomandevents/news/2015/march/global-energy-related-emissions-of-carbon-dioxide-stalled-in-2014.html.

Jackson, T. (2009). *Prosperity Without Growth: Economics for a finite planet*. London: Earthscan.

Johnson, B. (1998). Institutional learning and clean growth. In Tylecote, A. and Van der Straaten, A. (eds.), *Environment, Technology and Economic Growth*. Cheltenham: Edward Elgar.

Kovel, J. (2002). *The Enemy of Nature: The end of capitalism or the end of the world?* London, New York, Canada: Zed Books/Fernwood Publishing.

Krueger, A. (2004). *Letting the Future In: India's continuing reform agenda*. Keynote speech to Stanford India Conference, 4 June.

Lassen, C. (2010). Environmentalist in Business class: an analysis of air travel and environmental attitude. *Transport Reviews*, 30(6): 733–751.

Marx, K. (1993) *Grundrisse: Foundations of the critique of political economy*. Harmondsworth: Penguin.

Max-Neef, M. (1995). Economic growth and quality of life: a threshold hypothesis. *Ecological Economics*, 15, 115–118.

McDonough, W. and Braungart, M. (2002). *Cradle to Cradle: Remaking the way we make things*. New York: North Point Press.

Mills, J.H. and Waite, T.A. (2009). Economic prosperity, biodiversity conservation, and the environmental Kuznets curve. *Ecological Economics*, 68: 2087–2095.

Mol, A. (1995). *The Refinement of Production. Ecological modernization theory and the chemical industry*. Dublin: International Books.

Nadal, A. (2010). Is de-growth compatible with capitalism? *Triple Crisis*, 15 July. Accessed 23 July 2010 at http://triplecrisis.com/is-de-growth-compatible-with-capitalism.

Nielsen, P. (2011). *Velstandssamfundet* (Affluence society). Frederiksberg: Frydenlund.

Nørgaard, J.S. (2008). Avoiding rebound through a steady-state economy. In Horace Herring, H. and Sorrell, S. (eds.), *Energy Efficiency and Sustainable Consumption: Dealing with the Rebound Effect*, pp. 204–223. Basingstoke: Palgrave Macmillan.

OECD (2002). *Indicators to Measure Decoupling of Environmental Pressure from Economic Growth.* Paris: OECD.

Pricewaterhouse Coopers (2011). *Rare Earth Metals Scarcity: A "Ticking Time Bomb" for the World?, Asks PwC.* Accessed 19 June 2015 at http://press.pwc.com/GLOBAL/2011-News-releases/rare-earth-metals-scarcity-a-ticking-time-bomb-for-the-world-asks-pwc/s/7d5f3c30-79e8-4604-a4af-fd7d2de97b2c.

Rosa, H. (2010). *High-Speed Society: Social acceleration, power, and modernity.* State College, PA: Penn State University Press.

Schmidt-Bleek, F. (1993). *Wieviel Umwelt braucht der Mensch – MIPS, das Mass für oekologisches Wirtschaften.* Basel/Boston/Berlin: Birkhaeuser.

Sennett, R. (1999). *Det fleksible Menneske eller arbejdets forvandling og personlighedens nedsmeltning* (The flexible human or the transition of work and meltdown of personality). Høbjerg: Hovedland.

Spangenberg, J. (2001). The Environmental Kuznets Curve: A methodological artefact? *Population and Environment*, 23: 175–191.

Steigan, P. (2011). *Sammenbruddet* (The breakdown). Oslo: Spartacus.

Stern, D.I. (2004). The rise and fall of the Environmental Kuznets Curve. *World Development*, 32(8): 1419–1439.

Strannegård, L. (1999). *Black-boxing Eco-modernization. Nature and market discourses in leadership practice.* Stockholm: Centre for Advanced Studies in Leadership.

Tevie, J., Grimsrud, K.M., and Berrens, R.P. (2011). Testing the Environmental Kuznets Curve Hypothesis For Biodiversity Risk In the US: a spatial econometric approach. *Sustainability*, 3: 2182–2199.

Vetlesen, A.J. (2011). Technology, nature and ethics. In Bhaskar, R., Høyer, K.G., and Næss, P. (eds.), *Ecophilosophy in a World of Crisis: Critical realism and the Nordic contributions*, pp. 25–43. London and New York: Routledge.

Von Weizsäcker, E.U., Lovins, A.B., and Lovins, H.L. (1998). *Factor Four: Doubling wealth, halving resource use – a report to the Club of Rome.* London: Earthscan.

Woodward, D. and Simms, A. (2006). *Growth isn't working. The unbalanced distribution of benefits and costs from economic growth.* Series: Re-thinking Poverty 1. London: New Economics Foundation.

WWF (2014). *Living Planet Report 2014: Species and spaces, people and places.* Brussels: World Wildlife Foundation.

Xue, J. (2014). *Economic Growth and Sustainable Housing: An Uneasy Relationship.* London and New York: Routledge.

Young, S.C. (ed.) (2000). *The Emergence of Ecological Modernization: Integrating the environment and the economy?* London: Routledge.

11

CHINA AT THE CROSSROAD

Ecological modernization or ecosocialism?

Jin Xue

Introduction

The development in the history of modern China has been hailed in terms of poverty reduction and an increase in average living standard. This success has not been achieved without social and environmental costs. Widely acknowledged by the Communist Party of China is that the past development path is not environmentally sustainable and socially just, and there is an urgent call for change in the development trajectory. The need for changes is driven by multiple crises and challenges the country is facing, such as the resource limits to rapid economic growth, severe environmental pollution, polarization and inequality, political corruption, a moral decay in public life, food safety issues, and an aging population. China, as the most populous country, has become the world's largest economy and carbon emitter. Thus, the path that China will choose to respond to these crises and to move forward will bear a global significance. China's reforms since the 1970s have followed a development trajectory of the North and attempted at an integration into the global hegemony, both economically and culturally. However, when the global North is suffering from social, economic, and political crises as now, it is pertinent to ask whether China should continue to pursue the same development path. In addition, the finite natural resources are a real constraint that will have considerable influence on how the country can choose its future development.

In this chapter, I use the National Functional Zones Planning (NFZP) (National Development and Reform Commission of China, 2011) to illustrate that China's continuous reforms attempt to pursue the ecological modernization paradigm. I follow this with an analysis and critique of the pursuit of this paradigm as a hegemonic development path to sustainability in the Chinese context. Instead, I argue that economic degrowth in the affluent parts of China and a transformation toward an ecosocialist paradigm across the country is a precondition for obtaining long-term environmental and social sustainability nationally and globally. Lastly, I explore the socio-economic-political conditions enabling or hindering the ecosocialist restructuring.

China's development path: from a trickle-down strategy to ecological modernization

China's development strategy since the economic reform in 1978 can be characterized as a typical "trickle-down" policy, which encourages a proportion of the population and certain regions to become rich, assuming that those initially left out will catch up later. The country's limited resources and growth-stimulating measures have therefore been devoted to a few selected cities in the eastern coastal areas (Yao and Zhang, 2001). Specifically, from the late 1970s to the beginning of the 1990s, five cities were selected as special economic zones and fourteen cities were designated as coastal cities of open economy.[1] These cities were given preferential policies to encourage foreign investment. Some of these cities have gradually grown into metropolitan areas and evolved into national or regional growth centers making a vast contribution to the growth of the national economy.

After three decades of unprecedented economic growth and urbanization, despite a rising average affluence level, China is now in the predicament of resource scarcity, environmental degradation, and social inequality (Kanbur and Zhang, 2005). The trickle-down policy is not as effective as the central government had expected. Although absolute poverty across the country has been largely eradicated, the fruits of growth have not been evenly distributed among population groups and across regions. The Gini coefficient, which measures the inequality of pre-tax market income, demonstrated an increasing trend from 0.28 to 0.52 during the period 1980–2013 (Cevik and Correa-Caro, 2015). Inequality in China is not only confined to income but also applies to availability of educational resources, medical care, and a number of social welfares. Generally, the beneficiaries are those living in cities along the eastern coastline, where wealth is concentrated and polarized, accompanying an average higher per capita consumption levels and a widening gap with populations in impoverished regions in the inland and western China.

Accompanying massive increase in economic growth and living standards is a range of severe environmental problems, including resource depletion, urban water and air pollution, desertification, deforestation, biodiversity loss, soil erosion, cropland losses, ecological degradation, and, not least, greenhouse gas emissions. Environmental problems to some extent have been addressed in the process of economic growth tracing back to the early 1970s, several years before China's economic reform. Huan (2010) identified three phases of political ecologies responding to environmental problems in China, which are "environmental protection national policy from 1978 to 1991," "sustainable development strategy from 1992 to 2001," and "scientific concept of development since 2002." Despite the political discourse and strategies for environmental protection, the country's overall natural environment has been severely degraded, demand on resources increased, and pollution escalated.

In the face of the environmental and social crises in recent years, a shift can be observed on the Chinese political agenda. This shift reflects the central government's desire to address issues of sustainability, equity, and citizens' livelihood apart from maintaining economic growth. China's state government was trying to set a lower economic growth rate (for example, a reduced target for gross domestic product (GDP) growth of 7 percent for 2015), and to embrace more comprehensive goals which address changing economic structures, building an equitable society, and reducing environmental impacts. This overall shift can be illustrated by analyzing the National Functional Zones Planning issued in 2011 (National Development and Reform Commission of China, 2011). As strategic planning for national territorial development, NFZP represents the first of its kind in China's modern history. It is legally binding for local authorities, and is supposed to play an important role in forming a territorial spatial pattern that promotes the harmonious development between people, economy, and resources in the long run.

NFZP sets out the idea of pursuing efficient, balanced, and sustainable regional development through dividing the country's territory into four types of development zones. Within this frame, the spatial, economic, demographic, and land-use strategies are made for each zone. The four types of development zones, their key functions, and development principles are listed in Table 11.1.

For city regions designated by NFZP as development zones to be optimized, enhancing competitiveness to become a global player is emphasized as the goal of development. The government will change its role from growth stimulation to growth management focusing on enhancing the quality of growth. In order to achieve sustainability while remaining competitive, these city regions are expected to change the mode of economic growth by upgrading economic structures to less environmentally polluting and resource-intensive sectors and developing eco-efficiency technologies. Traditional industries will be outsourced to the lagging-behind regions. To achieve green growth, spatial planning strategies should contain urban sprawl, population growth, industrial areas, and scattered development of economic development zones; enlarge space for service sectors, transport, residences, and public infrastructures; promote compact land-use structure; and protect farmland and open areas between cities.

In NFZP, those areas designated as key development zones are located where the economy has been less developed but where there nevertheless exists the potential for further economic growth. Their goal is to accelerate industrialization and urbanization, through attracting industries outsourced from developed countries and the zones to be optimized. Growth stimulation continues to be the first priority, with the purpose of developing into the new growth centers in the country so as to shrink the gap in the affluence level among regions. In terms of spatial development, the plan allows for urban growth to accommodate the growth in urban population, manufacture, service sectors, transport, residences, and public facility in order to facilitate the process of industrialization.

TABLE 11.1 Types of development zones, functions, and development principles designated by NFZP (2011)

	Cover areas	*Functions*	*Development principles*
Development zone to be optimized	Three city regions along the coastal line, which are economically well developed[a]	Key regions for lifting the country's international competitiveness: • Locomotive of national social and economic development • Regions of national innovation • Influential regions capable of participating in global division of labor • Economic and population concentration area	• Upgrade economic structure and develop green economy • Optimize spatial structure, contain urban sprawl and industrial areas • Contain population size • Optimize spatial distribution of infrastructures • Optimize ecological patterns
Key development zone	Cities in middle and western part of China with potential for economic growth and concentrating population	• National economic growth center • Pivot that enhances balanced regional development • Economic and population concentration area	• Enlarge urbanized area • Speed up population concentration • Develop modern industries • Improve infrastructures • Protect the environment
Limited development zone	Major production areas of agricultural products, and areas with key ecological function	• Provide agricultural products • Important areas guaranteeing national ecological safety	• Limit extensive and intensive industrialization and urbanization
Prohibited development zone	Areas with representative ecological systems, endangered species, and valuable natural and cultural heritage	• Key conservation areas of national natural and cultural resources • Gene pool of endangered species	• Prohibit extensive and intensive industrialization and urbanization

[a] The three city regions are Bohai Economic Rim (economic hinterland surrounding Beijing and Tianjin), Yangzi River Delta region, and Pearl River Delta region.

Through this instrument of NFZP, the Chinese government aims to develop an efficient, balanced, and sustainable economy by 2020. It thus hopes to reduce inequality by extending economic growth from the east and south to the west and north, forming an economically and spatially polycentric structure. "Efficient" is interpreted in the NFZP as increasing the efficiency of space utilization measured as GDP per unit of urbanized area and population density. Compared with small-scale and scattered development, concentration of economic activities and population will be beneficial to pollution management and resource conservation. Harmonious development is assumed to be achieved through reconciling economic activities with the demographic distribution and the carrying capacity of the natural environment.

The plan clearly illustrates a departure from a single-minded pursuit of economic growth and a shift to a more comprehensive development strategy addressing environmental and social issues. Nevertheless, economic growth maintains its hegemonic position as indispensable to environmental and social sustainability. It can be said that China's development strategy follows the ecological modernization paradigm.

Ecological modernization tries to reconcile economic, environmental, and social sustainability within the capitalist organization of production and consumption. The adherents of ecological modernization believe that "there is no principle or theoretical argument making a 'modern' organization of production and consumption and its technology antithetical to sustainability" (Spaargaren, 2000). Key assumptions of the paradigm of ecological modernization are as follows:

1. It is necessary to institutionalize ecologically rational actions into the central social institutions of modernity (such as the economic sphere, the political sphere, the cultural sphere, etc.), i.e. we are required to "ecologize the economy."
2. Modern science and technology are central institutions for the environmentally induced rationalization of production and consumption (Fisher and Freudenburg, 2001; Jänicke, 2008). Environmentally friendly technologies are the main solutions to environmental problems.
3. Innovation and diffusion of eco-efficiency technologies should be carried on by economic agents through market forces, while the state takes the role of "enabler," providing incentives, standards, and regulations.
4. Ecologizing the economy through market mechanisms requires economizing environmental goods by placing economic values on the environment, characterized as the "economizing of ecology."
5. The above points suggest cooperation between business, government, and social movements in the decision-making process.

Indeed, NFZP explicitly states that "the building-up of the *development zone to be optimized* and *key development zone* relies on the market mechanisms" (National Development and Reform Commission of China, 2011). However, the question is: are ecological modernization policies capable of obtaining an ecologically and socially sustainable society all over the whole country, given the specific Chinese conditions?

Limits of ecological modernization as a path to sustainability

The discussion on the limits of ecological modernization as a path to sustainability will start from an ontological critique on this model and move to the specific conditions and challenges China is facing. Gowdy and O'Hara (1997) proposed a model of hierarchies of sustainability in the complex system composed by economy, humans, and nature, as shown in Figure 11.1. They consider the market economy to be a subsystem of the larger human world containing institutions, customs, social norms, historical contexts, and so forth. Furthermore, they see the human world as only a part of the even larger biophysical system. This model is commensurable with the critical realist concept of the stratification of reality, and precludes any reductionist analysis in dealing with economic, social, and environmental crises. A two-fold implication can be derived from this model.

First, the economic system relies on the natural environment. This is manifested through utilization of natural resources as a factor of production and emission of pollution into the natural environment. In accordance with the second law of thermodynamics, in any transformation of matter-energy there is always a tendency to increase in entropy (disorder), i.e. less useful energy to be available; hence, any economic activity cannot avoid production of pollution which needs to be assimilated by the natural environment (Georgescu-Roegen, 1981). The second law of thermodynamics also implies that any economic activity causes irreversible change in nature, and that 100 percent recycling is impossible. This phenomenon is more significant in a growing economy. Therefore, for several reasons, economic growth has a tendency to degrade the environment. The notion of decoupling economic

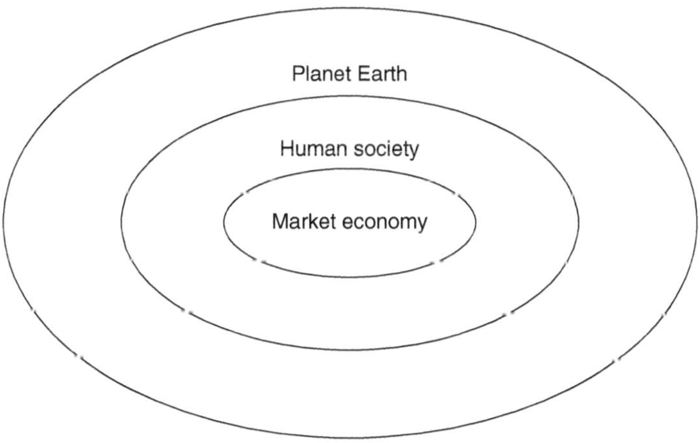

FIGURE 11.1 Hierarchies of sustainability
Source: Gowdy and O'Hara (1997)

growth from environmental degradation or dematerializing economic growth is thus a delusion (Nørgaard, 2009).

Second, this model demonstrates that resolving social problems (for example, social inequality) within the economic sphere by committing to economic growth only is a reductionism. The lower-order level has laws and powers at its own stratum that cannot be accounted for by the higher-order level (Bhaskar, 1975/2008). Therefore, the social problems cannot be solved solely by resorting to the economic sphere. This reductionist approach may explain the failures of the trickle-down strategy in reducing social inequality in China. Solutions should be found at the social sphere, for example social policies targeting the poor directly. This is particularly necessary in a society dominated by a capitalist market economy, because capital always seeks more profits and lets the profits accrue to the rich more than the poor.

These criticisms of ecological modernization in obtaining long-term sustainability apply not only to capitalist societies, which have an in-built growth compulsion (Gordon and Rosenthal, 2003; Fotopoulos, 2010; Harvey, 2010), but also to any growing economy in whatever societal paradigms (for example, productivist socialism), as the fundamental conflict lies between endless economic growth and environmental protection.

I have argued elsewhere that for global ecological sustainability, there is a limit to growth in the affluence level that China can reach (Xue *et al.*, 2012). That is mainly due to the country's large population. To use the estimates of the Global Footprint Network (2016), if China were to reach the average level of consumption and resource use efficiency of high-income countries in 2012, measured against ecological footprint per capita, then the total footprint of humanity would increase by 20 percent and we would need about two planets to maintain our consumption level (carbon footprint included). Due to the limited resources available within the borders of China, 57 percent of the total demand would have to be provided by the rest of the world. This means that, even though China may obtain a high eco-efficiency by following the ecological modernization model, the environmental gains from eco-efficiency would be counteracted by the high consumption level, resulting in huge pressure on the global environment.

As illustrated by certain indicators, some Chinese cities (those in the economically developed eastern area) have been able to couple economic growth with gains in sustainability (Urban China Initiative, 2012). Through an investigation of 112 Chinese cities, a positive correlation between income and environmental sustainability index is found, in line with the Environmental Kuznets Curve hypothesis (ibid.). There is, therefore, a tendency to draw the conclusion that China is heading for the decoupling between economic growth and environmental degradation. Nevertheless, a closer inspection finds that an increase in the environmental sustainability index, in the form of environmental impacts per unit of GDP, merely means an increase in eco-efficiency, hardly suggesting a decline in aggregate environmental impacts, i.e. absolute decoupling. Thus, a higher environmental sustainability index can only indicate that environmental impacts do not increase as fast as economic growth, which is relative decoupling. Economic growth in the already rich cities is still at the cost of environmental quality and resources, however with lower environmental costs than before due to efficiency improvement. This general conclusion is supported by an in-depth study on the housing sector in an affluent Chinese city, Hangzhou. Residential energy consumption and land use in Hangzhou in the past twenty years have increased, but at a slower rate than GDP growth in that building energy efficiency has been increased considerably (Xue, 2012).

That which is often taken as evidence of improvements in the environmental quality often takes place at the local level, for example reduction in water and air pollution. However, such improvements may have been achieved by outsourcing polluting industries to less developed regions. When measured at the national level, overall environmental impact has increased, despite localized improvements. To invoke Georgescu-Roegen's term, if total entropy will increase along with economic growth, increase in order in some places would imply more increase in entropy in other places. For some categories of environmental impacts, their effect is relatively minor at the local level, but they nevertheless have global consequences, such as the effect of greenhouse gas emissions on climate change. The ecological modernization model has shown little success at this level, as, for example, global CO_2 emissions have not been reduced despite attempts to do so (Galeotti *et al.*, 2006).

The aforementioned study of Chinese cities also points out that the correlation between eco-efficiency improvement and economic growth is not as strong in high-income cities as in low-income cities (Urban China Initiative, 2012). It indicates that growth in wealth in already rich cities may no longer expect further gains in sustainability. This can be attributed to the existence of more opportunities for achieving eco-efficiency when a city first sets out on a program of sustainability. Therefore, continual growth in rich cities or regions cannot be obtained without further degrading the natural environment. The idea that continual growth in wealthy cities would not undermine the future growth in the impoverished regions is implausible, if the national-scale environmental load is to be kept within acceptable limits.

Development in the rich regions has already exceeded their bioregion's capacity. It is because the Chinese state is aware of this that NFZP aims to avoid further population immigration, and encourages outsourcing resource-intensive industries in these cities. No doubt, the plan represents a departure from the previous strong commitment to economic growth in the decades since the 1970s. However, it remains committed to the growth paradigm, seeking a combination of competitiveness, equity, and sustainability. One strategy for these affluent regions for green growth is to convert the economy away from the material production of goods toward the service sectors, a substitution that is usually claimed to be less environmentally harmful. However, the environmental consequences of the service sectors are argued to be not as low as expected (Heiskanen and Jalas, 2003).

The above discussion has shown the limitations of ecological modernization for sustainability as a model *per se*, and as a pathway to sustainability in the Chinese context. Although it seems likely that some growth will be necessary to reduce poverty, there are simply not enough resources to support unrestricted growth for the country as a whole. A more viable model than ecological modernization for ecological restructuring of China based on the acknowledgment of ecological constraints is needed.

Ecological restructuring of China

In this section, I will explore how ecosocialism and degrowth can provide a viable model for China's ecological restructuring in a foreseeable future. An ecosocialist and degrowth society is first introduced with a discussion on its plausibility by drawing on the critical realist concept of four-planar social being, followed by an analysis of the Chinese socio-economic-political conditions enabling or hindering the ecosocialist and degrowth transformation.

Ecosocialism and degrowth

Ecosocialism is an ideological and theoretical field associated with Marxism and thus fundamentally challenges capitalist productivism. In contrast to ecological modernization, ecosocialists believe that ecodestruction is inherent within capitalism due to its relentless capital accumulation, which exploits nature wantonly, regardless of the long-term effects on the ecosystem's sustainability. If ecological breakdown is to be avoided, an ecologically viable alternative – socialism – should replace the capitalist mode of production, its institutions, and worldview (Kovel, 2007). Ecosocialism "seeks to subordinate exchange-value to use-value, by organizing production as a function of social needs and the requirements of environmental protection" (Löwy, 2005). Ecological rationality, rather than market rationality, becomes the principle of socio-economic organization, which implies that the economy must be integrated into the ecological, the social, and the political. As a society becomes embedded with ecological values, ecosocialism acknowledges ecological limits to growth, and insists that production should stay within these limits. As such, ecosocialism also criticizes productivist socialism that ignores the biosphere's limits. Production in an ecosocialist society is motivated by the satisfaction of social needs rather than driven by profit maximization. According to ecosocialist thought, a precondition for realizing ecological production is the collective ownership of the means of production, and democratic planning through which the society decides investment and production priorities. Radical changes should also be made to the consumption culture. Human needs should be altered toward authentic needs, and a capitalist consumerism based on hyperconsumption and positional goods should be abandoned (Löwy, 2007). As such, ecosocialism proposes a new civilization that is more humane and respectful of nature.

Highly relevant to the ecosocialist societal model is the concept of "degrowth." Degrowth is first and foremost a critique of growth as a social objective, and challenges the imaginary associating human progress with only growth. Instead, advocates of degrowth believe that human prosperity is possible without economic growth (Jackson, 2009). Partly as a response to the global ecological crisis, degrowth aims to reduce the society's throughput of resource and environment pollution to a level that is within the earth's biocapacity, through an equitable downscaling of production and consumption. The reduction in consumption level should first take place in the North, which will liberate ecological space for growth in the South. Underlying this are the moral premises of intra- and inter-generational equity (Xue *et al.*, 2012). Beyond that, degrowth emphasizes building a society with different socio-economic structures, values, and lifestyles. Degrowth, therefore, confronts the capitalist system, which has a growth imperative, and unavoidably increases impacts on the environment (Kallis *et al.*, 2015; Latouche, 2009).

It can be seen that ecosocialism and degrowth converge in many aspects. Both argue for a revolutionary change in society, downplay the importance of institutions of money, property, and market, and seek for a green, caring, and communal society. The difference may lie in how the role of state is conceived in the ecological restructuring. Early debates on degrowth tend to advocate institutional decentralization and self-government as a future sustainable society, while ecosocialists emphasize the importance of interference of the state in steering the restructuring. Nowadays, a multi-scalar transformation strategy is also addressed by some key degrowth proponents (Asara *et al.*, 2015). For several reasons, I consider the emphasis on state interference and multi-scalar strategy to be a more plausible alternative.[2]

In a world dominated by economic thinking and its ideological carrier of consumerism compelled by the need for endless capital accumulation, creating an alternative socio-economic paradigm is the only solution to replace the productive forces of capitalism driven by market dynamics and to eradicate the roots of the crises (Sarkar, 2010). In critical realist terms, ecosocialism provides a societal paradigm that takes into account the four planes of social being, therefore prefiguring the potentials of building up an environmentally benign and just human society.

According to Bhaskar (1993/2008), the four planes are: (a) material transactions with nature; (b) inter-/intra-subjective relations; (c) social institutions and structures; and (d) subjectivity of the agent. These four planes constitute a laminated and interrelated system. Each stratum should be situated in the context of the four planes. Ecosocialism respects nature, and acknowledges the reliance of human society on the natural environment. The acknowledgement of plane (a) leads to the prioritization of an ecocentric mode of production featured by collective ownership of the means of production and the dominance of ecocentric ethics over profiteering (b, c). As new property relations liberate labor from being a commodity for sale on the market, halt producers' alienation from nature, and eradicate the structural growth necessity, use value will predominate exchange value. This facilitates a transition along which consumerism will be significantly reduced and eventually vanish (d). This is in stark contrast to the capitalist market economy and its variants of neoliberalism, which, through promoting market forces, degrades the environment, precludes humans' real concern for nature (except its instrumental use), and distorts the real meaning of life (except materialism and consumerism).

Socio-economic-political conditions for the ecosocialist and degrowth transformation

If applied to China, ecosocialism and degrowth will constitute a more radical alternative to the dominant political ecology of ecological modernization. However, as the discussion above illustrates, the strategic choice for China's development has moved further away from an ideal ecosocialist society. In the following, I will elaborate on how China's development trend and on-going reforms may constitute institutional and cultural barriers to an ecosocialist transformation, and explore conditions that can be utilized to facilitate such a transformation.

An ecosocialist society adopts an ecocentric worldview, recognizing human beings as part of the nature. This worldview suggests that humans should respect the intrinsic value of nature, and that human activities should comply with the laws of nature. A harmonious relationship between humanity and nature is sought, whereas violating natural processes on a large scale through human activities should be avoided as much as possible. Although "harmony" has been emphasized as a goal in China's policies for ecological civilization, the actual development strategies seem to be in violation of this worldview. Instead, large-scale development projects, such as the Three Gorges Dam, South-to-North Water Diversion Project, and the ambitious plan for nuclear power plant construction, manifest a productivist and anthropocentric worldview that humans can dominate over nature through science and technology.

When ecocentric ethics is the main principle of organizing the human world, the role of economy will be repositioned as embedded within society rather than standing over society (Kovel, 2007). It means that economic growth should be socially meaningful and controllable, and is confined within the limits of the ecosystem. Ecological sustainability will replace economic growth as the priority of development. This is apparently not the current strategy in China, as evidenced by the 'Suggestions on the 13th Five-year National Socio-economic Development Plan (2016–2020)', where maintaining economic growth is addressed as the primary principle. However, it is difficult to judge whether China has taken an ecocentric ethic or not. After all, the prioritization of ecological consciousness does not necessarily mean growth should not be pursued at all. If economic growth still plays a vital role in alleviating poverty, it is reasonable to seek for growth with the awareness that growth is only a means to that end, and that there exists a limit. Indeed, given the fact that there are still 70 million people living below the poverty line (National Bureau of Statistics of China, 2015), economic growth in China is arguably necessary and morally acceptable.

Nevertheless, there are reasons to believe that if current trends continue, the economy of China will become increasingly difficult to be socially controllable. China's economic reforms have attempted to pursue a neoliberal agenda, introducing market mechanisms into different spheres of the economy, for instance in deciding investment, forming price, allocating labor, and economic resources. The introduction of market instruments has led to deregulation of the financial sector.

Meanwhile, the role of the state in terms of planning and controlling the economic development process has declined dramatically. The state and political means for capital accumulation are gradually replaced with free market mechanisms, leading to a shift from a state-led socialist economic growth to a market-led capitalist growth.

The former type of growth is driven by an ideology from the party bureaucrats, who made a deliberative political choice. In this sense, growth is an objective imposed from outside the economic system and is thus socially controllable in terms of determining growth for how long, for what, and for whom (Fotopoulos, 2005). However, the momentum of growth for the latter type emanates from within the system, characterized by a strong market competition, which exhibits a "grow or die" dynamic. The reform in the economic sphere in China toward deepening a free market economy will undoubtedly enhance the structure's dependency on growth. When growth becomes a structural necessity and imperative, it aims merely at profit maximization and is less concerned with human beings' well-being and environmental protection (Huan, 2010). Markets do not have the ability to decide the ecologically optimal size of economy and the production that is socially meaningful and environmentally accountable. In an ecosocialist society, the functioning of the market will be bound to be subordinated to the ecocentric mode of production coordinated by the state and civil society (Kovel, 2007). The weakening of the role of planning and state control, and the augmentation of markets through China's continuous reforms, undermine the necessary institutional settings for the ecosocialist restructuring.

An ecosocialist transformation has the collective ownership of the means of production as a structural prerequisite. Only when the means of production are controlled collectively is there potential to make decisions through democratic planning on what and how much to produce, and to direct the economy to serve society's common goods. However, this prerequisite, which used to be a key character of China's socialist regime, is being increasingly weakened. Along with marketization, waves of privatization have occurred since the late 1990s. Multiple forms of ownership have emerged, with state-owned enterprises accounting for a declining percentage of economic output and labor absorption (Wei, 2001). Years of neoliberal propaganda have turned private ownership into a doctrinal belief in China, even though it contradicts the country's self-claimed socialist identity (Chun, 2008).

Although inequality in income and welfare availability is increasing, a growth strategy can make redistributive conflicts less acute, as the worst off can hope to reach the present living standards of the wealthy through economic growth. However, in a world of finite resources that makes endless growth impossible, the distributive conflicts will increasingly become a pressing issue. This means that for China, the redistribution of the fruits from economic growth is much more important than just maintaining an overall high growth rate. Priority for growth should be channeled to poor regions in inland China and low-income population groups. A further increase in wealth accumulation in the already affluent regions cannot avoid taking up ecological spaces that are essentially necessary for the poor people to satisfy their vital needs.

Political willingness is important and necessary to pursue a transition toward degrowth in the affluent regions, and toward ecosocialism in general. However, whether or not the regional and local authorities will implement the national government's policy is in question. The decentralization of planning and decision-making to local authorities is a major component in China's economic reforms. As mentioned, the control and capacity of the central state in directing socio-economic development have declined dramatically due to the devolution of the fiscal systems, finance, investment, and management of state-owned enterprises (Wei, 2001). Local states have considerably increased their power in resource allocation, budgeting, project approval, investment decision, and many other areas. On the one hand, if local authorities show enthusiasm for high economic growth rates, the lack of proper macro-management mechanisms can make the implementation of national government's policy toward ecosocialism and degrowth difficult. On the other hand, if the local authority is willing to pursue a degrowth transition, it has great leeway and several policy instruments to do so. So far, economic growth is still regarded by provincial and municipal governments as the first priority. The inter-city competition for population growth, foreign investment, and industrial development has resulted in urban planning grossly over-dimensioning the areas set aside for future urban development – these areas are three times the size that could house the actual Chinese population (Chinadialogue, 2015). In order to incentivize the local government to focus more on social and environmental issues, the performance assessment system for officials and government agencies could be employed, where achievements of social justice and environmental sustainability are given more credits than GDP growth rates.

As pointed out above, leadership awareness and proper institutional settings are indispensable in establishing a degrowth and ecosocialist political agenda. However, to implement the policies in a democratic and efficacious way, the population's mental awareness and subjective readiness are paramount. As a result of China's striving for Western-style economic prosperity, the pursuit of money and material possession has become the predominant ideology among the majority of Chinese. At the national policy level, as indicated in the suggestions on the 13th Five-year Development Plan (2016–2020), domestic consumption is targeted as a major contributor to future economic growth. A rising consumer culture across the country and conspicuous consumption of certain social groups stand at odds with the ecosocialist priority of use value.

It can be seen that the trajectory that China is heading for is diverting from the degrowth and ecosocialist society. Having said that, we should also be aware of the conducive factors that China can utilize to trigger a transformation toward an ecosocialist society, if there is strong political willingness. It should be remembered that the Communist Party of China (CPC) during the past three decades has managed a deep societal transformation through a series of reforms. A one-generation-long reform has tremendously affected every corner of the society, ideologically, culturally, and in terms of economic and political structures. It is therefore possible to envision an ecosocialist reorientation of China's development led by the CPC in the next decades. The national planning system is a functional mechanism that can be employed to guide the development trajectory. Central government could employ the five-year social and economic development plan to demonstrate the strategic choice for China's near future. The NFZP, which focuses on the territorial and spatial dimension of development, can be made in accordance with the socio-economic development plan aiming in the direction of degrowth and ecosocialism.

Today, China's economic system still has certain socialist features, such as public ownership of land resources and a relatively higher contribution of state-owned enterprises to the country's economy compared with traditional capitalist societies. Instead of employing these institutions to maximize profits and privilege a certain social stratum, they can be used through democratic planning to control the volume and content of economy. In addition, materialism did not have a strong foothold in Chinese traditional values and philosophical thinking until recently; it has only gradually become dominant over the last three decades. The principles of degrowth and ecosocialism are inherent in ancient Chinese philosophy, which among others promotes frugality and the compliance of human activities with the law of nature (Pan, 2006; Xue *et al.*, 2012). Reviving traditional wisdom may provide the subjective resources to enhance the acceptance of a less materialist lifestyle.

Concluding remarks

In this chapter I have discussed the limits of the capitalist-based paradigm of ecological modernization pursued by China, and argued instead for an ecosocialist restructuring of the country, and economic degrowth in the affluent regions as an alternative path to a long-term sustainable future.

China aims to develop an affluent, green, and harmonious society. The pathway that it has selected to achieve these goals is the economic and technological paradigm of modern industrial civilization. However, the current crisis-ridden Western world seems to suggest the failures of this paradigm in solving economic, social, and environmental problems. The ideology of linear progress as indicated by the ecological modernization paradigm is highly challenged as a viable path to human prosperity. Furthermore, the harsh reality of limited natural resources and biocapacity may prevent China from reaching a global affluence level where it reaches the living standards of the wealthy countries. It is urgent to explore an alternative to the growth and ecological modernization paradigm for China's future development.

I have argued that since there is a limit to growth in China, priority for growth should be channeled to poor regions in inland China and low-income population groups, while degrowth should be applied to the more developed, wealthy regions. However, to achieve degrowth requires transformations in the capitalist economic structure, and marginal institutional adjustments are not able to overcome the contemporary crises. Ecosocialism as a societal paradigm that revolves around ecocentric ethics and mode of production can provide a radical and viable development path for China. Although China's current reform initiatives do not facilitate an ecosocialist reorientation, certain institutional and cultural elements are favorable if the CPC is determined.

Of the 'Two Century Goals' that the CPC has set for China's long-term development, the first goal of achieving a 'moderately prosperous society' (*xiaokangshehui*) will come true in 2021 – the year of the one hundred-year anniversary of the Communist Party of China. The second goal, which is planned to be realized in 2049 – a century after the foundation of new China – aims to build up "a prosperous, democratic, civilized and harmonious socialist modern society." When, by fulfilling the first goal, China's economy grows to the level such that its material living standards are comparable to those of the world average middle-income economies, a strategic choice of the pathway toward the achievement of the second goal is needed. As the chapter suggests, this strategic choice should look beyond the growth paradigm and seek the future prospects of degrowth and ecosocialism.

Notes

1 The five special economic zones are Shenzheng, Zhuhai, Shantou, Xiamen, and Hainan (province). The fourteen coastal cities of open economy are Dalian, Qinhuangdao, Tianjin, Yantai, Qingdao, Lianyungang, Nantong, Shanghai, Ningbo, Wenzhou, Fuzhou, Guangzhou, Zhanjiang, and Beihai.
2 For an elaborated argument, see Xue (2014).

References

Asara, V., Otero, I., Demaria, F. and Corbera, E. (2015). Socially sustainable degrowth as a social-ecological transformation: repoliticizing sustainability. *Sustainability Science*, 10(3): 376–384.

Bhaskar, R. (1975/2008). *A Realist Theory of Science*. London: Verso.

Bhaskar, R. (1993/2008). *Dialectic: The Pulse of Freedom. With a New Introduction*. Oxon: Routledge.

Cevik, S. and Correa-Caro, C. (2015). Growing (Un)equal: Fiscal Policy and Income Inequality in China and BRIC+. IMF Working Paper, WP/15/68. International Monetary Fund.

Chinadialogue (2015). New "ghost cities" typify out-of-control planning. www.chinadialogue.net/article/show/single/en/8239-New-ghost-cities-typify-out-of-control-planning. Accessed November 2015.

Chun, L. (2008). Against privatization in China: a historical and empirical argument. *Journal of Chinese Political Science*, 13(1): 1–27.

Fisher, D.R. and Freudenburg, W.R. (2001). Ecological modernization and its critics: assessing the past and looking toward the future. *Society & Natural Resources*, 14(8): 701–709.

Fotopoulos, T. (2005). The multidimensional crisis and inclusive democracy. IJID Publication.

Fotopoulos, T. (2010). The de-growth utopia: the incompatibility of de-growth within an internationalized market economy. In: Q. Huan (ed.), *Eco-socialism as Politics: Rebuilding the Basis of Our Modern Civilisation*. New York: Springer.

Galeotti, M., Lanza, A. and Pauli, F. (2006). Reassessing the environmental Kuznets curve for CO_2 emissions: a robustness exercise. *Ecological Economics*, 57(1): 152–163.

Georgescu-Roegen, N. (1981). Afterword. In J. Rifkin (ed.), *Entropy: A New World View*. New York: Bantam Books.

Global Footprint Network (2016). National Footprint Accounts, 2016 Edition.

Gordon, M.J. and Rosenthal, J.S. (2003). Capitalism's growth imperative. *Cambridge Journal of Economics*, 27(1): 25–48.

Gowdy, J. and O'Hara, S. (1997). Weak sustainability and viable technologies. *Ecological Economics*, 22(3): 239–247.

Harvey, D. (2010). *The Enigma of Capital and the Crises of Capitalism*. London: Profile Books.

Heiskanen, E. and Jalas, M. (2003). Can services lead to radical eco-efficiency improvements? – a review of the debate and evidence. *Corporate Social Responsibility and Environmental Management*, 10(4): 186–198.

Huan, Q. (2010). Growth economy and its ecological impacts upon China: an eco-socialist analysis. In: Q. Huan (ed.), *Eco-socialism as Politics: Rebuilding the Basis of Our Modern Civilisation*. New York: Springer.

Jackson, T. (2009). *Prosperity without Growth: Economics for a Finite Planet*. London: Earthscan.

Jänicke, M. (2008). Ecological modernization: new perspectives. *Journal of Cleaner Production*, 16(5): 557–565.

Kallis, G., Demaria, F., and D'Alisa, G. (2015). Introduction: degrowth. In D'Alisa, G., Demaria, F., and Kallis, G. (eds.), *Degrowth. A Vocabulary for a New Era* (pp. 1–17). Oxon: Routledge.

Kanbur, R. and Zhang, X. (2005). Fifty years of regional inequality in China: A journey through central planning, reform and openness. *Review of Development Economics*, 9(1): 87–106.

Kovel, J. (2007). *The Enemy of Nature: The End of Capitalism or the End of the World?* London: Zed Books.

Latouche, S. (2009). *Farewell to Growth*. Cambridge: Polity Press.

Löwy, M. (2005). What is ecosocialism? *Capitalism Nature Socialism*, 16(2): 15–24.

Löwy, M. (2007). Eco-socialism and democratic planning. *Socialist Register*, 43: 294–319.

National Bureau of Statistics of China (2015). *Bulletin of 2014 National Economic and Social Development Statistics*. Beijing: National Bureau of Statistics of China.

National Development and Reform Commission of China (2011). National Development Priority Zones Plan – Forming Efficient, Balanced and Sustainable Territorial Development Pattern (in Chinese).

Nørgaard, J.S. (2009). Avoiding rebound through a steady-state economy. In Herring, H. and Sorrell, S. (eds.), *Energy Efficiency and Sustainable Consumption*. London: Palgrave Macmillan.

Pan, Y. (2006). On socialist ecological civilization (in Chinese). *Green Leaf*, 10: 10–18.

Sarkar, S. (2010). Prospects for eco-socialism. In Huan, Q. (ed.), *Eco-socialism as Politics: Rebuilding the Basis of Our Modern Civilisation*. New York: Springer.

Spaargaren, G. (2000). Ecological modernization theory and the changing discourse on environment and modernity. In Spaargaren, G., Mol, A.P.J. and Buttel, F.H. (eds.), *Environment and Global Modernity*. London: Sage Publications Ltd.

Urban China Initiative (2012). *2011 Urban Sustainability Index*. Beijing: Urban China Initiative.

Wei, Y.D. (2001). Decentralization, marketization, and globalization: the triple processes underlying regional development in China. *Asian Geographer*, 20(1–2): 7–23.

Xue, J. (2012). Limits to decoupling strategies for sustainable housing development: the Hangzhou experience. *Journal of Environmental Planning and Management*, 55(8): 1004–1021.

Xue, J. (2014). Is eco-village/urban village the future of a degrowth society? An urban planner's perspective. *Ecological Economics*, 105: 130–138.

Xue, J., Arler, F. and Næss, P. (2012). Is the degrowth debate relevant to China? *Environment, Development and Sustainability*, 14(1): 85–109.
Yao, S. and Zhang, Z. (2001). On regional inequality and diverging clubs: a case study of contemporary China. *Journal of Comparative Economics*, 29(3): 466–484.

12

MAKING THE CRITIQUE OF CAPITALISM FIT FOR THE PRESENT CRISIS

Arne Johan Vetlesen

At the beginning of his book *Making Capitalism Fit for Society*, the political theorist Colin Crouch gives a summary of the state we're in: "Inequality is again becoming a major issue; the power of large corporations is producing a growing number of problems for consumers, workers and citizens; the neglect of collective needs is producing frightening problems of environmental damage" (2013: 1). He goes on to assert that "these are all areas where social democracy has strong positions, and where neoliberal capitalism is at its most vulnerable" (ibid.).

The first statement may appear uncontroversial, indeed unanimous, among political commentators these days; the latter less so. The role of social democracy vis-à-vis the triumph of neoliberalism in the last three decades is a complicated one; the former has certainly played a part in preparing for the hegemony enjoyed by the latter and thus cannot so easily be portrayed as its rival and corrective. In saying this, I am in fact echoing much of Crouch's analysis in his two earlier and much-read books, *Post-Democracy* and *The Strange Non-Death of Neoliberalism*.

Yet there is something strange about the position Crouch arrives at in the last book of his trilogy on the unexpected "non-death" of neoliberalism. In my view, he exaggerates the potential of "Third Way" social democracy to seriously challenge the reign of neoliberalism; he underestimates the former as an accomplice to the latter (see Hamilton 2004; Judt 2010). We need to go beyond Crouch's analysis to appreciate why the resistance to neoliberalism mustered by the political as well as intellectual left has been feeble at best and virtually absent at worst in the period dealt with in Crouch's trilogy. I will try to show that, to a large extent, this has to do with a stubborn predilection in Western Marxism for privileging the capital–labour relation over the capital–nature one. Given the nature of the present crisis and the kinds of conflicts, risks, and pathologies it produces, being ecological as they are, to hold on to yesterday's privileging may prove fatal.

While Crouch provides my point of departure, the substantial part of the discussion that follows will deal with the work of David Harvey, a leading critic of capitalism on the academic and political left for at least three decades. My emphasis will not be on the role of social democracy in the enduring reign of neoliberalism (though no doubt a key issue), but on what I argue are serious blind spots in the Marx-inspired account of the crises facing present-day capitalism offered by Harvey. The costs of privileging the capital–labour relation over the capital–nature one are not merely analytic or conceptual; they are becoming eminently empirical, and hence for all to see.

In a central passage in *Making Capitalism Fit for Society*, Crouch makes a distinction between "those who are willing to recognize and to act on the limits of market solutions" and "those who, because of the interests they represent, always push for more market and refuse to recognize its inadequacies" (2013: 60). He comments that "today only social democracy has a long political tradition that enables it wholeheartedly to represent the first set of positions" (ibid.), adding that when it comes to who to trust with the sustainability of human life on our planet, "only a coalition of social democratic and green movements can save us" (ibid.). Toward the end of the book, Crouch tells his readers (2013: 181):

> The general thrust of marketization should not be opposed as a matter of principle, but a sharp eye needs to be kept on the various inadequacies of the market and the damage it sometimes causes. These, whether they harm customers, workers or the third parties typically touched by such externalities as environmental damage, provide much of the stuff of twenty-first-century politics.

To be sure, this statement will come across as anything but remarkable. However, I shall seek to show that its having come to be thus considered is itself highly remarkable.

What is happening when a piece of analysis purporting to critique neoliberalism employs wording where that critique talks about the "inadequacies" of the market and the damage it "sometimes" causes? When "environmental damage" is depicted as an instance of "externalities" that "third parties are typically touched by"?

The question is whether critique can allow itself to take over the language distinctive of its object and its favored ways of perceiving the world, including what constitutes problems within it. I think not. I think that the practice demonstrated by Crouch's example, interestingly and subtly reinforced in the course of his three books, is part of the problem of the "non-death" of neoliberalism. Its well-documented failure to die, therefore, not only is evidence of the relative strengths of its advocates and the powers that be, it also reflects heavily on the practices – including linguistic ones – pursued by its proclaimed critics.

So much for the case of Crouch. If his is a wanting one, as I suggest, what about the case of David Harvey? If Crouch can be seen to lose more of his critical bite with each successive book, pinning his hope for an alternative to neoliberalism on a version of social democracy that arguably helped pave the way for its rise, and has since proved both unwilling and unable to oust it from power, then surely Harvey – never a social democrat, always a Marxist, and as such an exemplar of a near-extinct species these days – holds out the promise of a much more potent type of critique.

With an oeuvre as large as that of Harvey, I am unable here to do justice to his contribution to the critique of contemporary capitalism, dating back to his seminal *Limits to Capital* (first published in 1982). I shall confine my analysis to Harvey's two recent books, *Seventeen Contradictions and the End of Capitalism* and *The Enigma of Capital and the Crises of Capitalism*.

In the chapter of the former dealing with "contradiction 16," entitled "Capital's relation to nature," Harvey assesses the "widespread idea" that "capitalism is encountering a fatal contradiction in the form of a looming environmental crisis" (2014: 246). He considers this idea "plausible but controversial," and he reviews four reasons to cast doubt on it. The essence of these reasons, Harvey proposes, is that history shows that "it may be perfectly possible for capital to continue to circulate and accumulate in the midst of environmental catastrophes" (p. 249). If anything, environmental disasters create abundant opportunities for "disaster capitalism." As the popular notion has it, if there is a need for present-day capitalism to go green, it will. Environmental problems translate into so many new markets, so many business-meaning profit-opportunities. Who could be against a "Green New Deal"?

Of course, with, say, air quality deteriorating at an alarming pace in growth-obsessed countries like China and India, the more general problem of unfair distributions of environmental damages – where as a rule the poor and those least responsible for the damages are hit the hardest – is likely to add fuel to the worldwide environmental justice movement. For example, the Chinese government is known to worry that the higher the levels of pollution in the big cities, the higher the risk of social unrest that might lead to political protest and possibly revolt. But even though the social costs of accelerating environmental degradation do seem to be on the rise in many regions of the world, and thus constitute a valid cause of concern for the political regimes and the economic elites used to harvest the profits from degradations sold as "development" (or its inseparable price), Harvey is right to observe that "the resultant protests do not, as of now, constitute any major threat to the survival of capital" (2014: 250).

This prompts us to confront Harvey's question head on: What *is* capital's relation to nature?

Harvey speaks about "the contradictory unity between capital and nature" (ibid.). Capital "necessarily" views nature as nothing more than a "vast store of potential use values…that can be used directly or indirectly in the production and realization of commodity values." Accordingly, natural use values are monetized, capitalized, commercialized, and exchanged as commodities. And when the natural commons are privatized – when water is made into a commodity, for example – private individuals are free to extract social wealth from their ownership of a commodified nature.

Today the costs induced by capital's treatment of nature as a mere objectified commodity, one whose sole purpose is to facilitate neverending prospects for the twin imperatives of growth and profits, are of such a magnitude that they cannot be ignored. The question is how capital responds to its increasingly evident tendency to spoil the very elements of nature – the land, the air, the water – that capital, in conjunction with technologies and other factors, cannot do without, as expressed in the slogan: no planet, no business.

Harvey's response is worth quoting in extenso:

> Capital cannot, unfortunately, change the way it slices and dices nature up into commodity forms and private property rights. To challenge this would be to challenge the functioning of the economic engine of capitalism itself and to deny the applicability of capital's economic rationality to social life. This is why the environmental movement, when it goes beyond a merely cosmetic or ameliorative politics, must become anti-capital. The concept of nature that underpins various philosophies of environmentalism is radically at odds with that which capital has to impose in order to reproduce itself. The environmental movement could, in alliance with others, pose a serious threat to the reproduction of capital. But so far environmental politics has not, for a variety of reasons, moved very far in this direction.
>
> *(Harvey 2014: 252)*

Leaving aside the role of the more or less anti-capitalist-environmental movement, capital's favoured response to the "no planet, no business" scenario is to seize the environmental mantle for itself, working its old trick of exploiting crisis – regardless of what sort – for its own benefits so as to turn what critics consider a limit to profits into another means of making them. By "greening the economy" so that a win–win situation will be attained for all parties concerned, capital seeks to hijack the cause of environmentalism and to dominate the ecological discourse, hoping, as Harvey puts it, to "manage the capital–nature contradiction in its own broad class interests" (2014: 253).

The crucial question is whether this old-worn trick will actually work in the present situation, given that we are now at a key inflexion point in the exponential growth of capitalist activity such as to have "an exponential impact upon levels of environmental stress and distress within capital's ecology" (ibid.). Put in other terms than those used by Harvey, the central problem is systemic overshoot: production, distribution, and consumption the capitalist way, in a globalized mode, results in the world's natural resources being exploited at such pace and to such an extent that the resources in question are destroyed in their capacity to replenish (see Catton 1982). Thus, in 2014, what is known as Earth Overshoot Day was 19 August: in less than eight months, that is, humanity exhausts Earth's budget for the year. Every eight months we demand more renewable resources than the planet can provide for an entire year. Add to this that, as documented by WWF in September 2014, the number of wild animals (meaning individuals, not species) on Earth has halved in the last forty years. Creatures across land, rivers, and the seas are being decimated as humans kill them for food in unsustainable numbers, while polluting or destroying their habitats.

As we saw when discussing Crouch above, the instinct of capital is to treat harmful ecological effects as cost-shifting, or as what economists call "externalities," that is, an effect – in this case a negative one, one of degradation, depletion, and even extinction – that is produced by an economic activity – fishing, mining, oil production, industrialized agriculture – but that does not enter into the cost calculations of those responsible (the agents of capital) for the activity. This "not-paying", this not-compensating for what is only allowed to show up as negative by-effects *elsewhere*, meaning outside the profit-calculating matrix, explains why "externalities" is the preferred word. Crucially, the twin imperatives characteristic of capitalism, growth and profit, rely on the twofold tacit and till now unquestioned assumption that as far as the nature being incessantly commodified is concerned, there is always more for the taking, if not here, then somewhere else; and furthermore, that the nature-related consequences of the taking – exploitation – craved by growth–profit will always be a problem for others, not for the interests, let alone survival, of capital itself. For capital to externalize, then, in the strong sense of being what it is, and of thriving only by way of externalizing, means for it to rid itself of the havoc it is constantly wreaking, whereby the causing of the harm is not taken to endanger or delimit the reach of capital, but quite the opposite: to be its modus operandi.

Now, if this is the way that capital typically frames the problem of different sorts of ongoing ecological degradation, how does capitalism critic Harvey propose that we frame it?

As far as I can see, Harvey's key statement is the following one: "If capital does not successfully manage these contradictions [Harvey takes pollution to be a paradigmatic case in point] *it will not be because of barriers in nature*, but because of its own economic, political, institutional and ideological failings." Going on to cite climate change, Harvey contends that "the problem is the hubris and the vested interests of certain factions of capital...that have the power to dispute, disrupt and prevent actions that threaten their profitability, competitive position and economic power" (2014: 256). This being so, Harvey assures us that "there is nothing natural about so-called natural disasters and humanity knows just about enough to ameliorate or manage the threat of most (though never all) environmental catastrophes." He concludes by reiterating his claim that "the reasons problems persist are political, institutional and ideological and are not attributable to natural limits" (2014: 259).

I find this position unconvincing. Harvey's statements leave the impression that *either* there are barriers, or limits, "in nature," such as to be at the root of the "contradictions" of capital's relation to nature, resulting in such problems as pollution or climate change, *or* there are no such limits/barriers in nature, and the problems we witness are instead to be located solely on the part of capital, meaning – in principle – social agents.

This strikes me as a false either/or. As stated here, the two options involved both conflate and artificially pit against each other dimensions – amounting to root causes – that are in fact causally intertwined. I don't think Harvey would deny that this is indeed the case, were he to consider my claim. Even so, he is to be faulted for failing to identify the root causes of the problems in a sufficiently complex manner.

There is an ambiguity that needs to be addressed here. In asserting that the problems are "not attributable to natural limits," what position precisely is Harvey meaning to refute? One could of course say that insofar as a capitalist economy comes up against "natural limits," the limits in question will never be purely "natural"; rather, they will always be such – come across as limits – within the matrix of a specific "unnatural" and as it were historically contingent creation, namely the modus operandi of a capitalistic economy and the sort of institutions it helps sustain. To put it in a more Hegelian way, what we call "nature" is always mediated; and mediation reflects on human and social actors and on the perception of things – of anything – that their society induces in them.

Let there be no mistake. It is fine and well for Harvey to remind us that, say, climate change is a man-made disaster, as opposed to a nature-made one, if such a crude distinction makes sense. For lack of our current capitalist system and the practices upheld by the various social agents that populate that man-made system, there would be no such phenomenon as climate change, at least not in its current form and seriousness. Politically, this is an important point to make, especially as addressed to climate skeptics and downright deniers, of which there are plenty, doing their best to see to it that, far from being resolved, the problem seriously exacerbates.

This is fine, but the point I'm taking issue with is a different one, deeper and more substantial. As we shall see, it is in fact ontological.

To use Harvey's terms in contradicting his claim: there are indeed barriers in nature. Residing in *physis*, the barriers impose limits, meaning strict and non-relative limits, to what humanity, be it in the form of the operations of capital, can do to (or should I say against) nature. It is true that it is up to humanity (capital) to decide whether to respect these limits – or to ignore them, to pretend that they don't exist, or that failing to observe them as limits, as stop signs for humanity-induced exploitation, will carry no consequences worth taking into account.

There is a sense, then, in which acknowledging the nature-residing limits to our activities on Earth is optional for us: we can choose whether or not to heed them. What is not optional, and hence up to us to determine, are the limits as such. They exist whether we like it or not. We are in this sense free to ignore them, but in doing so in our exchanges with nature we will not be free from the consequences, however much the ideology of economics insists that they are but "externalities" affecting *others*, be they natural or social others.

Accordingly, Harvey's central claim, quoted above, should be reformulated as follows: if capital does not successfully manage the contradictions in its relation to nature, it will be because there are in fact barriers-cum-limits in nature, imposing absolute limits (say, in the form of the nine planetary tipping points identified in climate science) to the pace and extent with which capital may persist in exploiting nature, taken as so many commodities allowing for ever-accumulating, never-ending growth/profits. If the limits in question, being non-optional and non-removable, are not respected, this may be seen as a failure of capital's own economic, political, institutional, and ideological failings, to echo Harvey. But the ontological entity with respect to which capital thereby fails (if fail it does) is not of capital's own making; nor is it a purely cultural construct: it is nature as an entity that capital, encountering it as its "other," is dependent upon for there to be commodities to be sold, workers to produce them, and consumers to buy them. To put the contrast starkly, whereas nature expresses and embodies life and the interest residing in everything that lives to persist in its existence (conatus) and to allow the myriad other sorts of life, of species, etc., to thrive as well, constituting as X and Y and n… do the conditions of the existence of A, then capital, insofar as it can only intensify its pursuit of limitless growth, limitless profits (grow or perish), represents death, taken as the capacity to turn life into waste, to exploit so as to degrade, deplete, make go extinct nature treated as a mere means, as perfectly disposable, as unworthy of respect for its own sake, in short, as devoid of intrinsic value.

Therefore, Harvey does not in fact capture the fundamental contradiction in capital's relation to nature. In downplaying this dependence, Harvey scarcely fares better than the proponents of the kind of "social constructivism" widespread in sociology as well as in other work within critical human geography (see the critique in Benton 2001). By contrast, critical realism as pioneered in the work of Roy Bhaskar (e.g., 2012) acknowledges the reality of nature as well as the reality of social structures setting conditions for human interactions with nature, thus providing a much-needed contrast to many other contemporary philosophical positions that pass over the domain of nature in their ontology. In the case of Harvey, capital's contradictory relation to nature is merely implicit in his account, not stated as such: it is the contradiction that shows up in capital's non-optional, non-removable reliance on nature as a source of so much life, so many life forms and the elements constituting their *sine qua non* – air, soil, water (meaning non-degraded such); a reliance upon nature being what it is and being allowed to remain so (alive, thriving, reproducing, and repleting itself according to *its own* – as opposed to capital-dictated – mechanisms and rhythms), a reliance on its "other" that capital – therein the contradiction – cannot help take for granted and nonetheless undermine at one and the same time: capital's distinct way of relying on nature takes the form of incessantly spoiling that nature in its intrinsic qualities and elements. For this reason, when capital destroys nature, it also destroys itself. The hubris Harvey at one point referred to consists in the overreach thus at play, disrespecting what can be neglected only at capital's peril.

Against this critique it can be objected that I am using "nature" in a far too simple way; that I fail to do justice to the immense diversity of life forms and the full complexity of intertwined ecosystems. And what about the difference between non-renewable and thus strictly limited/finite natural goods and resources, on the one hand, and renewable ones on the other? Given current innovations within "green technologies" of various sorts, not to mention geoengineering, are we not witnessing a steadily enhanced potential for decoupling, allowing capital's growth/profit imperative to prevail into a new era, without risking to self-destruct like I claimed above?

To be sure, the notion of decoupling is intriguing; a godsend to neoliberals and Blairite social democrats alike, and most welcome to CEOs and shareholders, that there is no need for the boat called capitalism either to be rocked or to change its current course. The idea is that as economic output becomes progressively less dependent on material throughput, the economy can continue to grow and profits can continue to be had without breaching ecological limits or running out of (limited, irreplaceable) resources. Indeed, the constellation "more economic activity – less environmental damage" suggests a win–win situation.

As many scholars have pointed out, however, this notion, and the promise it carries on behalf of keeping capitalism and planet Earth both intact such that the one may thrive without endangering the other, does not hold up to closer scrutiny; empirically it is being falsified, not corroborated. As economist Tim Jackson points out in *Prosperity without Growth*, there is as yet no credible, socially just, ecologically sustainable scenario of continually growing incomes in a world of 9 billion people. It is entirely fanciful to suppose that "deep" emission and resource cuts can be achieved without confronting the very structure of capitalist market economies. Nowhere, Jackson maintains, is there any evidence that efficiency can outrun scale in the way it must do if growth is to become what it today demonstrably is not: compatible with sustainability. On current evidence, far from acting to reduce the throughput of goods, technological progress serves to increase productive output by reducing factor costs. The phenomenon known as "rebound" attests to this: money saved through energy efficiency gets spent on other goods and services (see Jackson 2010: 86ff.).

Certainly Harvey knows just as well as Jackson that what prevents decoupling from becoming a reality and ceasing to be mere rhetoric is the structural reliance of the market system itself on continued growth: on investments continuing to bring profits, on profits continuing to grow. As Harvey himself argues in a number of books, the twin objectives of growth and profit – whereby profit is both growth-dependent and growth-driving – are the system-immanent key characteristics of a capitalist economy; and they happen to be exactly the traits resulting in capitalism's incompatibility with the planetary key characteristics of limits and finiteness.

When it comes to the concept of natural resources, Harvey's position is that "they are so many technical, social and cultural appraisals, and so any apparent natural scarcity can in principle be mitigated, if not totally circumvented, by technological, social and cultural changes" (2010: 73). But can it really? What precisely does "in principle" amount to?

In the work I just quoted, *The Enigma of Capital*, and in keeping with his previous books, Harvey's position – which I take to be the predominant one among Marxist scholars – is that the "second contradiction of capitalism," referring to the barriers capital arguably comes up against in nature, is considered secondary in importance to the so-called first contradiction, residing in the capital–labour relation. This touches on a longstanding debate, dating back to how to interpret Marx himself as to the order of importance between the two contradictions, a debate I cannot review here. Suffice it to say that as far as Harvey is concerned, I take him to remain skeptical to any talk about "natural scarcities" and "natural limits/barriers." As far as I can tell, this skepticism is not exhausted in the commonplace reminder that nature – or anything at all encountered in nature, attributed to nature – is upon closer scrutiny cultural, i.e. always already brought into view, and put to practical use (exploitation), in ways shaped by the vantage points and interests of human societies, classes, and individuals. Rather, the gist of Harvey's skepticism seems to me to be of ontological kind – thus his warning that "there is always a danger in over-emphasizing supposedly 'pure' natural limits at the expense of concentrating upon the capitalist dynamics that force environmental changes in the first place and on the social (particularly class) relations that drive those dynamics in certain environmentally perverse directions" (2010: 77). He adds that "the capitalist class...is always delighted to have its role displaced and masked by an environmental rhetoric that lets them off the hook as the progenitors of the problem" (ibid.).

In my view, the Marxist legacy Harvey relies upon when he accords primacy to the contradiction – and hence potential for conflict, crises, and pathologies – identified in the capital–labour relation over the contradiction located in the capital–nature relation, is ill-suited to recognize the destruction now taking place in the latter, qualitatively as well as quantitatively. For a start, when Marx wrote about the sorts of crises he saw as the "first and foremost" ones that capitalism cannot help but produce, he did so in an historical epoch ignorant about the rapidity and extent to which capital in the twenty-first century destroys the natural world it crucially depends upon. At most, Marx had experience-based reasons to be concerned about, say, the smog in London, or the poisonous smoke from the factory pipes in Manchester – both serious enough, yet locally and temporarily so, and therefore a far cry from the abyss to which capitalism is bringing us today by way of depletion, degradation, and downright destruction, on a worldwide scale at that.

This is not to dispute that a present-day Marxist scholar such as Harvey will recognize the notion of planetary tipping points employed by state-of-the-art climate science, finding that as of 2014 the world has crossed four out of nine such. Nevertheless, Harvey's way of talking about the situation we are in strikes me as insufficient and imprecise, in fact seriously underestimating its gravity. In my view, what we witness today is *not* well caught as "capitalist dynamics that force environmental changes," as a case of class relations "that drive those dynamics in certain environmentally perverse directions."

Let me explain briefly the kind of criticism I am making here by invoking the analysis of capitalism developed by the Frankfurt School, a leading strand within Western Marxism (see Vetlesen 2015: 52–62). The attempt to control outer nature that Horkheimer, Adorno, and Marcuse saw as inseparable not only from capitalism as an economic system, but from Enlightenment thinking and modernity as such, crucially entails the domination of "man over man," of one social class over another. Moreover, and more subtly, the compulsion to rationally control the forces of nature is bought at the price of the repression of the inner nature of the human individual. If Marx is the precursor in the modern epoch of the first tendency, Freud is that of the second. In speaking about the "revenge of nature," the Frankfurters meant the revenge of human nature: the more mercilessly humans, by way of science and technology, exploit, subjugate, and alter outer nature understood as non-human species, life forms, and "resources," the more is human nature stifled, thwarted, and alienated in the process. To put it a bit – yes, just a bit – too simply, the exploitation of outer nature is criticized to the extent that, and for the reason that, it brings about the domination of one social class over another, and the alienation of humans from their full potential – for freedom, play, and needs – and fulfillment as humans.

My claim is this: something crucial is unsaid because underappreciated here. And what holds for the Frankfurters goes for Harvey as well, though the unsaid takes slightly different forms in the two cases.

In both, there is something that *could* – and I will argue *should* – have been said, but that isn't. The Frankfurters *could* have said that the phenomenon "revenge of nature" has a second form, playing out in the man–nature relation: the consequences of careless intervention into the ecosphere, distinct from the form and the relation they do address, namely the man-to-man one, the human-related and as such anthropocentric one. Once the obviousness of this form is stated, one is struck by its conspicuous absence in Horkheimer's and Adorno's classic, *Dialectic of Enlightenment* (1979). Surprisingly, apart from a few asides, that work contains no systematic discussion of the destruction of outer nature, be it from the point of view of humans affected by it or from the wealth of non-human creatures and life forms of which nature consists.

Likewise, Harvey *could* have said that given the present escalation in capital's ongoing destruction of the natural world, the contradiction between capital and nature is no longer secondary to that between capital and labour. Indeed, what Marx himself, as well as earlier generations of Marxists, could not have foreseen, but what we see unfolding now, is that the order of priority between the contradictions is *de facto* being reversed: if the slogan "no planet, no business" is true, and it is, then it follows that short of nature's intact capacity in facilitating, in the most basic manner, the relationship between capital and labour, that relationship would find itself in a vacuum; literally, it would not get off the ground.

I submit this claim as eminently concrete, fact-based, and reflecting empirical realities. Concretely, what my claim is referring to is the following: in many regions of the world, natural goods and resources that both parties to the capital–labour relationship have relied upon, and have taken for granted that they can continue to count on, are either becoming increasingly scarce, or downright depleted, or so degraded as to be unable to recover and replenish.

This is what overshoot is all about, what happens when a society goes beyond its carrying capacity. To appreciate the importance of this, consider that exploitation as constituting the *modus operandi* of capitalism is two-dimensional: when capital exploits labour, that labour is put to use so as to exploit nature in ways conducive to growth and profit. Short of a nature that provides the substrate at which labour directs its efforts in turning everything into commodities, the foundation for capital's interest in having those commodities sold would fall away. And it is not only that nature – being living and as such unfolding an intrinsic interest in reproducing itself – is invaluable to the process of making and selling commodities; nature is also invaluable to the reproduction of the human agents that make capital and labour as social classes. Humans are not a self-sufficient species; as humans we cannot, strictly speaking, feed ourselves – we can only successfully do so, and thereby help sustain humanity over time, by relying on the air, water, and soil that mother nature, and only mother nature, provides. Both humanity's and capital's existence depend on nature in this sense, absolutely and ineluctably so.

To echo my above criticism of the Frankfurters, Marx's analysis of capitalism and the kinds of crises and pathologies it cannot but bring about is so one-sidedly focused on the man-to-man exploitation as to ignore the man–nature one. To fail to recognize the full impact of the latter, not only on nature as such (as the over-exploited party) but in its capacity to remove the carpet as it were from under the capital–labour relation, is to be guilty of prolonging a blind spot in Marx the nineteenth-century thinker into the twenty-first century, a period whose distinct crises cannot be understood as long as the blind spot remains.

Now, for all the importance of the distinction between man's exploitation of man and man's exploitation of nature, my argument that in present times the latter is proving just as critical as the former, if not more so, should not mislead us into playing the one out against the other in the way of rivalry, let alone mutual exclusion. Ours must be a holistic perspective, not a partial one privileging one type of exploitation over the other. For all the dialectic promoted by Marx as well as Horkheimer and Adorno, the blind spot prevents the two dimensions in which exploitation takes place from being appreciated in their interconnectedness and interplay. Whereas human capital may be overused and overstretched so as to result in burnout in the human agents affected, natural capital may be (we should say is, of course) overexploited so as to result in overshoot within the ecosystems involved, the consequences being the disappearance of habitat, the erosion of the soil, the toxification of the seas, the pollution of the air, the extinction of species, the reduction of biodiversity, etc. What we need to recognize is the parallel and indeed interconnected ways in which the two absolutely essential and irreplaceable sources of value (profit) – the living nature that abounds in the natural world and the living nature that each human being exhibits throughout its life and in each instance of performing labour – tend to be brought to their respective critical limits by the sheer internal dynamics of an economic system that has no other method of sustaining itself than by way of overexploiting and so undermining the energies upon which its imperatives rest, namely growth and profit. It rests upon these sources in an exclusive sense, so that when the capitalist system tries to survive by way of the only route it recognizes, namely by exploitation-facilitated growth, it is bound to undermine the sources of value (profit) for which planet Earth, within which this system is bound to operate, has no substitutes – to put it in a way reminiscent of what Nicholas Georgescu-Roegen (1975) designates "the fallacy of endless substitution," attributed equally to the neoclassical school of economics and to the

Marxist one. In short, the sources of value that are factually undermined – taking the form of depletion and extinction in physical, non-human nature, and of burn-out and exhaustion in psycho-somatic human nature – cannot, once their undermining is set in motion, ever be fully restored.

At this point, it is worthwhile recalling Herman Daly's insistence that "the economy is a subsystem of the ecosystem, and that the containing ecosystem is finite, non-growing and materially closed" (Daly 2007: 2). The truth of this observation may appear so simple as to be grasped by any quick-minded child. And yet Daly, based on a long life in academic economics and politics, finds that it is a truth about which both fields are in stubborn denial. The question is: does this hold for a present-day Marxist critic of capitalism such as Harvey as well?

In Daly's terms, when the giants in eighteenth- and nineteenth-century thinking such as Smith, Ricardo, and Marx developed their theories, the world was relatively empty of humans and the artefacts, products, and waste of our activities; today it is increasingly full. In short, the pattern of scarcity has changed fundamentally. However, this change on the ground has not led to a corresponding change in the way we think about the economy: in Daly's words, we have not yet switched our thinking, let alone practices, from empty-world economics to full-world economics.

So what to do in a situation where manmade capital has become relatively plentiful, showing no signs of slowing down, while remaining natural capital is becoming more and more scarce? The answer will be decided by whether manmade and natural capital are viewed as substitutes or as complements (as indicated in Georgescu-Roegen's quote above). Received wisdom has it they are substitutes, and capitalism as we know it to this day continues to operate as if they are substitutes. But the truth is that they are not: they are complements instead. This implies that the factor in short supply is the limiting one (see Daly 2007: 27–28). Daly's argument goes like this:

> In yesterday's empty world man made capital and labour were limiting; in today's full world natural capital with its flow of natural resources and flux of natural services is limiting. [...] The fish catch is no longer limited by the number of fishing boats (manmade capital), but by the remaining populations of fish in the sea (natural capital). Cut timber is no longer limited by saw mills, but by standing forests. Energy from petroleum is no longer limited by pumping and drilling capacity, but by remaining geological deposits. Irrigated agriculture is limited not by pipes, pumps, and sprinklers, but by the amount of fresh water in aquifers and rivers. [...] the difficulty is that the condition of maintaining productive capacity intact has in the empty world been applied only to manmade capital. Natural capital has not been maintained intact by any depreciation or depletion set – asides. The unsustainable depreciation and depletion of natural capital has therefore been counted as income, as if it were sustainable consumption.
>
> *(Daly 2007: 252, 28)*

The last point bears repeating: it is perverse to continue practicing the gross domestic product (GDP) model of accounting where consumption of resources – even when it is a matter of taking the last fish in the stock, i.e. of resource depletion – is counted as income, hence as ensuring growth/profits, and so as desirable and rational.

Am I suggesting that Harvey would object to Daly's argument? Or am I suggesting that his own account of the contradictions we're now witnessing in capitalism largely ignores it, and is seriously lacking in explanatory power for doing so?

The latter. As for the former, I am not sure. Harvey does occasionally say things that would be compatible with Daly's insight into the change in what today causes scarcity and constitutes the limiting factor (natural capital, not manmade). But these observations, while factually relevant, never motivate Harvey to take wholly on board – conceptually, analytically, and diagnostically – the full implications of the change Daly points to. Contra what we have seen Harvey state, there are barriers in nature. Natural limits are not "potential" as such; they are all too real, becoming more so each year, in more and more dimensions (ecosystems) of natural capital and regions of the world.

That capitalism in its practices has not switched from an empty-world to a full-world model is clear. It is also clear that the neoclassical economics that continues to form the intellectual basis for those practices in today's world has not even begun considering making such a switch – truth be told, the leading proponents of the dominant school go out of their way to resist it (see Mirowski 2013); should it one day seriously start switching from empty to full world, its notions about the true sources of growth and profits would be challenged to their core (see Booth 2004; Spash 2002; Sedlacek 2011).

If this is only as might have been expected, how to explain that the leading critics – figures such as Harvey – of contemporary capitalism also fail to make the switch – to elaborate and exemplify it in theory so as to help encourage its taking place in practice?

Again, this raises the question of how Marx himself is to be understood on this issue. I already indicated that he cannot be criticized for not having foreseen that the limiting factor would change from manmade to natural capital; that is to say, that the world as a result of capitalism having become the only game in town (on Earth) is changing from empty to full world. Although I know a number of Marxist scholars will object and say that the key concepts and insights of how Marx understood the causes and symptoms of capitalism-induced crises still hold (see O'Connor 1998; Kovel 2007; Magdoff and Bellamy Foster 2011), I for one agree with Teresa Brennan's critique of Marx in a number of books (Brennan 1993, 2000, 2003) where she charges Marx with "the assumption that labour alone is living, and that nature is not." Marx, that is, not only identifies the "living factor" with subjective human agency, he endows the human subject alone with the capacity to give life. This, contends Brennan, is possible only where it is "assumed that nature gives nothing of itself; and that is only possible in a mode of production in which living nature is marginalized" (Brennan 2000: 94). Brennan's correction of Marx consists in her insistence that "all natural sources of energy entering production should be treated as variable capital and sources of surplus – value" (2000: 95).

It would require a more extensive review of Harvey's many books to establish whether the charge I take Brennan to correctly address to Marx can be validly addressed to Harvey as well. But my claim is that Harvey, when citing what is common knowledge about the devastation of nature (natural capital) currently taking place, at no place seems to seriously consider that the rising pace of this ongoing devastation makes necessary a rethinking of the Marxian framework. To pick an example, when Harvey (in *The New Imperialism*; 2003: 145ff.) makes his case for the current relevance of Marx's account of "accumulation by dispossession," the long list of processes the reader is presented with is clearly more concerned with the pressures affecting manmade capital (labor, often in the form of slavery) than those affecting nature (natural capital). At one point, Harvey does speak about "the wholesale commodification of nature in all its forms," understood as the form now assumed by the sum of the processes of primitive accumulation listed (2003: 146). But – and this is the point – when Harvey does pay attention to the ways in which capital now exploits nature, the casualties he is concerned with are not those located in the natural world, making it up *qua* so many non-human species and life forms; instead, the parties granted status and so attention as actual or potential casualties of the nature-devastation at hand always tend to be human agents, showing up the social costs of the devastation as opposed to the nature-specific, nature-immanent ones. To the extent that ecosystems are being brought to the point of critical breakdown, Harvey's focus is exclusively on the ways in which such breakdowns are likely to play out in that most conventional of crises frameworks, be it Marxian or neoclassical: the relations between classes, affecting asymmetries of power, wealth, and positions between them. To pick a typical passage: having mentioned "the escalating depletion of the global environment commons (land, air, water) and proliferating habitat degradations," Harvey points out that "biopiracy is rampant," as is "the pillaging of the world's stockpile of genetic resources." And what interests Harvey in this connection? How this development will be "to the benefit of a few pharmaceutical companies" (2003: 148).

Sure it will. But what justifies taking it for granted that this is the only aspect of the devastation, let alone the only affected party that deserves mention?

Harvey's fondness for Karl Polanyi's classic work *The Great Transformation* is worth considering here. First published in 1944, Harvey holds that it "remains landmark text to this day" (2014: 56). Harvey approvingly cites Polanyi's much-elaborated point that a market economy must comprise all elements of industry (or production), including labour, land, and money. These elements, Polanyi maintains, must be organized into markets, "forming an absolutely vital part of the economic system." He then goes on to say, in the passage Harvey likes to quote:

> But labour, land, and money are obviously *not* commodities… Labour is only another name for a human activity which goes with life itself, which in its turn is not produced for sale but for entirely different reasons, nor can that

> activity be detached from the rest of life, be stored or mobilized; land is only another name for nature, which is not produced by man. (…)The commodity description of labour, land, and money is entirely fictitious.
>
> *(Polanyi 2001: 75; see Harvey 2014: 56)*

Harvey also cites Polanyi's warning that "to allow the market mechanism to be the sole director of the fate of human beings and their natural environment… would result in the demolition of society" (Polanyi 2001: 76; see Harvey 2014: 56). Ultimately, considers Polanyi, no society could stand the effects of such a system of crude (commodity) fictions "even for the shortest stretch of time unless its human and natural substance as well as its business organization was protected against the ravages of this satanic mill" (ibid.). The upshot of transforming labour, land, and money into commodities in order to keep production going (and profits growing), observes Polanyi, is that "human society becomes an accessory of the economic system" (2001: 79).

Once again we note that the party found worthy of mention is human society, not the natural world. Degradation of the latter – in Polanyi's account, land – is accounted for, and criticized, insofar as it harms human society, i.e. the future of humans on Earth and the prospects of their well-being. Harvey's gloss on this at the end of his discussion of Polanyi is that "the commodification of nature has certain limits because some things (like the atmosphere and the restless oceans) are not easily privatized and enclosed. While the fish extracted from the oceans can easily be commodified, the waters in which they swim pose a different problem" (Harvey 2014: 59).

While it is true that privatization is one of the limits that the commodification of nature comes up against, it is hardly the most fundamental one. Rather, the commodification of nature we are currently seeing around the world has the well-documented effect of spoiling nature, of degrading nature to such a degree that in one area after the other there is nothing to commodify, nothing to sell, nothing to convert into profits. Capitalism's exploitation of nature has become so wholesale as to destroy and eliminate that which is being exploited at its core, in its capacity to reproduce itself and replenish. This is what I referred to above as the ontological dimension, absent in Harvey's account. Among recent philosophically informed critiques of capitalism twentieth-century style, no one has caught this dimension better than the late Teresa Brennan, who ended what was to be her last book with the following observation:

> As the biosphere and species are destroyed, and human quality of life is degraded, the owl of Minerva points to the natural laws governing and regulating the survival of what has been or is being destroyed. *One learns what a necessary condition of life was as that condition ceases to exist.* This diabolic experiment with the Earth and its creatures reveals how individual human organisms depend like other organic life on the diversity of the whole biosphere.
>
> *(Brennan 2004: 161, my italics)*

References

Benton, Tim, 2001. "Why are Sociologists Naturephobes?". In J. Lopez and G. Potter, eds., *After Postmodernism: An Introduction to Critical Realism*, pp.132–145. London: Athlone Press.

Bhaskar, Roy (2012). "Critical realism in resonance with Nordic ecophilosophy." In R. Bhaskar, K.G. Høyer and P. Næss, eds., *Ecophilosophy in a World of Crisis*. London/ New York: Routledge.

Booth, Douglas E., 2004. *Hooked on Growth. Economic Addictions and the Environment*. Lanham, MD: Rowman & Littlefield.

Brennan, Teresa, 1993. *History After Lacan*. London: Routledge.

Brennan, Teresa, 2000. *Exhausting Modernity: Grounds for a New Economy*. London: Routledge.

Brennan, Teresa, 2003. *Globalization and its Terrors*. London: Routledge.

Brennan, Teresa, 2004. *The Transformation of Affect*. Ithaca, NY: Cornell University Press.

Catton, William R., 1982. *Overshoot. The Ecological Basis of Revolutionary Change*. Urbana, IL: University of Illinois Press.

Crouch, Colin, 2004. *Post–Democracy*. Cambridge: Polity Press.

Crouch, Colin, 2011. *The Strange Non–Death of Neoliberalism*. Cambridge: Polity Press.

Crouch, Colin, 2013. *Making Capitalism Fit for Society*. Cambridge: Polity Press.

Daly, Herman E., 2007. *Ecological Economics and Sustainable Development*. Cheltenham: Edward Elgar.

Georgescu-Roegen, Eugen, 1975. "Energy and Economic Myths," *Southern Economic Journal*, 41, 347–381.

Hamilton, Clive, 2004. *Growth Fetish*. London: Pluto Press.

Harvey, David, 2006 [1982]. *Limits to Capital*. London: Verso.

Harvey, David, 2003. *The New Imperialism*. Oxford: Oxford University Press.

Harvey, David, 2010. *The Enigma of Capital and the Crises of Capitalism*. London: Profile Books.

Harvey, David, 2014. *Seventeen Contradictions and the End of Capitalism*. London: Profile Books.

Horkheimer, Max, and Theodor W. Adorno, 1979 [1947]. *Dialectic of Enlightenment*. London: Verso.

Jackson, Tim, 2010. *Prosperity without Growth*. London: Earthscan.

Judt, Tony, 2010. *Ill Fares the Land*. London: Penguin.

Kovel, Joel, 2007. *The Enemy of Nature*. London: Zed Books.

Magdoff, Fred, and John Bellamy Foster, 2011. *What Every Environmentalist Needs to Know About Capitalism*. New York: Monthly Review Press.

Mirowski, Philip, 2013. *Never Let a Serious Crisis Go to Waste. How Neoliberalism Survived the Financial Meltdown*. London: Verso.

O'Connor, James, 1998. *Natural Causes. Essays in Ecological Marxism*. New York: Guilford Press.

Polanyi, Karl, 2001 [1944]. *The Great Transformation*. Boston, MA: Beacon Press.

Sedlacek, Tomas, 2010. *Economics of Good and Evil*. Oxford: Oxford University Press.

Spash, Clive L., 2002. *Greenhouse Economics*. London: Routledge.

Vetlesen, Arne Johan, 2015. *The Denial of Nature. Environmental Philosophy in the Era of Global Capitalism*. London: Routledge.

INDEX

www.ingramcontent.com/pod-product-compliance
Lightning Source LLC
LaVergne TN
LVHW021125300926
849160LV00010B/870

* 9 7 8 0 4 1 5 8 1 8 7 4 2 *